BANKING REGULATION AND SUPERVISION

Banking Regulation and Supervision

A Comparative Study of the UK, USA and Japan

Maximilian J. B. Hall

Senior Lecturer in Economics
Loughborough University of Technology

Edward Elgar

© Maximilian J. B. Hall 1993

Published by
Edward Elgar Publishing Limited
Gower House
Croft Road
Aldershot
Hants GU11 3HR
England

Edward Elgar Publishing Company
Old Post Road
Brookfield
Vermont 05036
USA

British Library Cataloguing in Publication Data
Hall, Maximilian
  Banking Regulation and Supervision:
  Comparative Study of the UK, USA and
  Japan
  I. Title
  332.1

Library of Congress Cataloguing in Publication Data
Hall, Maximilian.
    Banking regulation and supervision: a comparative study of the
UK, USA, and Japan/by Maximilian J.B. Hall.
      p. cm.
    1. Banking law—Great Britain.   2. Banking law—United States.
  3. Banking law—Japan.   I. Title.
  K1066.H35 1994
  346'.082—dc20
  [342.682]   93–15392
                                                                                CIP

ISBN 1 85278 129 7
Printed and bound in Great Britain by
Hartnolls Limited, Bodmin, Cornwall

Contents

v

Exhibits

Tables

Abbreviations

ABA	American Bankers Association
ACB	Adjusted capital base
ATS	Automatic transfer of savings
BA	Bankers acceptance
BCCI	Bank of Credit and Commerce International
BCMA	Bank Capital Markets Association (USA)
BHC	Bank holding company
BHCA	Bank Holding Company Act 1956 (USA)
BIF	Bank Insurance Fund (USA)
BIS	Bank for International Settlements
BOJ	Bank of Japan
BSD	Banking Supervision Division of the Bank of England
CCC	Competition and Credit Control (UK)
CDs	Certificates of Deposit
CFSR	Committee for Financial System Research (Japan)
CP	Commercial paper
DIC	Deposit Insurance Corporation (Japan)
DIDMCA	Depository Institutions Deregulation and Monetary Control Act 1980 (USA)
DTI	Department of Trade and Industry (UK)
EC	European Community
ERM	Exchange Rate Mechanism of the European Monetary System
FAIR	Foundation for Advanced Information and Research (Japan)
FASB	Financial Accounting Standards Board
FBAJ	Federation of Bankers Associations of Japan
FDIA	Federal Deposit Insurance Act 1966 (USA)
FDIC	Federal Deposit Insurance Corporation (USA)
FDICIA	Federal Deposit Insurance Corporation Improvement Act 1991 (USA)
FFIEC	Federal Financial Institutions Examination Council (USA)
FHC	Financial holding company
FIRREA	Financial Institutions, Recovery, Reform and Enforcement Act 1989 (USA)
FOMC	Federal Open Market Committee (USA)
FRB	Board of Governors of the Federal Reserve System (USA)
FRNs	Floating Rate Notes

FRS	Federal Reserve System (USA)
G10	Group of Ten
GAAP	Generally accepted accounting principles
GAO	General Accounting Office (USA)
HLTs	Highly-leveraged transactions
HMSO	Her Majesty's Stationery Office (UK)
IACERC	Inter-Agency Country Exposure Review Committee (USA)
IBA	International Banking Act 1978 (USA)
IBFC	Investment Bank Finance Company (USA)
IBJ	Industrial Bank of Japan
JCIF	Japan Centre for International Finance
JMB	Johnson Matthey Bankers
Joint Group	Joint Japan-US *Ad Hoc* Group on Yen-Dollar Exchange Rate, Financial and Capital Market Issues
LBOs	Leveraged buy-outs
LDC	Less developed country
MLR	Minimum Lending Rate
MMC	Monopolies and Mergers Commission (UK)
MMCs	Money market certificates
MOF	Ministry of Finance (Japan)
MPT	Ministry of Posts and Telecommunications (Japan)
NOW	Negotiable order of withdrawal
OBS	Off balance sheet
OCC	Office of the Comptroller of the Currency (USA)
OECD	Organisation for Economic Co-operation and Development
OFT	Office of Fair Trading (UK)
OTS	Office of Thrift Supervision (USA)
QFBO	Qualified foreign banking organisation (USA)
RAR	Risk asset ratio
SEC	Securities and Exchange Commission (USA)
SIA	Securities Industry Association (USA)
SIB	Securities and Investments Board (UK)
SICAFC	Savings Insurance Corporation for Agricultural and Fishery Co-operatives (Japan)
SROs	Self-regulatory organisations
TBs	Treasury bills
TCSC	Treasury and Civil Service Committee
TIRAL	Temporary Interest Rate Adjustment Law 1947 (Japan)
TOWRA	Total of weighted risk assets
TSE	Tokyo Stock Exchange
UK	United Kingdom
USA	United States of America

Preface

This book is concerned with the regulation and supervision of commercial banks. It provides a detailed assessment of the regimes currently operating in the UK, the USA and Japan and contrasts their operation from monetary policy and prudential standpoints. The likely future course of developments in each country is also discussed and suggestions for improving the cost-effectiveness of policy are provided.

The choice of countries for the study reflects not only the need to accommodate the systems governing the operations of most of the world's largest banks but also the desire to secure a geographical spread – European, North American and Far Eastern – and, above all, one which takes in economies whose financial systems are at different stages of development and which are subject to differing intensities of regulation and supervision. For these reasons, the banking sectors of the UK, the USA and Japan were chosen for analysis.

The format of the book is straightforward. Part I sets out the institutional framework obtaining in the financial sector of each economy, focusing on the central and commercial banks. This serves to put the analysis contained in the rest of the book firmly within an institutional context, thereby facilitating discussion and comparison. The detailed analysis of the current regulatory and supervisory regimes is contained in Part II. Finally, the comparative analysis provided in Part III includes both a general overview and a more detailed discussion of two issues assuming particular importance at the present time – the implementation of the G10 agreement on capital adequacy assessment and the breakdown of barriers between 'banking' and 'securities' activities.

It is readily apparent from a cursory glance through the book that a disproportionate amount of time is devoted in Parts I and II to coverage of the Japanese position. This is intentional. The decision to adopt this approach was taken in the light of the dearth of up-to-date texts in English on the Japanese financial system and in the belief that many readers will be unfamiliar with the operations of Japanese financial markets and institutions. The background to the current programmes of financial liberalization, deregulation and internationalization being conducted in Japan is included so that the reader is fully appraised of the pressures, both internal and external, which are likely to be brought to bear on any government harbouring aspirations to an enhanced status within the world economy for its indigenous markets and institutions.

As soon becomes apparent from a reading of the book, common problems afflict both banks and regulators alike, whatever the distinctiveness of local arrangements. The former, for example, are all labouring under: an intensification in competition – partly the result of deregulation and liberalization – which is pressing down on margins; the loss of traditional corporate business as their prime borrowing customers exploit the opportunities arising from securitization; rising bad debts, as a result of the bursting of asset bubbles (for example, in respect of land, property and stock prices), the relaxation of lending standards in the boom years and the cyclical downturn in local and global economies; increasingly burdensome capital requirements, as regulators move to underpin the soundness and stability of the local and international banking communities; and a more general intensification in supervision as governments react to the public outcry over the highly publicized excesses of the late 1980s and supervisors respond to the deficiencies in both domestic and international supervisory practice revealed by major bank collapses (such as the Bank of Credit and Commerce International). The regulators and supervisors, in turn, have to deal with the consequences – for both monetary and prudential policy – of the deregulation programmes instituted by their governments, of the growing interdependencies arising from the internationalization of banking and conglomeration, and of the banking industry's innovation in the light of these and other pressures.

At the end of the day, the regulators and supervisors have to conduct monetary policy in an efficient manner and operate cost-effective supervisory regimes. The arrangements best suited to achieving these goals are not always clear, however. Nevertheless, there is sufficient agreement on some of the underlying principles which should guide the actions of the regulatory fraternity to allow for an objective critique of current arrangements.

This does not mean, of course, that all issues have been resolved to the satisfaction of the informed majority. Far from it. But it is to be hoped that, by highlighting the continuing areas of controversy – such as the best way of reducing opportunities for regulatory arbitrage, the wisdom of persisting with a flawed methodology for the assessment of capital adequacy, the case for retaining direct monetary controls, the desirability of moving towards a universal banking style of operation, and the role of moral suasion, to name but a few – I shall serve to stimulate further debate on what I regard as significant public policy issues.

Acknowledgements

First, I should like to acknowledge gratefully the finanacial support received from the British Academy, the British Council and the Nuffield Foundation which enabled me to visit the shores of the United States of America and Japan in order to collect material and interview interested parties. The latter – comprising regulators, practitioners, trade associations and academics – must also be thanked for their willing co-operation. In this respect, Professor Jun'ichi Senda of Nagoya University and Professor Sadao Katayama of Shiga University deserve a special mention for opening doors for me in Japan and for guiding me through the maze of an unfamiliar Japanese financial system.

Secondly, I should like to apologize, once again, to my family for having to endure the interruptions to normal family life necessitated by immersion in the project. Thirdly, I should like to thank Su Spencer and Gloria Brentnall for their tireless efforts on my behalf on the word processor. And, finally, I wish to thank Edward Elgar for his patience in waiting for the delivery of the manuscript. I hope he finds the wait worthwhile.

PART I

THE INSTITUTIONAL FRAMEWORK

1   The banking sector in the UK

The UK financial sector

As you would expect in an economy with a highly developed financial system, the UK financial sector comprises a wide range of depository and non-depository institutions (see Exhibit 1.1). Discussion, however, will focus on the activities of the central bank and the commercial banks it regulates as it is these which form the subject matter of this book. (For a discussion of the activities of the other financial intermediaries, see, for example, Pawley, Winstone and Bentley, 1991; Goacher *et al.*, 1987; Drake, 1989; and Kay, 1990.)

Exhibit 1.1   The UK financial sector[a]

Central bank – the Bank of England
Banking sector
Non-bank depository institutions
    Building societies
Other non-bank financial intermediaries
    Non-bank credit companies
    Insurance companies (life and general)
    Pension funds
    Portfolio institutions (i.e., unit trusts and investment trusts)
    Special investment agencies
    Venture capital funds

Note: [a] Ignoring public sector bodies, such as local authorities, which are active in most of the UK's financial markets, and the National Savings movement.

Central banking

The central bank in the UK is called the Bank of England (henceforth termed 'the Bank'). Its functions are many and various. First, it is responsible for the issue of banknotes (more precisely, it is the Issue Department of the Bank, which in the national accounts is included as part of the public sector, that performs this task). Secondly, it is responsible for advising the government on and the implementation of monetary policy which, of course, involves management of the national debt and intervention in financial markets – bill, bond and foreign exchange – to secure the government's financial goals. Thirdly, through its Banking Department, it performs a range of commercial banking functions, acting as banker to the government, commercial banks, overseas central banks, some international financial organizations, a few private-sector customers and its staff. Fourthly, it is responsible for the prudential regulation and supervision of the UK banking system under the Banking Act of 1987, and for ensuring the wellbeing of the UK financial sector more generally, which involves the operation of the traditional lender-of-last-resort facility. And finally, it is responsible for a range of other miscellaneous duties such as running the clearing system, managing the nation's stock of gold and foreign currency reserves (which are held in the Exchange Equalization Account at the Treasury) and acting as registrar for government stock.

Constitutionally, the Bank is not independent of government: under Clause 4 of the Bank of England Act of 1946 the Treasury has the formal power to issue directions to the Bank. The chain of command is thus clear: ministers (that is, the Cabinet) instruct the Treasury what to do and the Treasury instructs the Bank of England what to do. Although the Governor of the Bank has a statutory right to be consulted prior to the issue of a direction, he has no power to veto it. In practice, however, this formal power to issue directions has never been used, the Bank and the Treasury enjoying a very close working relationship even if opinions differ occasionally on the optimal course for policy (see HMSO, 1980, ch. 25, for a more detailed assessment of the independence and accountability of the Bank). Under the same Clause 4 the Bank is also given the statutory power to issue directions to the commercial banks, although, once again, this has never proved necessary to ensure compliance with the Bank's wishes.

The managing body of the Bank is the Court of Directors, which comprises the Governor, the Deputy Governor, four full-time Executive Directors and twelve part-time Directors. All are appointed by the Crown (in practice, by the Prime Minister). The Governor and Deputy Governor hold office for five years (at least in the first instance), and the Directors for four years, four of them retiring each year (although they are eligible for reappointment).

As for the future, and irrespective of whether or not the Bank gains its independence, its autonomy will be severely circumscribed by the advent of a European System of Central Banks, as called for by the Committee of Governors of the Central Banks of the Member States of the European Economic Community in 1990 (see Goodhart, 1991).

Commercial banking
The structure of the UK (commercial) banking sector is presented in Exhibit 1.2, which also provides some balance sheet data as at the end of 1991. The

Exhibit 1.2   The UK banking sector:[1, 2] balance sheets at end December 1991

	£m
Retail banks[3]	445,827
British merchant banks[4]	54,138
Discount houses[5]	11,857
'Other' British banks	51,983
Overseas banks	
American	78,949
Japanese	226,300
'Other'[6]	336,559

Notes
1. This is the classification system used by the Bank of England since December 1983 in respect of United Kingdom banks (formerly 'monetary sector' institutions).
2. For supervisory purposes the Bank of England also distinguishes UK-incorporated banks from overseas-incorporated banks, and large British banks from smaller UK banks.
3. Broadly speaking, the retail banks group comprises those intermediaries which have extensive branch networks in the UK and participate in a UK clearing system. Formally, the group is defined to comprise: the London and Scottish clearing banks; the Northern Ireland banks; the National Girobank; the Co-operative Bank; the Yorkshire Bank; and the Banking Department of the Bank of England.
4. This group broadly comprises banks whose majority ownership is British and whose main business is primarily concerned with corporate finance and mergers.
5. This group comprises those institutions authorized under the Banking Act 1987 which have a money-market dealing relationship with the Bank of England.
6. Includes consortium banks.

Source: Bank of England (1991) pp. 99–100. Bank of England (1993) Tables 2.4, 2.5, 2.7, 2.10, 2.11, 2.13 and 4.

classification system used is that adopted by the Bank of England in the presentation of its statistics for United Kingdom banks.

While a detailed analysis of the activities undertaken by the various groupings is not provided here (see, for example, Pawley, Winstone and Bentley, 1991, ch. 4, for such a discussion), it is worth noting at this juncture that the main focus of attention in this book, in so far as it relates to the UK scene, is on the regulatory environment governing the operations of the retail banks and, more especially, the clearing banks which dominate this group. Other texts (for example, Hall, 1989, Appendix 1; and Kay, 1990, ch. 15, in respect of discount houses and merchant banks respectively) must be consulted if a detailed discussion of the regulation of the banks in the other groupings is required.

This grouping of banks comprises those banks which participate in the UK clearing system (Molyneux 1990: ch. 6, pp. 62–5). In the past this meant the membership of the London Bankers' Clearing House (Sayers 1967: Appendix 1, pp. 301–8) but today the group comprises the so-called 'big four' (that is, Barclays Bank, Lloyds Bank, Midland Bank and National Westminster Bank), plus the three Scottish clearing banks, four Northern Ireland banks, the Trustee Savings Bank, the Co-operative Bank, the Yorkshire Bank, the Girobank and Abbey National plc, the recently-converted building society. Together these institutions dominate the payments system, handling the bulk of the UK's cheque and credit clearing.

By tradition retail deposit-takers and lenders to the personal and corporate sectors, the clearing banks were obliged to become major providers of funds to the British government during the Second World War. This situation continued in the early post-war years under the influence of lending constraints so that by 1950 around sixty per cent of deposits held were directly or indirectly invested in British government debt (Lewis and Davis 1987: p. 5). Their traditional retail banking roles were, however, resumed during the 1960s although, towards the end of the decade, they did move into 'wholesale banking' as the so-called 'parallel' money markets developed in London (Shaw 1975: Part III). This, in turn, led to a dramatic expansion in the scale and significance of their interbank transactions and to the development of 'liability management' – the 'funding of loans' as opposed to the traditional 'lending of deposits' – in the early 1970s, the source of much disquiet for the domestic monetary authorities (Hall 1983: chs 3 and 4).

Today the UK clearing banks are among the best capitalised banks in the world and their operations span most parts of the globe and the full spectrum of financial services. Their traditional areas of activity, such as money transmission services, cash distribution, personal and corporate banking, leasing, factoring, instalment credit, trade finance, tax consultancy and executor and trustee services, have been complemented in recent years by wide-scale diversification. These new activities embrace, *inter alia*, international banking, investment banking, credit and debit card operations, mortgage lending, financial services for small businesses and a range of non-banking financial service operations (most notably, insurance brokerage but also insurance underwriting and financial advisory and estate agency services). The clearing banks, typically located in the high streets of most of the towns and cities in the UK, have thus become multi-product and multi-functional financial conglomerates, distinguished, in part, by the high percentages of their assets and liabilities which are denominated in foreign currency. They are also heavy users of advanced payments technology in the provision of automated teller machines (ATMs) and electronic funds transfer at point of sale (EFT/POS) and 'home banking' facilities.

Despite their financial strength and experience in both domestic (they still dominate the retail and corporate banking markets) and international financial markets, however, the clearing banks' diversification strategies have not always proved successful. Their mixed experience with the finance house instalment credit market in the early eighties for example was crowned by their plunge into the third world sovereign lending market, the results of which forced some (that is, Lloyds and Midland) to break new ground by declaring pre-tax losses for the financial year 1989. While the potentially-disastrous (from a systemic point of view) consequences of this foray into sovereign lending have successfully been avoided, the associated provisions for bad and doubtful debts continue to eat into recorded profits for most (the last to join their ranks – the Trustee Savings Bank and the Abbey National – are not affected) of the clearing banks. Moreover, having exorcised this ghost the clearers are now facing renewed threats, predominantly from their domestic operations.

Apart from the continuing difficulties experienced by some (that is, Midland and National Westminster) in overseas (especially North American) markets, the major problems currently facing the clearing banks are home-grown. All are beset by bad loan experiences on their domestic books as a result of the recession and the depressed property market; and some (most notably National Westminster) are still striving to extract adequate returns from capital, if not profits, from their investment banking operations, which were established in the run-up to the 'Big Bang' on the London stock exchange in 1986 (see Hall 1987: ch. 3). These difficulties resulted in poor results for the majority in the financial years 1990–1992; and a significant recovery in profits is unlikely to materialise until the second half of 1993 at the earliest.

References

Bank of England (1991), 'Bank groupings in statistical presentations', *Bank of England Quarterly Bulletin*, February, pp. 99–100.

Bank of England (1993), *Statistical Abstract 1992: Part 1*, March.

Drake, L. (1989), *The Building Society Industry in Transition* (London: Macmillan).

Goacher, D. J. *et al.* (1987), *British Non-Bank Financial Intermediaries* (London: Allen and Unwin).

Goodhart, C. A. E. (1991), 'The draft statute of the European System of Central Banks: A commentary', Special Paper no. 37 (London: London School of Economics, Financial Markets Group).

Hall, M. J. B. (1983), *Monetary Policy Since 1971: Conduct and Performance* (London: Macmillan).

Hall, M. J. B. (1987), *The City Revolution: Causes and Consequences* (London: Macmillan).

HMSO (1980), *Committee to Review the Functioning of Financial Institutions*, Cmnd 7937 (London: Her Majesty's Stationery Office).

Kay, W. (ed.) (1990), *Clay and Wheble's 'Modern Merchant Banking'* 3rd ed. (London: Woodhead Faulkner).

Lewis, M. K. and Davis, K. T. (1987), *Domestic and International Banking* (London: Philip Allan).

Molyneux, P. (1990), *Banking: An Introductory Text* (London: Macmillan).

Pawley, M., Winstone, D. and Bentley, P. (1991), *UK Financial Institutions and Markets* (London: Macmillan).
Sayers, R. S. (1967), *Modern Banking*, 7th ed. (Oxford: The Clarendon Press).
Shaw, E. R. (1975), *The London Money Market* (London: Heinemann).

2 The banking sector in the USA

The US financial sector

Because it is at the centre of a highly developed financial system, the US financial sector naturally comprises a diverse set of institutions, both depository and non-depository (the full list is presented on Exhibit 2.1 – for further details, see Kidwell and Peterson, 1981, ch. 2). The focus of this study, however, is confined to the operations of the central bank and the commercial banks, which will now be briefly considered.

Exhibit 2.1   The US financial sector

Central bank – the Federal Reserve System
Banking sector
    Commercial banks
Non-bank depository institutions
    Savings and loan associations
    Mutual savings banks
    Credit unions
    Postal savings system
Other non-bank financial intermediaries
    Insurance companies (life and casualty)
    Pension funds
    Real-estate investment trusts
    Federally-sponsored credit agencies and
    mortgage pools
    Public authorities
    Mutual funds
    Money market funds
    Securities brokers and dealers
    Finance companies

Central banking

The central bank in the USA is called the Federal Reserve System (FRS). It was established in 1913 primarily to prevent the financial sector causing economic crises. It operates autonomously of the Federal government.

Because of the federal nature of the USA, the FRS in fact comprises twelve district Federal Reserve Banks, each one situated in a major financial centre. The three largest are located in New York, Chicago and San Francisco, the first-mentioned acting as agent for the other eleven in all market transactions of the FRS and as official correspondent of foreign central banks and the international institutions of which the United States is a member. These twelve institutions represent the organs through which national monetary policy is implemented. They also provide a range of services, such as custodial services and discount window lending, to their (bank) membership and are required to represent the interests of their local communities at national policy-making sessions.

The body responsible for formulating regulatory and supervisory policy and monitoring and co-ordinating the activities of the district Federal Reserve Banks is the Board of Governors of the FRS, which is headquartered in Washington. It comprises seven individuals each of whom is elected by the President of the US and subject to Senate approval. The chairman, too, is appointed by the President and, by tradition, he is also the chairman of the Federal Open Market Committee, the main organ for formulating national monetary policy (see Young, 1973, chs 1 and 3 for further details).

Apart from providing services to the membership, the FRS carries out the usual range of central bank functions such as: formulating and implementing monetary policy (after taking advice from the Treasury and the Federal Advisory Council, see Young, 1973, ch. 1); designing and implementing prudential policy (in respect of bank holding companies, state member banks and others, see Chapter 5); overseeing the operation of the national payments system; intervening in the foreign exchange market; acting as banker to the federal government and member banks and as fiscal agent for the Treasury Department. It is not, however, responsible for the note issue or the minting of coin or for managing the nation's international reserves; these are functions of the Treasury Department.

Commerical banking

As can be seen from Exhibit 2.2, the US commercial banking sector is both fractured and diverse. One way to categorize such institutions is to divide them into those which are members of the FRS and those which are not. All national banks, that is those with federal charters, have to belong to the FRS, but those with a state charter ('state banks') have the freedom to choose. Since enactment of the Depository Institutions Deregulation and Monetary Control Act in 1980, which allowed the FRS to extend reserve requirements to non-member banks, the balance of advantage has swung back in favour of membership, which explains why the majority of state banks (see Exhibit 2.2) are now members.

Another distinction which can be drawn is between FDIC-insured and non-FDIC-insured banks (see Chapter 5 for a discussion of federal deposit

Exhibit 2.2   *The US commercial banking sector*

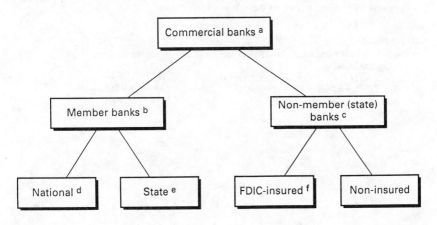

Notes
a   12,528 in total at the end of 1989 comprising national banks, state member banks, FDIC-
    insured non-member banks and non-insured non-member banks. Domestic deposits to-
    talled $2,193,604,976 at end-1989.
b   5188 in total at the end of 1989, accounting for 73% of the domestic deposits of the US
    commercial banking sector.
c   7340 at the end of 1989, accounting for 27% of the domestic deposits of the US commer-
    cial banking sector.
d   4163 at the end of 1989, accounting for 59% of the domestic deposits of US member
    banks.
e   8365 at the end of 1989, accounting for 41% of the domestic deposits of US member
    banks.
f   99.9% of all commercial banks are FDIC-insured now.

Source: Board of Governors of the Federal Reserve System.

insurance arrangements). Again, while national banks are required to secure
FDIC insurance for their depositors, state banks are left to choose. The
benefits of federal insurance are now so high, however – few depositors will
voluntarily forgo the protection afforded – that virtually all banks are covered in this way.

Final distinctions which can be drawn are between so-called 'reserve city'
member banks, 'regional' member banks and 'country' member banks. The
first grouping comprises the larger ('money centre') commercial banks sited
in the major financial centres; the second group are sited in the regional (as
opposed to national) financial centres and most maintain correspondent banking relationships with money centre banks; the last-mentioned, though the
largest in number, are smaller concerns scattered throughout the countryside

and often engaged in 'correspondent banking' (see Kidwell and Peterson, 1981, pp. 178–80 for further details).

References

Kidwell, D. S. and Peterson, R. L. (1981), *Financial Institutions, Markets and Money* (Hinsdale, Ill.: Dryden Press).

Young, R. A. (1973), *Instruments of Monetary Policy in the United States: The Role of the Federal Reserve System* (Washington, DC: International Monetary Fund).

3   The banking sector in Japan

Introduction

Historical background.
The roots of the present-day structure can be traced back to the beginning of the Meiji Restoration period in 1868. The system set up at that time was based on the national banking system of the US, characterized by the existence of a large number of issuing banks. Accordingly, under the National Bank Act of 1872, a number of privately owned national banks were permitted to start operations, functioning largely as issuing banks. By 1879, the date at which a halt was called to the establishment of national banks, there were over 150 such banks in existence and they operated side by side with other types of company also engaged in banking business. Indeed, it was from the latter group's ranks that the first private bank emerged when the Mitsui Gumi company formed the Mitsui Bank in 1876. This bank, along with most of the other private banks and banking companies formed after 1876, subsequently converted to ordinary bank status in accordance with the Banking Act of 1890. For the national banks, this process was accelerated by their loss of issuing authority following the founding of the Bank of Japan in 1882. The result was that the Japanese banking system operated along the lines of the British system, rather than that of the US, before the turn of the nineteenth century.

Another important historical feature of the Japanese banking system is the absorption of the savings bank system into the banking system proper. The savings bank system was established as long ago as 1890 under the Savings Bank Act, and the savings banks were initially protected by the Savings Bank Law of 1921 which prohibited ordinary banks from engaging in savings banking business (that is, the taking of small deposits, their investment in securities – primarily government bonds – and the payment of compound interest). This prohibition remained in force until 1943, but by the end of the Second World War only five savings banks remained. And by 1949 each of these five institutions had either converted into or merged with an ordinary bank, marking the demise of the species as a separate entity. After 1949 savings banking business became the preserve of the ordinary banks, a position formalized in 1981 with the revision of the Banking Law which, for the first time, gave official blessing to the joint offering of commercial and savings banking business.

Structural features

As noted earlier, the post-1890 banking system of Japan possessed many of the features of the British system, although a notable difference was the absence of merchant banks in the former, the functions of which were largely performed by securities companies and money market dealers. A number of additional distinguishing features exist today, however. Most noticeably, the Japanese banking sector is characterized by a high degree of specialization. Thus, some banks specialize in long-term finance while others specialize in finance for small and medium-sized businesses, in serving specific industries (especially agriculture, forestry and fisheries), or in trust business. Such specialization is symptomatic of the highly segmented Japanese financial system where banking and securities business is separated by the prohibition, in principle, on banks engaging in securities business,[1] where restrictions are imposed on the concurrent operations of (ordinary) banking and trust business, and where a clear distinction is drawn between short-term and long-term finance.

This distinction between short- and long-term finance first appeared in the 1880s when 'long-term' institutions were set up to channel long-term funds into both the agricultural and industrial sectors to facilitate their modernization. By 1944, however, all these special institutions had been absorbed by the Nippon Kangyo Bank, and after the war the special banking system was abolished. The Nippon Kangyo Bank subsequently assumed ordinary bank status together with the Industrial Bank of Japan – an institution set up in 1901 to provide long-term funds to industry, using securities as collateral – but the latter went on to convert to a long-term credit bank in 1952 following the enactment of the Long-term Credit Bank Law. The feature currently distinguishing short-term credit institutions (including ordinary banks, *sogo* banks and *shinkin* banks – see below) from long-term ones (that is, long-term credit banks and trust banks) is that the latter group alone can borrow funds for up to five years. The others are restricted by Ministry of Finance (MOF) administrative guidance to a two-year-to-maturity threshold for their time deposits, and are prohibited from issuing debentures, the exclusive preserve of the long-term credit banks.

A classification system

Banking institutions in Japan may be categorized according to the system adopted in Exhibit 3.1. Under this approach, the central bank, ordinary banks, specialized banks and government-owned banks are separately identified. Even this list, however, does not embrace all deposit-taking intermediaries operating in Japan: credit co-operatives (including the National Federation of Credit Co-operatives), agricultural co-operatives (and their credit federations) and fishery co-operatives (including their credit federations)

Exhibit 3.1   The Japanese banking system

Central bank	The Bank of Japan
Private banks	
Ordinary banks	City banks
	Regional banks
	Foreign banks
Specialized banks	
in foreign exchange and foreign	The Specialised Foreign
trade	Exchange Bank (i.e., the
	Bank of Tokyo)
long-term financial institutions	Long-term credit banks
	Trust banks
in finance for small and medium-	*Sogo* banks
sized corporations	*Shinkin* banks/*Zenshinren* Bank
	Labour banks/*Rokinren* Bank
	Shokochukin Bank
in serving the agricultural, forestry	*Norinchukin* Bank
and fisheries industries	
Public (non-depository) sector banks	Japan Development Bank
	Export-Import Bank of Japan

Sources: Federation of Bankers Associations of Japan, 1989, ch. 1; Suzuki, 1987, ch. 5.

from the private sector, and the Post Office from the public sector, all play their part (see Federation of Bankers Associations of Japan (FBAJ), 1989, pp. 27–35; and Suzuki, 1987, ch. 5, for further details); and it includes three institutions (that is, the central bank and the government-owned banks) which do not accept deposits from the general public. Nevertheless, for illustrative purposes, it is perhaps the most sensible taxonomic approach to adopt, although clearly historical precedent further reduces the degree of functional separation secured.

The central bank
The Bank of Japan (the 'Bank') was established as the central bank of Japan in October 1882 and currently operates under the Bank of Japan Law of 1942. Legally, it functions as a special corporation outside the framework of government, with 55 per cent of its capital held by the government and the remainder by the private sector. Control over the Bank is exercised by a Policy Board comprising the Bank's Governor and representatives from industry, private sector banks, the Economic Planning Agency and the MOF.

As prescribed in Article 1 of the above-mentioned Law, the main role of the Bank is to ensure the smooth and efficient functioning of the financial system so as to promote economic development. This is to be achieved primarily through appropriate manipulation of the money supply and money market conditions, the proximate goals of which are a stable currency and price stability. The other traditional macroeconomic goals – full employment, economic growth and external balance – are also considered important, however.

Apart from conducting monetary policy (for further details, see Part II, chapter 6), the Bank also performs a range of other duties traditionally expected of a central bank. These embrace, *inter alia*: note issuance; banker to the government; banker to the banking system; foreign exchange market intervention; and government bond and money market activities.

Private banks

The first group of privately owned banks, the ordinary banks, operate in accordance with the Banking Law under license from the MOF. They concentrate on the provision of short-term finance facilities, operating as traditional western-style deposit bankers in both domestic and foreign markets. Their customer base embraces small, medium-sized and multinational corporations, together with private individuals.

Statistically, the ordinary banks are broken down into three separate groupings: city banks; regional banks; and foreign banks.

The city bank grouping   This group comprises the ten[2] nationwide branching institutions. Traditionally suppliers of short-term funds to large corporations, they have recently focused on developing the longer-term end of their business. Additionally, they have been forced to cultivate clients from amongst the smaller corporate fry and the personal sector because of the downturn in their traditional customers' demand for bank credit. This downturn arose for a number of reasons, chief among which were an increasingly liquid trading situation and the opportunities created by developments in the capital market – the so-called process of securitization – which were themselves partly the result of official deregulatory moves (for example, to allow for the establishment of a commercial paper market and to open up the corporate bond market during the 1980s). Apart from borrowing from the Bank of Japan (see chapter 6), they fund themselves in the deposit and short-term financial markets. They are widely engaged in securities-type operations – despite the legal restrictions separating commercial banking and securities business in Japan (see Part II) – at both home and abroad, and most have a significant international dimension to their operations (the largest are the largest banks in the world, by deposit or asset size).

Despite their size, however, the city banks are currently facing serious pressures on a number of fronts, apart from the declining loan demand of their traditional customers alluded to earlier. First and foremost, they are having difficulty in meeting the capital standards required of them under the Group of Ten (G10) central bank governors' agreement of 1988 (see Part II). This is largely due to the downturn in the Tokyo stock market (which fell by over 40 per cent in nominal terms at one stage during 1990) that has: (i) reduced the availability of Tier 2 capital in the form of latent gains on securities holdings; (ii) made rights issues more difficult and expensive; and (iii) reduced the supply of capital emanating from conversions to equity by convertible bond holders. The fall in the value of the yen against the US dollar has exacerbated their problems – a high proportion of their assets are denominated in dollars whereas their capital is almost exclusively denominated in yen – as has the secular decline in profits, which has retarded retained earnings.

The drop in recorded profits experienced by most in the financial years 1990/91 and 1991/92 can be attributed to a number of factors. First, the steep declines in asset values witnessed in local markets – especially the stock and property markets as land values tumbled – have dented associated portfolio returns and worsened bad-debt experience for those (the majority) exposed to those sectors of the economy, leading to the recording of valuation losses and rising provisions and write-offs. Secondly, and despite the benefits deriving from the new business opportunities created (for example, enhanced access to funds management and advisory services – see chapter 6), the official programme of financial deregulation has impaired the banks' lending margins as a result of the lifting of deposit rate ceilings on all except 'small' time and demand deposits.[3] Thirdly, many are still heavily exposed to third world countries in spite of increased provisions, with only meagre tax relief being received on the volume of provisions. And fourthly, the persistent high interest rate policy pursued by the monetary authorities in recent years in an attempt to damp down asset markets has led to a further squeezing of margins and to some incurring running losses on their traditional maturity-transforming borrowing and lending activities because of the temporary inversion of the yield curve. These factors, taken together with the more competitive trading environment and the defection of part of their corporate customer base to the capital markets for funds, go a long way to explaining the banks' poor returns.

Although such pressures have led to downgradings by international rating agencies of some of the banks' debt ratings, the outlook is not entirely bleak. Further deregulatory moves – especially those associated with a lowering of the barriers between banking and securities and insurance activities – are likely to bestow net benefits on the city bank fraternity, even if conducted on a strict *quid pro quo* basis; the local stock market appears to have bottomed out following the rescue package announced in August 1992[4] and the rate of decline in land and property prices has decelerated markedly; the fall in the yen against the US dollar has partly been reversed, thereby improving capital ratios; bad debt experience, on both domestic and foreign loan books, is likely to improve in line with the international trading environment; and lending margins improved during 1991–2 largely because of falling interest rates. And whatever the extent of the cyclical turnaround in profits, the recent hiatus is likely to prove invaluable to the long-term fortunes of this and other sectors of the banking industry by forcibly demonstrating how important it is to focus on rate of return on equity rather than size as one's measure of success in the market-place. (For a discussion of city banks' financial strategies post-liberalization, see Kawada, 1991.)

The regional banks   The second grouping of ordinary banks comprises some 60 members that are smaller in scale than the city banks and usually confine their operations to the principle cities of the prefectures in which their head offices are located. Accordingly, their local ties are strong, with the bulk of their lending going to small or medium-sized companies in the locality. The bulk of their deposits are time deposits of an initial term of one year or more, with over 50 per cent accruing from individuals. Apart from making business loans they invest heavily in the stock market and are important lenders in the local money market.

In spite of their secure local customer bases many of the regional banks are experiencing similar trading difficulties to their city bank competitors, with combined pre-tax profits for the financial year 1990–1 falling by 2.4 per cent. This was the second consecutive fall experienced, with business profits – a proxy for profits from banking operations – declining by 9.8 per cent over the two-year period 1990–1. The general problems relate to a narrowing of spreads, declining corporate demand for bank loans, excessive geographical loan concentration, and increasing competition from other financial institutions, especially the city banks as a result of their recent aggressive move to increase market share in the small to medium-sized company and individual loan markets where interest margins are higher. To this can be added the downturn in profitability of property and stock portfolio investment and related lending activities. They are also experiencing difficulties in complying with the BIS capital ratio requirements, although the MOF has alleviated their problems somewhat by allowing them to tap the trust banks for subordinated loans. The larger institutions have, nevertheless, curtailed ambitions for further international expansion, and the recent merger between Sanin-Godo Bank and Fuso Bank may set a trend for the future in this sector as medium-sized banks strive to achieve a 'critical mass' and offer a wider range of services to their customers. Striking agency agreements with securities firms and other financial groups is an alternative means of achieving the same end.[5]

Foreign banks There are more than 80 foreign banks forming the third and final grouping of ordinary banks. Licensed by the MOF in respect of their branching operations (prior notification suffices in the case of representative offices), they have traditionally been heavily involved in foreign currency transactions and trade finance and so have also had to acquire the status of authorized foreign exchange banks. Their share of the Japanese banking market has always been small, at roughly 3 per cent in recent years, but this may pick up in the next few years as a result of the customer shake-out by Japanese banks as they restructure their operations to comply with the BIS capital adequacy requirements. While presenting opportunities this, however, also poses new problems for the foreign banks in the form of credit control and risk management. Margins are also likely to remain low on corporate lending activities and this has led some to eschew the new opportunities and instead to focus on investment banking and risk management, both for themselves and for clients. Other advisory services offered relate to foreign real-estate investment and mergers and acquisitions; leasing and securitization activities are also regarded as potentially profitable. For tax reasons, however, incentives remain for the banks to book outside the country the deals agreed in Japan. On the liabilities side, they are forced to rely heavily on eurocurrency borrowings from their main branch offices as their limited branch networks (the source of the city banks' major funding advantage), like the local money market, fail to deliver funds in sufficient quantity. Despite deregulation – which, although ending their monopoly on the provision of foreign currency loans to Japanese residents, did provide them with access to trust banking and broadened their funding base through a broadening of the interbank market, the establishment of an offshore market and expansion in the yen swap market – foreign banks still find it difficult to penetrate domestic markets.

Specialized banks
The first of the specialized banking institutions listed in Exhibit 3.1 is the *Specialized Foreign Exchange Bank*. Established in 1954 under the Foreign Exchange Bank Law, this bank, like the other authorized foreign exchange banks, specializes in foreign exchange transactions and trade finance. It does, however, receive preferential treatment when it comes to establishing overseas operations and receiving deposits from the government of its foreign exchange balances and, since 1962, has been allowed to issue debentures – either three-year interest-bearing debentures or one-year discount

debentures – currently up to a maximum of ten times the value of shareholders' equity. On the domestic front, however, its lending activities are confined to foreign exchange and trade operations, and branches may only be established in cities which are important centres for such activities. It is, though, allowed to undertake the same range of securities activities that ordinary banks may engage in.

Long-term financial institutions   comprise both long-term credit banks and trust banks. The long-term credit banks, of which there are three in number, were established under the Long-Term Credit Bank Law of 1952 to engage in long-term finance in order to achieve a separation between short- and long-term finance and to reduce the long-term funding burden imposed on the ordinary banks by the demands of industry. They are distinguishable from ordinary banks in their funding operations, their lending operations and in the size of their branch networks. On the funding side, they alone are permitted to issue debentures – either five-year interest-bearing debentures or one-year discount debentures – up to a maximum of 30 times their own capital, but must confine their deposit-taking to their borrowing clientele, public bodies, corporations who entrust bond subscriptions to them, and other clients; on the lending side, the average term to maturity of their loans is considerably longer (partly because of the limitation placed on their provision of short-term working capital for industry: it cannot exceed the volume of deposits solicited); and the size of their branch networks is considerably smaller.

Partly because of their specialist role – providers of long-term finance to industry, particularly the heavy industries – the long-term credit banks are suffering more than most from the decline in corporate loan demand. Initially, this caused them to expand overseas and to diversify domestically into lending to the wholesale and service trades and to financial companies satisfying the personal sector's demand for housing finance and consumer credit. Apart from the reverses experienced in these markets, which have increased bad-debt provisions, they have also suffered from the slowdown in euromarket activity, particularly eurobond underwriting, the fall in property and stock prices, which has reduced related portfolio returns, LDC loan exposures, and from maturity-transforming lending under an inverted yield curve. As a result, their credit ratings are under attack by the major rating agencies, although in the longer term they are well placed to benefit from any further removal of the barriers separating banking from securities business (although other deregulatory moves are likely to count against them). Their peculiar difficulties, however, have already led the president of one of the institutions – the Industrial Bank of Japan – to declare publicly his interest in merging with another banking institution if a suitable partner can be found. In the near term, the banks are looking to fee income, off-balance-sheet transactions and foreign exchange and public bond trading profits to improve their balance sheets. (For a more detailed discussion of how long-term credit banks have coped with financial liberalization, see Watanabe, 1991.)

The other group of long-term banking institutions are the trust banks. These institutions are ordinary banks established under the Banking Law but given extended powers in accordance with the 1943 law permitting concurrent ordinary bank and trust operations (that is, the Law Concerning Joint Operation of Ordinary Banks, Savings Bank Business and Trust Business) as revised in 1981. Excluding the subsidiaries of foreign banks – nine were admitted in 1985 by the MOF on condition that they incorporate locally – there are currently seven institutions operating as trust banks in Japan. They obtain most of their funds from trusts (particularly the loan trusts peculiar to Japan – see Suzuki, 1987, ch. 3) and, in respect of their trust accounts, satisfy much of the large Japanese corporations' capital investment finance needs. They also offer savings and deposit accounts and tap the money markets. Apart from their trust and banking operations, they are active in funds management (especially *tokkin* funds,[6] but also pension funds), and provide real-estate broking and stock transfer services. Following an easing of the restrictions on the proportion of trust assets which can be invested outside Japan[7] they have become significant investors in overseas markets where they are also engaged in securities underwriting and distribution as well as lending operations.

As a group, the trust banks have not escaped the chill winds blowing through the Japanese banking sector. Combined pre-tax profits for the year to end-March 1991 fell by 37.5 per cent, with profits from banking operations falling even more sharply (business profits, a proxy for banking profits, declined steeply by 53.9 per cent); and a further fall of 38.8 per cent was recorded for the 1991–2 financial year. These results, following the previous year's disappointing figures, demonstrate the sector's vulnerability to high interest rates – they are unable to fund their fixed rate investment portfolio at fixed long-term rates – and to weakness in domestic and overseas property and stock markets, because of their related exposures. Domestic deregulation has also hit the sector hard by intensifying competition in many areas of activity (especially pension fund management and discretionary investment portfolio management – see below), leading most of the international credit rating agencies to downgrade the senior debt ratings of some of the trust banks. Despite these problems and the loss of business resulting from the numerous stock market scandals (see ch. 6, note 46), however, the trust banks' capital ratios are holding up comparatively well (see Part II), and many hope the opportunities afforded by commodity funds management, first sanctioned in 1991, will go some way to offsetting their declining fortunes. (For a more detailed discussion of the future of trust banks, see Kinya, 1991.)

Finance for small and medium-sized companies is the domain of a third group of specialized banks. This group comprises the *sogo* banks, the *shinkin* banks (including the *Zenshinren* Bank), the labour banks (including the *Rokinren* Bank), and the *Shokochukin* Bank. The *sogo* banks, in fact, no longer exist as a distinct class of specialized intermediary as they had all converted to ordinary bank status by the end of 1989 in accordance with the Law Concerning Amalgamation and Conversion of Financial Institutions of 1968. Given their continuing focus on the small to medium-sized company sector, however, it is legitimate to single out the ex-*sogo*s for special attention, at least for the immediate term, before their former identifying role completely vanishes.

The *sogo* banks emerged from Japan's traditional mutual loan company sector and used to be regulated according to the *Sogo* Bank Law of 1951. This Law was frequently amended to allow them to diversify their activities outside their traditional area of mutual instalment savings (*kakekin*) and lending business and they soon came to resemble ordinary banks, particularly regional banks, in their style of operation, despite the restrictions aimed at confining activities to their specialized role of servicing the small to medium-sized company sector. Once the opportunity to escape from those remaining onerous restrictions (for example, restrictions, in principle, on the make-up of their customer base) presented itself in February 1989, however, the majority (52 of the 68-strong membership) immediately seized upon it and converted to ordinary bank status, the remainder following by the end of the year. The move was also seen as a means of improving their image in the market-place, the majority believing that they were previously perceived by the general public as second-rate institutions. Accordingly, they hoped to be able to reduce funding costs and broaden their funding base, as well as their range of business activities, following conversion and to attract a more highly qualified workforce.

In spite of these benefits, however, conversion has not solved all of the sector's problems. Although the restrictions may have been eased, the competition has certainly not waned. Already, it is clear that the city and regional banks are making significant inroads into the ex-*sogo*s' loan customer base; and the liberalization of the interest rates payable on small deposits is putting increasing pressure on their margins as they strive to retain their funding base. Unable to achieve the economies of scale and scope of the larger city banks and possessing only a limited distribution network of branches they, like other small banks, are not ideally placed for the deregulated environment of the future.

This state of affairs has already led to significant and accelerating rationalization within another group of small intermediaries, the *shinkin* banks, although combined pre-tax profits for the financial year to end-March 1991 actually rose by 16.5 per cent, largely as a result of the influx of small companies turned away by the city banks. And in March 1991 Tokai Bank, a city bank, took over Sanwa Shinkin Bank after the latter's survival became threatened by its over-exposure to the property and stock market sectors of the economy. This is likely to herald further takeovers and mergers within the sector, although an alternative open to some *shinkin*s, judging by the tie-up agreed between the largest city bank Dai-Ichi Kangyo and the Jonan Shinkin Bank, the country's biggest community bank, may be a link-up with a larger commercial bank. The advantage for the latter, as in the tie-up cited above, is likely to lie in a cost-effective extension of regional penetration.

The *shinkin* banks, operating in accordance with the 1951 *Shinkin* Bank Law (as last revised in 1981), are non-profit-making co-operatives with a strong local bias. Their membership comprises local residents and small to medium-sized companies (that is, those with a capitalization of up to Y400 million and employing up to 300 staff), and the minimum subscription per member is fixed by law. Their business comprises the taking of deposits and instalment savings from both members and non-members, lending and discounting bills for members, as well as effecting funds transfers and engaging in foreign exchange operations. The amount of lending to non-members which they can undertake is limited to 20 per cent of their total lending (excluding lending to financial institutions), and a single loan limit of 20 per cent of net worth (or Y800 million, whichever is smaller) applies. They are also allowed to undertake certain ancillary operations, the most important of which are securities-related.

Each *shinkin* bank is a member of the *Zenshinren* Bank which acts as the national federation of *shinkin* banks. As stipulated in Article 54 of the *Shinkin* Bank Law, this bank may engage in: deposit-taking, lending and funds transfer for its members; deposit-taking and lending with non-members, as permitted by the MOF; deposit-taking for national and regional government bodies and other non-profit-making organizations; and, as ancillary business, securities-related activities and agency services for public financial institutions. Since 1981, the *Zenshinren* Bank has also been allowed to undertake foreign exchange operations and to accept short-term surplus funds from its members. Like its members it, too, is subject to loan exposure rules – loans to one borrower may not exceed 25 per cent of net worth, with a lower limit of 20 per cent applying if the borrower is a non-member.

The final group of specialist bank institutions (that is, with the term 'bank' used in their title) serving the small to medium-sized company sector in Japan are the *labour banks*. These institutions operate along co-operative lines in accordance with the Labour Bank Law of 1953. Their raison d'être is to raise the living standards of labourers by promoting the activities of bodies such as labour unions and consumer co-operatives. They are relatively unsophisticated intermediaries, mainly involved in deposit-taking, the generation of instalment savings and lending. Ceilings are placed on the extent to which they can fund themselves from outside their membership (20 per cent of total deposits) and on the amount of their lending to non-members (20 per cent of total loans, excluding loans to financial institutions). Surplus funds are usually lent to affiliated associations or invested in public corporation bonds.

Like the *shinkin* banks, the labour banks have their own central national organization, the *Rokinren* Bank, which was set up in 1955. Its major activities of deposit-taking and lending mirror those of its member institutions, although it has also developed systems to maximize efficiency in funds transfer and management for the benefit of its members.

The final specialist institution involved in servicing the small to medium-sized company sector in Japan is the *Shokochukin* Bank. Founded in 1936 under the *Shokochukin* Bank Law to provide financial assistance to the unions of small and medium-sized companies and to rectify temporary local fund imbalances between them, the bank is currently involved in lending to and taking deposits from its subscribers, their members and others, including individuals, non-profit-making organizations, government bodies, financial institutions, foreign enterprises and electricity, power and gas companies. Its chief source of funds, however, is debenture issues – it is allowed to raise up to 20 times its net worth through this medium – some of which are underwritten by the government. A revision to the governing law in 1985 also allows them to undertake certain securities-related activities.

The fourth area of operation for the specialist Japanese banks is the servicing of the financial needs of the *agricultural, forestry and fisheries industries*. The most powerful institution operating in this field, and the only one with the term 'bank' included in its title, is the *Norinchukin* Bank. This bank's capital was subscribed by private agricultural, forestry and fishery organizations according to its founding law (the *Norinchukin* Bank Law of 1923), and its funding base comprises deposits (mainly taken from its subscribers, especially agricultural organizations) and the proceeds from debenture issues (limited to 30 times its net worth). In principle, these funds are to be used for the purpose of lending to subscribers, although surplus funds are also lent to non-subscribers that are eligible to subscribe and to a range of other organizations and individuals. Surplus funds are invested in short-term securities, and securities-related (sanctioned under an amendment of the Law in 1981) and money market activities have assumed a greater significance in recent years. Indeed the *Norinchukin* Bank is an important provider of funds to the interbank markets and is the largest institutional investor in the private sector through its securities holdings.

So much then for the private sector banks in Japan; but what of their public sector counterparts?

Public sector banks
In fact, there are just two wholly publicly owned banks operating in Japan today – as explained above, the government also holds stakes in the *Shokochukin* Bank and the *Norinchukin* Bank – the Japan Development Bank and the Export–Import Bank of Japan. Neither, however, is permitted to take deposits as this would breach the prohibition in principle on competing with private-sector institutions. (This has not stopped their share of total intermediation from rising dramatically in recent years, however.) For this reason, it is unnecessary to delve further into their roles and functions as it is the deposit-taking function that gives rise to the systemic interest of regulation, the major focus of attention in this book. (Further information is contained in Suzuki, 1987, pp. 291–4.)

Notes

1. As is explained in Part III (chapter 9), this does not preclude banks from underwriting or trading in public bonds nor from investing in equities and other securities on their own behalf.
2. Until recently there used to be 12 but in April 1990 the Taiyo Kobe Bank merged with the Mitsui Bank to become the second largest city bank – later named the Sakura Bank – after the Dai-Ichi Kangyo Bank. And in April 1991 the Kyowa and Saitama banks merged to form the Kyowa Saitama Bank, which now ranks as the eighth city bank by deposit size.
    The logic behind the first-mentioned merger apparently lay in the complementary nature of the banks' business operations, with Mitsui's strengths lying in corporate finance and overseas activities and Taiyo Kobe's in its domestic retail branch network. The merger was also expected to produce economies of scale and scope and to better position the banks for the deregulated environment of the future in the banking and securities markets both at home and abroad. The second merger can also be viewed as an attempt to secure 'critical mass' with the future very much in mind.
3. Sanwa Research Institute has estimated that full liberalization of interest rates would have reduced the pre-tax profits recorded by city banks in the financial year 1988–9 by 18 per cent. For the other banks, more heavily dependent on retail deposits, the situation would have been much worse, with estimates of the fall in pre-tax profits for the regional and *shinkin* banks coming out at 56 per cent and 70 per cent respectively (the figures for small credit co-operatives and agricultural co-operatives were worse still).
4. On 1 August 1992 the government announced an emergency package of measures aimed at supporting the beleaguered banking system, which was suffering from the combined effects of an enormous bad debt burden, declining profitability and inadequate capital. The measures formed part of the government's larger emergency economic package announced on 28 August 1992 and represented the first public acknowledgement that the banking sector was facing serious difficulties.

The measures announced embraced, *inter alia*, the following: (a) exhortation to banks not to sell their stock holdings in order to realize capital gains in advance of publication of interim profits at the end of September; (b) as a *quid pro quo* for toeing the MOF line set out in (a), banks would be spared from having to comply with accounting requirements relating to the setting aside of provisions against unrealized losses on securities holdings and the reporting of such valuation losses in the profit and loss account; (c) exhortation to banks to ease their internal restrictions on real estate lending; (d) the lifting of rules limiting the distribution of dividends to 40 per cent of net profits (this would allow them to maintain payment levels without the necessity of realizing capital gains on securities holdings); (e) enhancing the banks' ability to meet the BIS capital adequacy requirements without curtailing lending growth by sanctioning new forms of Tier 2 capital (e.g., perpetual subordinated loans, perpetual FRNs and convertible bonds with mandatory conversion) and new forms of securitization; and (f) assistance, including tax incentives, in the orderly disposal of the banking industry's problem loans.

These measures were subsequently reaffirmed in the economic rescue package announced later in the month, which also committed the government to drawing up by the end of 1992 schemes to help the banks remove bad debts from their books. Direct benefits to the banking industry would also derive from the government's plans to step up the level of public-sector investment in the local stock market, which should help raise the value of the banks' share portfolios; and indirect assistance should be forthcoming from the stimulus to bank profits provided by the higher economic growth planned for. It was also confirmed that, despite the possible 'moral hazard' created, public funds would be used to help the banks dispose of their non-performing loans. In the interim, however, the banks are proceeding with a plan to establish a joint body which would purchase from them property (and, possibly, non-performing property loans) held as collateral against non-performing loans.

5.   For example, in June 1990 the Joyo Bank secured agreements with Nikko Securities, Mitsubishi Trust and Banking, Nippon Fire and Marine, and Daihyaku Mutual Life (all of them shareholders in the bank) to market the bank's customer services. The bank's partners, in turn, were seeking to establish a presence in northern Tokyo through the arrangement.

6.   That is, special investment trusts, managed only by the trust banks, which represent funds which companies wish to invest in the stock market. Tax incentives induce companies to invest such funds through this medium.

7.   Since July 1986 the trust banks have been allowed to invest up to 3 per cent (the previous limit was 1 per cent) of their loan assets in foreign bonds and, since August 1986, to invest up to 30 per cent (the previous limit was 25 per cent) of their pension fund assets in foreign-currency-denominated securities.

References

Federation of Bankers Associations of Japan (1989), *The Banking System in Japan* (Tokyo: FBAJ).

Kawada, H. (1991), 'City banks' comprehensive financial strategy', in *Japan's Financial Markets* (Tokyo: Foundation for Advanced Information and Research (FAIR)), pp. 352–64.

Kinya, N. (1991), 'Future of trust banks', in *Japan's Financial Markets* (Tokyo: FAIR), pp. 378–88.

Suzuki, Y. (ed.) (1987), *The Japanese Financial System* (Oxford: Oxford University Press).

Watanabe, T. (1991), 'Financial deregulation and the long-term credit banks' response to it', in *Japan's Financial Markets* (Tokyo: FAIR), pp. 365–77.

PART II

THE CURRENT REGULATORY AND SUPERVISORY FRAMEWORKS

4 Bank regulation and supervision in the UK

THE CURRENT REGULATORY AND SUPERVISORY FRAMEWORK

Regulations employed for monetary policy purposes

The demise of direct controls

The dismantling of the post-Second World War panoply of direct controls used to support official UK monetary policy is charted in Exhibit 4.1. As can be seen, since the abolition of hire-purchase terms control in July 1982 the UK authorities have managed to make do without any form of direct control (apart from the occasional use of an *administered* discount rate that is,

Exhibit 4.1   The dismantling of monetary controls in the UK

Date effective	Reform measure
October 1971	Under the *Competition and Credit Control* regime (see Hall, 1983, chs 1–4) the following reforms were implemented: • the clearing banks' *interest rate cartel* was abolished; • the 8 per cent *cash ratio* and the 28 per cent *minimum liquid assets ratio*, both imposed on clearing banks alone, were replaced by a $12^1/_2$ per cent *minimum reserve assets ratio* to be applied to clearing banks, secondary banks and 'large'[a] finance houses; • a $1^1/_2$ per cent *minimum cash ratio* was imposed upon the clearing banks; • *lending ceilings* were abolished; • *hire-purchase terms control* was abolished.
October 1972	Bank Rate, the Bank of England's traditional rediscount rate, was replaced by a market-determined *minimum lending rate* (MLR).
September 1973	An *interest rate ceiling* of $9^1/_2$ per cent was imposed on the amount banks could pay on sterling deposits of less than £10,000.

Date effective	Reform measure
December 1973	*Hire-purchase terms control* was reintroduced; and a 'supplementary special deposit scheme' (the *corset*) was introduced for the first time.
February 1975	The $9^{1}/_{2}$ per cent deposit *interest rate ceiling* was removed. The *corset* was taken off.
November 1976	The *corset* was reimposed.
August 1977	The *corset* was taken off again.
May 1978	*MLR* was set by administrative action, that is, the market-related formula was overriden.
June 1978	The *corset* was re-imposed again.
October 1979	*Exchange control* was abolished.
June 1980	The *corset* was finally abolished.
August 1981	A new monetary control regime was introduced under which: • the *minimum cash ratio* and minimum *reserve assets ratio* were abolished; • *MLR* was suspended; • a $^{1}/_{2}$ per cent[b] of 'eligible liabilities' *non-operational cash ratio requirement*[c] was imposed on all monetary sector institutions with liabilities averaging at least £10 million over a selected period.
July 1982	*Hire-purchase terms control* was finally abolished.
January 1985	*MLR* reappeared for one day.
September 1992	*MLR* reappeared again.[d]

Notes

[a]   That is, those with deposits totalling at least £5 million. For these institutions, the minimum reserve assets ratio requirement was set at 10 per cent.

[b]   The current level is 0.4 per cent.

[c]   It is important to note that this ratio requirement plays no part in the conduct of policy. It is simply a device for securing interest free loans to the Bank of England which can be used to defray its running costs.

[d]   As the UK authorities fought, unsuccessfully, to keep sterling within the Exchange Rate Mechanism of the European Monetary System.

Source: Hall, 1983, ch. 4, Table 4.2; Hall, 1987, ch. 2, Table 2.5.

Minimum Lending Rate). This reflects an acknowledgment of the costs (competitive distortions created, misallocation of resources and so on) associated with their usage and a recognition of their spurious benefits (for example, they may assist in the attainment of monetary targets but only by destroying the statistical linkage between such targets and the ultimate goals of policy, such as those for inflation, nominal income growth and son on). (For a detailed appraisal of these issues, see Hall, 1983, chs 4, 5 and 7; and Hall, 1991.) The special deposits instrument, however, which is a device for freezing banks' excess cash reserves,[1] is retained within the monetary authorities' armoury, although it remains in abeyance.

The Bank's ability to conduct policy without prescribing a reserve ratio requirement (the fulcrum for open market operations is provided by the balances held *voluntarily* by the clearing banks at the Bank – see Hall, 1983, ch. 9) is facilitated by the convention requiring the clearing banks to inform the Bank, on a daily basis, of their target clearing balances. This enables the Bank, through its money market operations (see Bank of England, 1988), to determine the desired level and structure of short-term[2] interest rates in a predictable fashion.

The future

Given the UK's continued membership of the European Economic Community, which limits the circumstances in which exchange controls may be reintroduced, it is difficult to conceive of a scenario, particularly under the present administration, where the clock might be turned back in respect of the use of direct controls to support monetary policy (see Llewellyn and Holmes, 1992). The most that is likely to happen is continued occasional *ad hoc* use of an *administered* discount rate plus, perhaps, the occasional use of moral suasion to influence the direction of bank credit, probably for prudential rather than economic reasons.

Prudential regulation and supervision

The Bank of England's supervisory style and approach

The Bank's supervisory philosophy, as pertaining to the banking sector, was once described by a Head of Banking Supervision in the early 1970s as 'personal, participative, progressive and flexible' (Cooke, 1986). Since that time, the Bank has sought to preserve this approach in the face of emerging statutory frameworks (in the guise of the 'home grown' 1979 and 1987 Banking Acts and legislative provisions associated with the EC's single market programme – Hall, 1989, ch. 9), and ever-increasing litigiousness and competition. While this has not always proved easy, the Bank still prides itself on its flexible approach, which is accommodated by the 1987 Banking

Act because it leaves the Bank with plenty of scope in the interpretation and implementation of the legislative provisions, most especially in the setting of prudential requirements and in carrying out day-to-day supervisory activities (Quinn, 1991). Accordingly, moral suasion retains its place alongside the rule of law, and prudential requirements, which are promulgated following extensive consultation with representatives of the banking industry, are tailored to the needs of individual banks. Such an approach is still espoused as the most cost-effective approach because it is believed to address the issues (among others) of cost, effectiveness, competitive equity and adaptability in an optimal manner (see Hall, 1991, for a critique). Significant changes, however, in both form and substance, are due for implementation in the wake of the *post mortem* on the Bank of Credit and Commerce International affair (see below).

Supervision itself centres on the management interview – the inspection-based approach adopted in the US and elsewhere is eschewed – at which the Bank's analysis of the vast amount of statistical information collected beforehand through the medium of prudential returns serves as a starting point for discussions. Other issues likely to be discussed are the bank's future business plans and profitability forecasts and the reporting accountants' (and possibly auditors') reports on accounting procedures, the keeping of records, internal control systems and so on. Making full use of quantitative analytical techniques where relevant (for example, in the assessment of capital and liquidity adequacy and the adequacy of provisions against third world debt – see below), subjective evaluations as to the adequacy of prudential safeguards on a variety of fronts are eventually produced. These evaluations also embrace judgements on management competence and expertise. Where deficiencies have been identified, advice will be given on the form and duration of the remedial action to be taken. Close monitoring would then ensue to ensure compliance with the Bank's requests in the time elapsing before the next interview.

Apart from relying upon the work of auditors and reporting accountants (in practice, the former act in the latter capacity also), whose supervisory roles have been extended considerably in recent years, and the management interviews, the Bank is also able to draw upon the combined wisdom and expertise of its own staff and that of the Board of Banking Supervision (see Hall, 1989, ch. 5) to enhance the effectiveness of its supervision. It also has close working relationships with other supervisory bodies, both domestic and foreign, which can on occasions be used to good advantage.

All of these resources and techniques are employed to secure the Bank's prudential objectives, which comprise the protection of depositors' (existing and potential) interests, as enshrined in the Banking Act 1987, and the preservation of financial stability.

The regulatory and supervisory framework[3]

Authorization procedures   In order to secure authorization to act as a bank in the UK an institution has to satisfy the Bank that it meets the minimum criteria for authorization set out in Schedule 3 of the Banking Act 1987. These minimum criteria comprise the following: (i) a requirement for a bank to conduct its business in a 'prudent manner' (which involves the institution, *inter alia*, in satisfying the Bank that it has 'adequate' capital, liquidity and provisions, that it maintains 'adequate' accounting and other records and adequate systems for controlling its business and records, that it generally behaves in a prudent manner, and that it is effectively directed by at least two individuals); (ii) a requirement relating to the composition of the board of directors; (iii) a requirement for the business to be carried out with 'integrity and skill'; (iv) a requirement for the institution to have minimum net assets of £1 million at the time of authorization;[4] and (v) a requirement for directors, controllers and managers to be 'fit and proper' persons.

As required under Section 16 of the Banking Act 1987, the Bank has published (Bank of England, 1988c)[5] a statement of the principles it uses in interpreting the minimum authorization criteria (and, indeed, the grounds for revocation (or restriction) specified in Section 11). This greatly assists applicants in their attempts to ensure compliance with the criteria.

Capital adequacy assessment   The Bank has assessed the capital adequacy of UK-incorporated banks on a risk-based basis since 1980. The G10 agreement on the measurement and assessment of capital adequacy was implemented in full at the end of June 1989, and the modifications necessitated by compliance with the EC's 'Own Funds' (EC, 1989a) and 'Solvency Ratio' (EC, 1989c) Directives were adopted in January 1991 (see Chapter 8 for full details). The G10 approach, as modified for compliance with EC legislation, is not however the sole focus of attention.

In assessing capital adequacy, the Bank seeks to take account of *all* the possible risks of loss to which an institution may be exposed. These embrace *credit risk, foreign exchange risk, interest rate risk, position risk, operational risk, concentration risk* and *contagion risk*. As a result, the Bank takes account of an institution's on- and off-balance-sheet activities, as well as the nature of its relationships with group and other connected parties. Risk analysis is undertaken on both a consolidated and unconsolidated basis, the former to capture exposures arising in subsidiaries and other connected companies and the latter to determine whether there is an appropriate distribution of capital within the group. Some of the risks are subject to formal measurement (that is, credit risk and foreign exchange risk); and special reporting arrangements are deployed to facilitate the monitoring of other risks (such as those relating to 'large exposures' (see below) in connection with the monitoring of concentration risk).

At the end of the day, the Bank's main objective is to ensure that each and every bank is able to identify and manage each of the risks to which it is exposed; the Bank's formal capital requirement – in the shape of an individually-agreed 'trigger' risk asset ratio (see Chapter 8) – reflects the Bank's overall subjective evaluation as to the nature and size of a bank's exposure to risk and the ability of its management to handle this risk. The latter part of the assessment exercise requires the Bank to assess the expertise, experience and track record of an institution's management, its internal control and accounting systems, its future business plans, its size and position in the chosen markets and any other factors (such as future business prospects) which the Bank may deem relevant.

Because 'trigger' risk asset ratios are 'agreed' with senior management on an individual basis, the diversity of business mix and other characteristics can be accommodated. The eschewal of 'norms', however, does not mean that 'standardization' does not take place; 'peer group assessment' ensures that, to a degree, it does. Nevertheless, the Bank's approach is conducive to maximizing its flexibility of operation and hence to minimizing competitive distortions. (For details of the actual capital ratios recently run by the UK clearing banks, see Exhibit 4.2.)

Exhibit 4.2   Capital ratios for UK Clearing banks, 1989–91

	Capital ratios (%)					
	End 1989		End 1990		End 1991	
	Risk asset ratio	Tier 1 ratio	Risk asset ratio	Tier 1 ratio	Risk asset ratio	Tier 1 ratio
Barclays Bank	8.3	5.7	9.0	5.8	8.7	5.9
Lloyds Bank	7.4	4.4	8.5	5.2	9.7	6.2
Midland Bank	10.0	5.4	9.8	5.4	10.3	5.5
National Westminster Bank	9.1	5.2	9.1	5.3	9.6	5.5

Source: Annual Reports.

Liquidity adequacy assessment The Bank's current approach on this front is still based on the principles established in July 1982 (Bank of England, 1982).[6] Its main concern is with funding rather than interest rate risk (see Hall, 1988, pp. 56–60) and to this end it seeks to ensure that each bank is able to meet its commitments as they fall due, on both sides of the balance sheet. To achieve this objective, the Bank is concerned to ensure that a 'prudent' mix of liquidity sources – cash, readily liquefiable assets, asset maturity monies, retail deposits, wholesale deposits and other borrowing sources – is adopted and that this mix is appropriate to the business engaged in by the bank. This necessitates frequent reappraisal of the bank's position. Additionally, the Bank will be keen to ensure that appropriate maturity-matching policies are adopted, and that the bank has in place internal control and monitoring systems which allow management to ensure that such policies are pursued on a continuing basis.

As in the assessment of capital adequacy, a judgement on the 'quality' of management (for example, their ability to manage risk using derivatives) features in the equation; and the individual characteristics of the banking firm are fully accommodated in the assessment exercise.

Although the overall evaluation of liquidity adequacy is necessarily subjective, an important component of the assessment process is the analysis of the maturity transformation undertaken by the bank. Although the overall level of maturity transformation is monitored by the Bank it is not subject to a formal requirement; that undertaken in the period up to one year is, however.

The requirement, in the form of an agreed guideline, relates to the bank's 'net cumulative mismatched position' (Bank of England, 1982), which represents the accumulation of the 'net mismatch positions' (that is, liabilities minus assets) recorded in the sub-periods from sight to eight days, eight days to one month, one month to three months, three months to six months and six months to one year. Assets and liabilities are slotted into the maturity ladder according to a pre-specified set of rules;[7] and sterling and currency mismatches are usually considered alongside the combined mismatch figure. Although the guidelines, which are agreed individually with a bank's senior management and monitored continuously by the Bank, relate only to the cumulative net mismatch positions up to one year, particular attention is also devoted to the period up to one month.

Liquidity adequacy is usually monitored on a consolidated basis for those UK-incorporated banks whose affiliates operate mainly in the UK.[8] For those which operate extensively overseas, either through branches or affiliates, the Bank is likely to monitor closely the bank's arrangements for monitoring and controlling its worldwide liquidity needs. Finally, in respect of the UK branching operations of overseas banks, the Bank is likely to monitor closely the *sterling* liquidity position, taking due account of the relationship between the branch and its head office and of its exposure to 'country risk' (see Bank of England, 1984b, p. 238).

Measures to limit exchange rate risk   The approach adopted by the Bank towards the assessment of a bank's foreign exchange position risk is set out in its papers of April 1981 and April 1984 (Bank of England, 1981 and 1984a). In assessing such exposures, which are considered in relation to the other risks incurred by the institution and to its capital base, the Bank takes account of *all* exposures arising from uncovered foreign currency positions including, since April 1984, those resulting from the writing of options business.[9] Net positions in single currencies, including sterling, are considered alongside the aggregate net position in all currencies.

While acknowledging that a bank's management has primary responsibility for controlling foreign currency exposures, the Bank nevertheless will agree, on an individual basis, 'dealing position'[10] guidelines with each bank. It will also seek to ensure that each bank's internal controls allow for effective and continuous monitoring of exposures so as to ensure that the guidelines are not breached. The management factor also features in the assessment process as the agreed guidelines are designed to accommodate not only the business characteristics of a bank but also its relative expertise in managing foreign currency exposures.

Typically, two guidelines are agreed with each bank: one relating to exposures in individual currencies and one covering the aggregate level of exposure incurred. UK-incorporated banks which are experienced in foreign exchange operations can expect to face the following guidelines: (i) a limit on the net 'open'[11] dealing position in any one currency of 10 per cent of the 'adjusted capital base';[12] and (ii) a limit on the net 'short' open dealing positions (covering both spot and forward transactions)[13] of all currencies taken together of 15 per cent of the adjusted capital base.

The guidelines apply to the domestic and overseas branching operations of all UK banks. Their subsidiaries are monitored on a separate basis with a view to eventually allowing for a consolidated assessment for capital adequacy purposes of banks' foreign currency exposures. In line with the revised Basle Concordat (see Hall, 1989, ch. 3), the foreign currency operations of the UK branches of overseas banks will also be monitored; and guidelines, in the form of absolute limits on exposure, will be agreed in those instances where the Bank is unhappy about the internal controls administered by the branches themselves, or by their head offices, or is otherwise concerned with the monitoring arrangements adopted by the banks' home supervisory authorities.

Measures to limit concentration risk   As a direct response to the Johnson Matthey Bankers débâcle (see Hall, 1987(b)), the Banking Act 1987 requires all UK-incorporated banks and banking groups to notify the Bank of any exposure[14] to a single non-bank party or group of 'closely related' non-bank parties which exceeds 10 per cent of the bank's 'adjusted capital base'.[15] In addition, institutions are required to provide the Bank with prior notice of proposed transactions which would raise exposure to over 25 per cent of the adjusted capital base.

As outlined in the Bank's paper on the subject (Bank of England, 1987b), there is a presumption that such exposures should not normally exceed 10 per cent of the adjusted capital base, and that only in exceptional circumstances[16] should exposures exceed 25 per cent of the adjusted capital base. It should be appreciated, however, that *no* statutory limits currently apply;[17] the only statutory element of control relates to the reporting requirements.

Institutions running a number of exposures in excess of 10 per cent of the adjusted capital base or any in excess of the 25 per cent threshold will usually be obliged to hold additional capital, the amount depending on the standing of the borrower, the nature of the bank's relationship with the borrower, the nature and extent of security taken against the exposure, the bank's expertise in the particular type of lending, and the number of such exposures, their individual size and nature.

The notification requirements formally apply only to UK-incorporated banks, although similar policies are likely to be adopted by the Bank in respect of the UK branches of overseas banks. For UK subsidiaries of overseas banks, the Bank will agree with the parent bank supervisor 'appropriate' levels of exposure in the light of the extent of consolidated supervision exercised by the latter authority. Finally, the overseas subsidiaries of UK banks are expected to conform to local regulatory requirements although the Bank, as part of its consolidated supervision, will want to identify those which run significant exposures.

Assessment of the adequacy of provisions   In assessing the adequacy of its provisions (against bad and doubtful debts, expected losses on contingents and tax liabilities), a bank is, of course, bound by the Companies Act 1985 requirements apart from any requirements specified by the Bank. The latter, however, are significant, not least because the maintenance of adequate provisions is part of the 'prudent conduct' criterion for authorization.

Apart from requiring banks to observe the accounting standards embodied in the *Statements of Standard Accounting Practice* when valuing assets and liabilities and determining provisions, the Bank has indicated how it attempts to assess the adequacy of a bank's provisions for the purposes of determining whether a bank fulfils the 'prudent conduct' criterion. Additionally, it gives guidance, via a matrix, as to how a bank should determine the *minimum* level of provisions appropriate for exposures to third world countries. These issues will now be addressed in turn.

The Bank's general approach to the assessment of the adequacy of provisions is spelt out in its *Statement of Principles* (Bank of England, 1988c, p. 7). It has regard to a bank's 'provisioning policy, including the methods and systems for monitoring the recoverability of loans,[18] the frequency with which provisions are reviewed, the policy and practices for the taking and valuation of security and the extent to which valuation exceeds the balance-sheet value of the secured loans'.

In contrast to this subjective approach, the Bank's line on the adequacy of provisions against sovereign and other country risk exposures is more objective. Here, the Bank has devised a formal matrix to assist banks in determining the *minimum* levels of provisions which should be held against such exposures.

The matrix (see Bank of England, 1990) identifies a range of factors (16 in all) which influence the likelihood of partial or total failure to repay. The factors are split into three groups: those which provide evidence of a borrower's inability or unwillingness to meet its debt service obligations, whether at the due date or thereafter; those which provide evidence of a borrower's current debt service problems; and those, economic or other, which provide an indication of likely future debt repayment difficulties. The factors are also weighted to reflect their relative significance in the determination of the appropriate levels of provisions to be held against country risk exposures. Each country to which a bank is exposed is then 'scored' by simply summing the individual scores for each factor. The country scores, in turn, are to be used to determine the appropriate (minimum) levels of provisions which should be maintained, on a moving average basis (for further details on how the scores translate into provisioning levels, see Bank of England, 1990, p. 4). The provisioning percentages yielded by application of the matrix are typically to be applied against all claims on a country unless the Bank can be satisfied that a particular claim or class of claims will be repaid in full.

Apart from the relevance of the matrix to the Bank's supervisory process, it plays an important role in a bank's discussions with its auditors and the Inland Revenue concerning its accounts and tax liabilities respectively.

Measures to limit country risk   Country risk refers to the risks involved in cross-border lending, of which there are two main kinds: 'sovereign risk' and 'transfer risk'. The former is the risk that foreign governments will be either unable or unwilling to service their debts; while the latter is the risk that a government willing to repay its debt may be unable to do so because of a lack of foreign exchange necessary to allow it to discharge its debt service obligations

The Bank's approach to the subject of country risk is set out in Bank of England (1984b). While acknowledging that the primary responsibility for measuring, assessing and controlling country risks resides with a bank's management, the Bank nevertheless will seek to ensure that suitable risk assessment systems are in place and that adequate resources are devoted to the task; that adequate systems for weighing the risks and controlling exposures through the setting of limits are in place; and that these limits are appropriate and continuously monitored for compliance. As ever, an assessment of management will also feature in the overall evaluation of the adequacy of a bank's assessment and control procedures.

Given the importance of a bank's exposure to country risk for its overall soundness, the Bank will consider such exposures in relation to the bank's capital and provisions.[19] In general, the larger the bank's exposure to country risk and the smaller its provisions, the greater will be the bank's 'trigger' risk asset ratio.

Finance industry 'support'   Apart from its traditional rediscount facility, the Bank has, in the past, called upon the banking community (and especially the major UK clearing banks) to limit any feared spread of contagion. Its preference is for the formation of 'lifeboats', whereby the major banks, creditors and the Bank itself contribute to a fund which can then be used to effect the rescue of ailing yet fundamentally sound institutions. Support has not, as yet, been extended beyond the banking sector, although a serious crisis in some of the other sectors of the financial services industry, such as the securities, insurance or building society sectors, would be likely to necessitate such a shift in policy because of the substantial systemic risks associated with the financial operations currently conducted in such markets. The emergence of financial conglomerates has exacerbated the problems facing the Bank in this respect.

The most recent example of such a bail out was the rescue of Johnson Matthey Bankers in 1984 (see Hall, 1987b and 1987c). And before this, in the early 1970s, a more extensive lifeboat support operation was mounted to stem the loss of confidence associated with the secondary banking crisis (see Reid, 1982).

Merger restrictions   Apart from satisfying European Community law,[20] potential merger parties may also have to allay the anxieties of the Monopolies and Mergers Commission and, if there are competitive concerns, the Office of Fair Trading. The Office of Fair Trading is responsible for advising the Trade Secretary on whether or not proposed mergers or bids (Lloyds Bank's bid for Midland Bank was referred to the Monopolies and Mergers Commission in May 1992) should be so referred on competition grounds.

'Ownership' controls Apart from the Monopolies and Mergers Commission and the Office of Fair Trading, both HM Treasury and the Bank have powers enabling them to influence the ownership and control of UK-incorporated banks. In addition, informal guidelines, practices and 'understandings' between the Bank and the relevant government departments (for example, the Department of Trade and Industry in respect of links with insurance companies) govern the 'permissible' degree of interlocking ownership with non-bank financial intermediaries. (EC requirements, as laid down in the proposed Takeovers Directive – see Berger, 1991 – will also govern the conduct of takeovers once the Directive is implemented.)

The Bank's powers in this respect derive from the Banking Act 1987 which gives the Bank considerable discretion in determining who may or may not control a UK-registered bank. Prospective 'shareholder controllers',[21] for example, have to satisfy the Bank that they meet the 'fit and proper' criterion which entails, *inter alia*, a consideration of the likely degree of influence the person will bring to bear on the conduct of the institution's affairs and whether the financial position, reputation or conduct of the person is likely to damage the institution through contagion.[22] Prospective 'indirect controllers' also have to meet requirements for fitness and probity; the greater the influence exerted on the authorized institution the higher the threshold will be for the fulfilment of the criterion.[23]

Once over the 'fit and proper' hurdle, prospective shareholder controllers are well on their way to achieving this status unless they go for full control, when both the Office of Fair Trading and the Monopolies and Mergers Commission may move to block the move, the former on competitive grounds and the latter on 'national interest' grounds, the basis of the rejection of the Hong Kong and Shanghai Banking Corporation's bid for the Royal Bank of Scotland in 1982 (HMSO, 1982).[24] There remains, however, one remaining possible impediment to their securing their objective: the reciprocity clause inserted into the Banking Act 1987 to allow the Bank, on the direction of the Treasury, to block any moves made by institutions from a country which does not give reciprocal rights to UK residents and firms. The circumstances in which the Treasury would so act are unclear, however.

The Bank's view of stakebuilding by foreign financial concerns in the UK banking sector – currently acquisitions of stakes of over 5 per cent have to be notified to the Bank, and the Bank's prior consent has to be obtained by those wishing to acquire 15 per cent or more of a bank's voting power[25] – is that while it is not in principle opposed to such moves[26] it nevertheless would withhold approval unless a number of provisos were met (see Bank of

England, 1987c). These provisos would appear to embrace the following: (i) that all shareholders and indirect controllers satisfy its 'fit and proper' test; (ii) that the Bank is satisfied as to the nature and scope of the supervision exercised by the home authority and has received adequate assurances from the latter as to the institution's soundness; (iii) that such moves are not designed to put the banks 'into play' nor to lead to the break-up of the bank or group; (iv) that developments do not proceed to the point where a strong and continuing British presence in the UK banking system is threatened; and (v) that UK institutions enjoy, or are likely to enjoy in the near future, reciprocal rights of action in the predators' own countries.

While stakebuilding by foreign *financial* concerns is thus accepted in principle by the Bank, such manoeuvres by non-financial concerns, domestic[27] or foreign, are likely to receive a less than enthusiastic response. This is because of the Bank's overriding concern to avoid the conflicts of interest that are likely to ensue and the risks and consequences (for example, for 'lender of last resort' policy) of contagion inherent in such moves. In this sense, the UK approach is more akin to that adopted in the USA and Japan than in Germany, in that a degree of functional separation between commerce and 'banking' is thought desirable.[28]

Deposit protection arrangements   Apart from complying with various forms of consumer protection legislation,[29] UK-authorized institutions (including the foreign contingent since 1987) also have to contribute to a fund which provides compensation to depositors if institutions default. Under the statutory Deposit Protection Scheme administered by the Deposit Protection Board, which is chaired by the Governor of the Bank of England, authorized institutions contribute periodically to a freestanding fund according to the size of their sterling deposit bases. The minimum contribution is currently £30,000 and the maximum £300,000. Supplementary arrangements exist for raising such further and special contributions as prove necessary, although calls on institutions remain subject to a statutory limit of 0.3 per cent of their sterling deposit bases.

Under the scheme, (non-bank) depositors with sterling-denominated deposits of an initial term of less than five years to maturity receive protection to the tune of 75 per cent of the first £20,000 of such deposits per authorized institution.

The future

UK banking supervision post-BCCI
Apart from accommodating recent EC law (most notably that associated with the implementation of the 'single market' programme in financial ser-

vices, the bulk of which took effect on 1 January 1993 – see Hall, 1992a, Part II), the Banking Act 1987 is also due for amendment to take account of those changes in supervisory practice, recommended by Lord Justice Bingham in the light of the Bank of Credit and Commerce International (BCCI) affair, which require legislative action. The full BCCI story is told in some detail in Lord Justice Bingham's report (HMSO, 1992b) and need not detain us

Exhibit 4.3   A summary of Lord Justice Bingham's recommendations for reform of UK banking supervisory arrangements

---

- The Bank should develop a high degree of alertness and inquisitiveness in its supervisory staff.
- The Bank should improve its internal communications.
- The Bank should ensure that the Board of Banking Supervision is better informed.
- The Bank should proceed with its plans to enhance the efficacy of its investigation function through the establishment of a Special Investigations Unit within the Banking Supervision Division.
- The Bank should proceed with its plans to strengthen the Banking Supervision Division's legal unit.
- The Bank should, if necessary, be given an explicit power to refuse or revoke authorization on the grounds that the applicant or bank cannot be effectively supervised.
- The Bank should, if necessary, be given an explicit power to require banks to locate their effective head office in the country of incorporation.
- A duty should be imposed on auditors of financial institutions to report suspicions of fraud or malpractice to the relevant supervisory authority.
- There should be a review of the circumstances in which public bodies – regulators and others – may and should pass information to each other about a bank's activities.
- All 'small' banks should be subject to a full-scope review by reporting accountants on an annual basis.
- The Bank should give consideration to the imposition of a specific duty on a bank's management to disclose and provide information on any organization under common control.
- The Bank should be given the power to require separate audits for the UK branches of non-EC banks.
- All companies in a banking group should have the same accounting dates.

Source: HMSO, 1992b.

longer here, but it is important to appreciate the significance of his recommendations, which were accepted in full by both the government and the Bank, for reform of domestic supervisory practice.[30] The recommendations are thus summarized in Exhibit 4.3 and a summary of the Bank's response is presented in Exhibit 4.4.

Exhibit 4.4 The Bank of England's response to the Bingham Report

---

To implement the Bingham Report Recommendations:

- The Bank is creating a new Special Investigations Unit, to be headed by Ian Watt FCA, who joins the Bank from KPMG Peat Marwick. This will be specifically responsible for pursuing any indication of fraud or malpractice affecting banks.
- The Bank will extend its on-site examination of banks in the UK.
- The Bank is creating a new specialized Legal Unit, to be headed by Peter Peddie, formerly a partner in Freshfields.
- The Bank has strengthened systems for internal communication, and for communication with the Treasury.
- The Bank will strengthen procedures for involving the Board of Banking Supervision.
- The Bank will continue to press for adoption of the new minimum standards of supervision by overseas regulators; and the Treasury is taking steps to encourage better exchanges of information with overseas supervisors.
- At the Bank's request, the Treasury will introduce a change in the Banking Act to give the Bank an explicit power to refuse or revoke authorization of banks with group structures that cannot be properly supervised.
- At the Bank's request, the Treasury will introduce a change in the Banking Act to place auditors of banks under a duty to pass relevant information to the Bank of England.
- The Bank will be actively involved in the new machinery announced by the Chancellor to co-ordinate action against fraud.

Source: Bank of England, 1992b.

As is evident from a brief perusal of these exhibits, the Bank has committed itself, *inter alia*, to extending its on-site examination of banks and to strengthening its procedures for communicating internally, with other government departments, with relevant non-regulatory agencies (such as the police, Customs and Excise, the securities services and the National Drugs Investigations Unit)[31] and with the Board of Banking Supervision. Such measures should enhance co-operation and co-ordination of action in future investigations. It is also moving to strengthen its in-house legal and investigations units, and has requested that the Banking Act be amended, first, to impose a *duty* on auditors to pass on suspicions of fraud or malpractice to the Bank; and secondly, to give it powers to refuse or revoke a bank's authorization on the grounds that a group's structure or other factors[32] preclude effective consolidated supervision. The Treasury has acceded to both of the Bank's requests and will seek due amendment of the Banking Act 1987 at the earliest opportunity.[33]

Issues outstanding
While these changes should certainly increase the effectiveness of banking supervision in the UK, at least in terms of increasing the chance of early detection of any future fraud or malpractice, a number of important issues remain to be resolved. The first of these relates to the design of the Deposit Protection Scheme. At the minimum, this should be redesigned to reduce the degree of co-insurance (currently 25 per cent up to the £20,000 cut-off point) asked of the depositor and to raise the basic level of protection given (currently £15,000), which should then be indexed. Additionally, a study on the feasibility of switching to 'risk-related' levies, a system which is due to be operational in the US from the middle of 1994, should be conducted. (For further details, see Hall, 1987d.)

Deposit protection issues aside, the cost effectiveness of supervision might also be improved if the Bank: (i) paid less attention to the use of the 'risk asset ratio' methodology in the assessment of capital adequacy, notwithstanding its duties under EC law; (ii) relied less heavily on the 'lead regulation' principle in discharging its supervisory responsibilities (this may involve a fundamental re-assessment of the merits of 'functional' *vis-à-vis* 'institutional' regulation; and (iii) clarified, at least for its own benefit, the basis on which it is willing to activate its lender of last resort facility and the scope of this part of the safety net.

Notes

1. Calls for special deposits have in the past been expressed as a percentage of 'eligible liabilities' (roughly speaking, sterling deposits with an initial term of up to two years) and involved the banks in depositing such amounts at the Bank of England. Such 'blocked' accounts, however, did receive a market rate of interest (linked to the average discount rate on treasury bills).
2. The focus of policy is usually on the commercial bill rate in the 0 to 14 day maturity band, but, quite frequently the Bank is concerned with bill yields stretching out to the one month to maturity threshold and even beyond that, that is, to the three months to maturity threshold.
3. For a more detailed exposition, see Hall, 1989, Part 2.
4. Under the EC's Second Banking Coordination Directive (EC, 1989c), which took effect on 1 January 1993, a minimum (initial and continuing) capital requirement of ECU 5

million will apply. For EC institutions licensed before 1 January 1993, however, implementation of this requirement may, at the discretion of national authorities, be delayed until end-December 1996.

5. This is to be revised (see below) in the light of the Bank's experience in the supervision of the Bank of Credit and Commerce International.

6. The idea of introducing a formal 'high quality liquidity stock' requirement to ensure liquidity adequacy in 'difficult' trading conditions (Bank of England, 1988b) was eventually abandoned following opposition from foreign banks operating in London.

7. For example, deposits are included according to their *earliest* maturity, although account is taken of the stability and diversification of the deposit base when the guidelines are established; and the marketable assets receive special treatment. The latter are to be placed at the start of the maturity ladder, irrespective of their maturity dates, although account is taken of their varying marketability and susceptibility to price volatility by the application of varying discounts – the more marketable and the less susceptible to price volatility the asset, the *lower* the discount – against the (normally market) value of the assets. The position of other assets in the maturity ladder in dictated by their maturity. (For full details of the rules, see Bank of England, 1982.)

8. Under the *Basle Concordat*, as revised in 1983 (see Hall, 1989, ch. 3), the supervision of liquidity is the *primary* responsibility of *host* supervisory authorities although parent supervisors are given a monitoring role for the group's activities as a whole.

9. For more details, see Hall (1989, ch. 15, n. 31).

10. 'Dealing' positions, which create exposures as a result of normal, day-to-day operations, can be distinguished from 'structural' positions, which create exposures of a longer-term nature. Although structural positions are not considered under the guidelines they are, nevertheless, captured within the Bank's assessment of capital adequacy, which takes account of both dealing and structural positions when deriving 'aggregate foreign currency positions' for inclusion within the risk weight framework (see Chapter 8).

11. That is, the difference between assets and liabilities.

12. As defined for the purpose of computing a bank's risk asset ratio – see Chapter 8.

13. That is, the net foreign currency *liability* positions.

14. Broadly defined as the sum of all claims plus undrawn facilities, contingent liabilities, other counterparty risks and equity holdings. For further details, see Bank of England (1987a) as amended by Bank of England (1987b).

15. Again, as defined for the purpose of calculating a bank's risk asset ratio.

16. The main exceptions are: exposures to other banks with a maturity of up to one year; exposures of up to one year to group financial companies; exposures to overseas central governments; exposures secured by cash or by an OECD guarantee or by British government stock; underwriting exposures incurred by 'experts' (see Bank of England, 1988a); and, in the case of bank subsidiaries, exposures guaranteed by the parent bank. Limits, however, do have to be agreed with the Bank, on an individual basis, for each of these items.

17. Under EC law, however, it is likely that a 25 per cent limit on such exposures will apply from 1 January 1994. This is because the draft Large Exposures Directive includes such a clause, together with requirements relating to the reporting of individual exposures which amount to at least 10 per cent of a credit institution's 'own funds'. All such exposures, when aggregated, would also be subject to an overall limit of 800 per cent of 'own funds'. Exceptions to the limits, however, are provided for; and transitional arrangements will allow for the phasing-in of the requirements where exposures in existence at the time the Directive is adopted are concerned.

18. For example, the monitoring of the financial health of counterparties, their future prospects, the prospects of the markets and geographical areas in which they operate, arrears problems and credit scoring techniques.

19. For the UK branch of an overseas bank, such exposures will also be considered in relation to the liquidity of the branch. Close attention will also be paid to the scale of the

branch's lending to its country of origin and to its dependence on the wholesale money markets for the funding of such lending.

20. The EC's policy on mergers took effect in September 1990. The Mergers Regulation provides for mandatory prior notification of 'qualifying' mergers to the Commission, which will involve a short suspension of the implementation of the merger and a rapid clearance procedure. It also ensures a clear division of responsibility between the Commission on the one hand and Member States on the other – the Commission only deals with mergers with a community-wide dimension. To help clarify this situation, a number of criteria are established to determine the instances in which the Commission would normally become involved. (For further details on this and on the Commission's approach to assessing the merits of prospective mergers in the financial services field – only 'competition' issues are considered – see Donnelly, 1991.)

21. Someone who either alone or with associates is entitled to exercise or control the exercise of the voting power in the authorized institution or its parent.

22. For further details on how the Bank assesses whether or not this criterion is satisfied, see Hall (1989, pp. 110–11).

23. Again, see Hall (1989, pp. 65–6), for further details.

24. Somewhat ironically the Hong Kong and Shanghai Banking Corporation's takeover of Midland Bank was actively encouraged in 1992.

25. From 1 January 1993, in line with the requirements of the EC's Second Banking Co-ordination Directive (EC, 1989b), supervisory control over major shareholders will involve the following: (i) disclosure to the competent authorities, prior to the grant of authorization, of the identity and interests of shareholders who hold 10 per cent or more of the capital (or voting rights) of the credit institution or who otherwise exert a significant influence over the credit institution; (ii) prior reporting of the size of their prospective stakes to the competent authorities by shareholders and associates contemplating the acquisition of stakes in credit institutions; and (iii) prior reporting to the competent authorities by persons intending to increase their 'qualified participation' which would result in their participation passing the 20 per cent, 33 per cent and 50 per cent of capital (or voting rights) thresholds, or which would result in the credit institution becoming their subsidiary.

26. As testimony to this, in recent years the National Australia Bank has acquired the Northern Bank and Clydesdale Bank (a clearing bank in its own right); Equiticorp, the New Zealand financial services company, and later the Bank of Yokohama, a Japanese regional bank, acquired controlling stakes (in the case of the latter, eventually outright ownership) in the small merchant bank Guinness Mahon; Deutsche Bank acquired the major merchant bank Morgan Grenfell; and the Hongkong and Shanghai Banking Corporation acquired Midland Bank, one of the major UK clearing banks.

27. A recent (September 1987) example of the Bank's line on this is provided by the sharp rebuff received by the advertizing agency Saatchi and Saatchi which had designs on Midland Bank in the heady days of the local stockmarket boom before Black Monday. (Robert Maxwell is rumoured to have suffered a similar fate.)

28. Under the EC's Second Banking Co-ordination Directive (EC, 1989b), which took effect on 1 January 1993, a bank's holdings in non-financial companies will also be limited according to the following: (i) a credit institution should not normally hold a 'qualifying participation' (that is, a direct or indirect holding in an undertaking representing 10 per cent or more of the capital or of the voting-rights or making it possible to exercise significant influence over the undertaking's management) exceeding 15 per cent of its 'own funds'; and (ii) the total value of such participations should not exceed 60 per cent of its 'own funds'.

29. For example, the Consumer Credit Act of 1974, the Cheques Act of 1992, and so on (see National Consumer Council, 1983, esp. Section 6, for further details.)

30. Lord Justice Bingham's recommendations are contrasted in Hall (1992b) with those emanating from earlier studies of the BCCI affair – see Hall (1993) and HMSO (1992a).

31. A new inter-agency group is to be established with a view to providing an effective co-ordinated response to complex fraud covering both the exchange of information and

agreement on which body should lead an investigation when malfeasance is suspected (Bank of England, 1992a).
32. Such as having an active branch presence in secretive jurisdictions.
33. The introduction of the duty to report on bank auditors will follow extensive consultation with the accounting profession, not least with a view to clarifying the circumstances in which the duty should be exercized.

References

Bank of England (1981), 'Foreign currency exposure', *Bank of England Quarterly Bulletin*, June.

Bank of England (1982), 'The measurement of liquidity', *Bank of England Quarterly Bulletin*, September.

Bank of England (1984a), *Foreign Currency Options*, (London: Bank of England).

Bank of England (1984b), 'Supervisory aspects of country risk', *Bank of England Quarterly Bulletin*, June.

Bank of England (1987a), *Large Exposures Undertaken by Institutions Authorised Under the Banking Act 1979*, consultative paper, February.

Bank of England (1987b), *Large Exposures Undertaken by Institutions Authorised Under the Banking Act 1987* (BSD/1987/1), September.

Bank of England (1987c), Governor's speech to the President's Banquet of the Northern Ireland Chamber of Commerce on 13 October 1987, reprinted in *Bank of England Quarterly Bulletin*, November, pp. 525–6.

Bank of England (1988a), *Large Underwriting Exposures* (BSD/1987/1.1), February.

Bank of England (1988b), *Proposals for a Stock of High Quality Liquidity*, consultative paper, March.

Bank of England (1988c), *Banking Act 1987, Section 16: Statement of Principles*, May.

Bank of England (1988d), 'Bank of England operations in the sterling money market', *Bank of England Quarterly Bulletin*, August.

Bank of England (1990), *Country Debt Provisioning*, notice issued to UK-incorporated authorized institutions with exposures to countries experiencing debt-servicing and repayment difficulties (London: Bank of England Supervision Division, January).

Bank of England (1992a), *The Bank's Response to the Treasury and Civil Service Committee's Second Report on BCCI*, 8 July.

Bank of England (1992b), Press Notice issued by the Bank of England in response to the Bingham Report, 22 October.

Berger, K. P. (1991), 'The proposed EC Takeover Directive: balancing investor protection with the need for regulatory flexibility', *Journal of International Banking Law*, vol. 6, no. 1, pp. 11–27.

Cooke, P. W. (1986), 'Self-regulation and statute – the evolution of banking supervision', in E.P.M. Gardener (ed.), *UK Banking Supervision: Evolution, Practice and Issues* (London: Allen and Unwin).

Donnelly, M. (1991), 'Competition in finance services: a new environment for mergers and acquisitions', presentation at the *Institute for International Research Conference on EC Financial Regulation and Compliance* (London, 24 October).

European Community (EC) (1989a), *Own Funds Directive*, 89/229/EEC, April.

European Community (EC) (1989b), *Second Banking Coordination Directive*, 89/646/EEC, December.

European Community (EC) (1989c), *Solvency Ratio Directive*, 89/647/EEC, December.

European Community (EC) (1991), Draft *Large Exposures Directive*, EEC, April.

Hall, M. J. B. (1983), *Monetary Policy Since 1971: Conduct and Performance* (London: Macmillan).

Hall, M. J. B. (1987a), *Financial Deregulation: A Comparative Study of Australia and the United Kingdom* (London: Macmillan).

Hall, M. J. B. (1987b), 'UK banking supervision and the Johnson Matthey affair', in C. A. E.

Goodhart, D. Currie and D. T. L. Llewellyn (eds), *The Operation and Regulation of Financial Markets* (London: Macmillan), pp. 3–30.

Hall, M. J. B. (1987c), 'The Johnson Matthey Bankers affair: have the lessons been learnt?', inaugural issue of *Journal of International Securities Markets*, pp. 59–71.

Hall, M. J. B. (1987d), 'The Deposit Protection Scheme: the case for reform', *National Westminster Bank Quarterly Review*, August.

Hall, M. J. B. (1988), 'Managing liquidity', in J. S. G. Wilson (ed.), *Managing Bank Assets and Liabilities* (London: Euromoney Publications).

Hall, M. J. B. (1989), *Handbook of Banking Regulation and Supervision* (London: Woodhead-Faulkner).

Hall, M. J. B. (1991), 'Financial regulation in the UK: deregulation or reregulation?', in C. J. Green and D. T. Llewellyn (eds), *Surveys in Monetary Economics* (Oxford: Basil Blackwell).

Hall, M. J. B. (1992a), *Towards Better Banking Regulation and Supervision*, consultancy report prepared for the International Federation of Commercial, Clerical, Professional and Technical Employees (FIET) (Geneva: FIET).

Hall, M. J. B. (1992b), 'A review of the Bingham Report', mimeo., November.

Hall, M. J. B. (1993), 'BCCI: the lessons for bank supervisors', *International Journal of Regulatory Law and Practice*, vol. I, no. 2, February.

HMSO (1982), *Hong Kong and Shanghai Banking Corporation, Standard Chartered Bank Ltd and the Royal Bank of Scotland Group Ltd: Monopolies and Mergers Commission Report on the Proposed Mergers*, Cmnd 8476 (London: Her Majesty's Stationery Office).

HMSO (1992a), *Banking Supervision and BCCI: International and National Regulation*, Fourth Report of the Treasury and Civil Service Committee (London: Her Majesty's Stationery Office).

HMSO (1992b), *Inquiry into the Supervision of the Bank of Credit and Commerce International* [the Bingham Report], House of Commons, 22 October (London: Her Majesty's Stationery Office).

Llewellyn, D. T. and Holmes, M. (1992), *Competition or Credit Controls?*, Hobart Paper no. 117 (London: Institute of Economic Affairs).

National Consumer Council (1983), *Banking Services and the Consumer; a Report* (London: Methuen).

Quinn, B. (1991), 'The influence of the Banking Acts on the Bank of England's traditional style of banking supervision', in J. J. Norton (ed.), *Bank Regulation and Supervision in the 1990s* (London: Lloyds of London Press).

Reid, M. (1982), *The Secondary Banking Crisis 1973–75* (London: Macmillan).

5 Bank regulation and supervision in the USA

THE CURRENT REGULATORY AND SUPERVISORY FRAMEWORK[1]

Regulations employed for monetary policy purposes

Deregulation
Following the abolition of Regulation Q in 1986 the only major regulation left to support monetary policy is that concerned with the implementation of reserve requirements: the Federal Reserve Board's (FRB) Regulation D. Before looking at Regulation D in detail, however, it is worth charting the demise of Regulation Q because such a discussion serves to highlight the problems involved in employing *any* control device for monetary policy purposes.

Regulation Q was the means by which the FRB implemented the provisions of the Banking Act of 1933 which prohibited the payment of interest on demand deposits by member banks and limited the rates of interest they could pay on time and savings deposits. The restrictions reflected the then prevailing view that 'destructive' interest risk competition had contributed to the bank failures of the 1920s and early 1930s, although evidence to support this hypothesis is conspicuous by its absence (see Cox, 1966). The general prohibition on the payment of interest on demand deposits and the interest ceilings on time and savings deposits remained unchallenged until the passage of the Depository Institutions Deregulation and Monetary Control Act of 1980 (DIDMCA) which sought, *inter alia*, to remove the impediments to competition for funds by depository institutions and to allow small savers a market rate of return on their investments.

Under DIDMCA, Regulation Q was required to be phased out by the end of 1986 (in accordance with Title II), and the prohibition on the payment of interest on the demand deposits of individuals and non-profit making organizations – but not corporations – was abolished (Title III). The rationale for both moves was the same: the restrictions were inequitable, distortive and resulted in a serious misallocation of resources.

As far as the interest rate ceilings were concerned, perhaps the most serious criticisms levelled at their usage related to the costs associated with the evasion and avoidance industry which they spawned. In the early 1960s, for example, active liability management by US banks, keen to circumvent the controls, resulted in the development of the 'negotiable CD' market and an upsurge in eurodollar borrowing, both of which, at least until the regulators caught up with the banks' new practices, lay outside the area of regulated liabilities. In the 1970s, money market mutual funds, money market certificates, 'NOW' (negotiable order of withdrawal) accounts, 'share drafts' (issued by credit unions), and ATS (automatic transfer of savings) accounts were the media through which (small) savers were accommodated in the face of the constraints.

Apart from the real resources consumed by this avoidance industry and the regulatory response to it, the controls also distorted financial markets, leading to disintermediation from both the banking and thrift industries. In the former case, this distorted the significance of monetary indicators thereby complicating monetary management of the economy, and in the latter case it destabilized the housing market.

On top of all this, other inefficient practices were induced as banks (and thrifts) engaged in non-price competition. A burgeoning branch network (as far as regulations allowed) and the offering of non-cash premiums to new account holders were the result.

In short, the interest rate ceilings had seriously distorted financial markets, complicated monetary management of the economy, discriminated against small savers and seriously misallocated resources, all on account of the dubious hypothesis that freedom of competition would destabilize the financial system.

Similar criticisms can, of course, be levelled at the continuing prohibition on the payment of interest on *corporate* demand deposits (here the avoidance industry has come up with devices such as repurchase agreements, subsidized loan rates, the provision of 'free' gifts and services and so on to circumvent the restriction), although to date the administration has not seen fit to campaign for its abolition.

Reserve requirements
Since 1980 and the enactment of DIDMCA, all depository institutions (including Edge Act and 'agreement' corporations and the US branches and agencies of foreign banks) have been required to observe reserve requirements, as set out in the FRB's Regulation D. Previously only member banks were affected. Currently, these reserve requirements are levied against net 'transaction accounts', 'non-personal time deposits' and 'eurocurrency liabilities' (see Exhibit 5.1). Additionally, the FRB may, after consultation with the Board of Directors of the FDIC, the Director of the Office of Thrift Supervision and the National Credit Union Administration Board, impose a supplementary reserve requirement of up to 4 per cent of transaction accounts if this is deemed 'essential for the conduct of monetary policy'.

Exhibit 5.1 Reserve ratios imposed on US depository institutions (as at end-September 1992)

Category of liability	Reserve requirement (%)	Date effective
Net transaction accounts		
$0–$42.2 million[a]	3	17.12.91
Over $42.2 million	0[b]	4.2.92
Non-personal time deposits	0[c]	27.12.90
Eurocurrency liabilities	0	27.12.90

Notes
[a] This cut-off point is increased each year to reflect 80 per cent of the percentage change in total transaction accounts of all depository institutions during the previous year ending 30 June.
[b] This can vary between 8 and 14 per cent under statute.
[c] This can vary between 0 and 9 per cent under statute.

Source: *Federal Reserve Bulletin*, September 1992, Table A9.

All reserve requirements must be held in the form of non-interest-bearing balances with the Federal Reserve or in vault cash. Deficiencies in required reserves during a reserve period are subject to penalties at a rate of 2 per cent per year above the lowest rate in effect for borrowings from the Federal Reserve Bank on the first day of the calendar month in which the deficiencies occurred.

Other direct controls
Apart from prescribed variable reserve requirements, which many assert (for example, Goodfriend and King, 1987, esp. pp. 6–16) are unnecessary for the successful conduct of monetary policy (one argument in favour of their retention is the possibility that different interest rate effects are associated with variations in reserve ratios as compared with open market operations), the only other direct controls which impinge on monetary policy are the administered official discount rate and some state usury laws. The former instrument, which may be retained in administered rather than market-determined form because of its associated 'announcement effects' which might on occasions prove beneficial to the conduct of policy, affects both the level of banks' borrowing from the Federal Reserve (and hence reserves) and market expectations about the future course of monetary and economic policy. State usury laws, in contrast, where they have not been overridden by

federal law in the form of DIDMCA (Title V) (Federal Reserve Bank of Chicago, 1987, pp. 20–2), have considerably less impact because in practice they tend to be non-binding.

Prudential regulation and supervision

Institutional arrangements

The current institutional framework governing the regulation and supervision of US banks is extremely complex, with both federal and state agencies playing a role. The major[2] *federal* agencies involved comprise the Office of the Comptroller of the Currency (OCC), the Federal Reserve System (FRS) and the Federal Deposit Insurance Corporation (FDIC), an independent agency managed by three directors appointed by the President and subject to congressional approval. The OCC is responsible for the supervision of federally chartered national banks (all of which are required to be members of the FRS); the FRS for the supervision of state-chartered member banks (membership of the FRS is voluntary for state banks) and all US bank holding companies; and the FDIC for the supervision of non-member state-chartered banks in the main. Superimposed on this network of federal regulation and

Exhibit 5.2   The structure of federal bank regulation in the USA

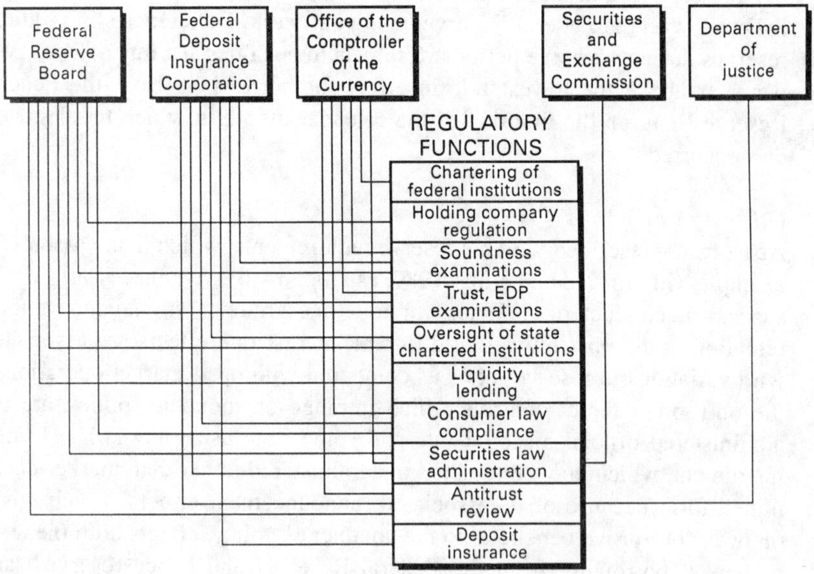

Source: The Report of the Task Group on Regulation of Financial Services, Office of the Presidency, 1984.

supervision (see Exhibit 5.2) is the state system, comprising 50 state banking agencies responsible for the award of charters to those opting for the state route and for their supervision.

The OCC, which was established in 1863 by the National Bank Act, although technically under the direction of the Secretary of the Treasury, enjoys in practice a high degree of autonomy from federal government. Apart from the granting of charters, its regulatory responsibilities embrace the examination of national banks, approval of branch office applications (where allowed by state law), enforcing operating regulations, evaluating merger applications (where the surviving bank would be a national bank) and, when necessary, declaring national banks insolvent. Operational policy is determined in the Washington D.C. Office and put into effect via a network of 14 regional offices.

The FRS, which was created in 1913 primarily to ensure the stability of the US financial system, performs a number of regulatory and supervisory functions. It sets legal reserve requirements for depository institutions (in accordance with Regulation D – see below); it has sole responsibility for approving the formation of, or banking and non-banking acquisitions by, bank holding companies (in accordance with Regulation Y); it determines the non-banking activities in which bank holding companies and foreign banking organizations may engage either directly or through a subsidiary (in accordance with Regulation Y); it regulates US banking organizations' overseas activities and foreign banks' non-banking operations in the US (in accordance with Regulation K); it charters, regulates and supervises Edge Act corporations; it specifies pre-notification requirements for changes in the control of state member banks and bank holding companies (in accordance with Regulation Y); and it is responsible for examining state member banks, approving mergers in which the surviving institution is a state member bank, authorizing their new branch offices and, when necessary, declaring them insolvent.

Finally, the FDIC, which was set up in 1933 to prevent the spread of bank failures by insuring deposits at commercial and mutual savings banks, is involved in the examination and supervision of FDIC-insured state non-member banks. Although not directly involved in the chartering of banks, the FDIC nevertheless strongly influences the process through its deliberations on banks' applications for deposit insurance.[3]

By way of contrast with their federal counterparts, state banking authorities generally engage in the same range of activities – examination, authorization of branches and so on – in respect of state-chartered banks as those undertaken by the OCC in respect of national banks. The quality of supervision is variable, however. Moreover, the states are generally more permissive in the range of activities banks are permitted to engage in, a fact which

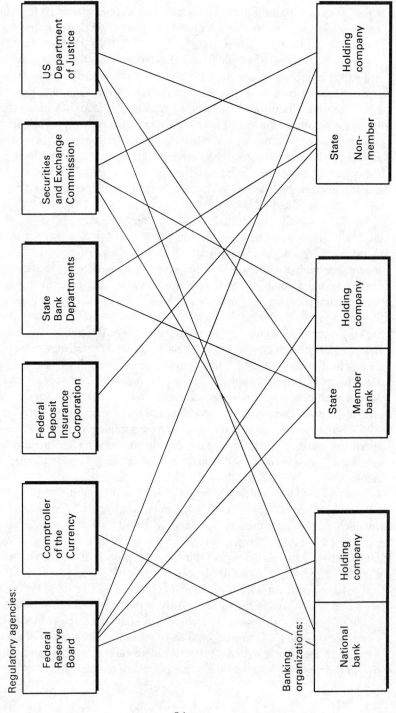

Exhibit 5.3   The 'dual' system of banking regulation and supervision in the USA

Regulatory agencies:

Federal Reserve Board

Comptroller of the Currency

Federal Deposit Insurance Corporation

State Bank Departments

Securities and Exchange Commission

US Department of Justice

Banking organizations:

National bank

Holding company

State Member bank

Holding company

State Non-member

Holding company

helps to explain the continued popularity of state charters. (Bank holding company status is also valued as it allows for avoidance of restrictions on inter-state branching as well as permitting a wider-range of permissible activities (see below), factors, along with tax advantages, which explain why most large US banks are owned by holding companies.)

Such a 'dual' regulatory system, involving side-by-side state and federal regulation (see Exhibit 5.3), is justified by some as the best means of promoting change and innovation in the banking industry, competition between regulators for custom being assumed to secure this goal. Others, however, question the merits of allowing 'regulatory arbitrage', fearing a lowering of supervisory standards as a result of 'competition in laxity'. Moreover, the problems associated with co-ordinating the supervisory effort cast doubt upon the cost-effectiveness of the current supervisory framework (see below).

The regulatory framework
In an excellent review of the regulatory burden borne by US commercial banking organizations the American Bankers Association (ABA, 1989) divided regulations into four groups: (i) those employed for 'bank safety and soundness' reasons; (ii) those employed for 'consumer protection' reasons; (iii) those employed to secure a 'fair' distribution of credit; and (iv) those employed for 'government convenience' reasons. A similar taxonomic approach is adopted below, although groupings (ii) and (iii) are subsumed together under the 'consumer protection' banner, whilst group (iv) items are listed in the miscellaneous section.

Regulations employed for 'safety and soundness' reasons
This list embraces regulations, both federal and state, which are designed to reduce systemic risk. It covers, *inter alia*, federal deposit insurance arrangements; functional separation; chartering and branching restrictions; bank ownership controls; lending restrictions (including margin requirements); capital adequacy requirements; the prohibition of payment of interest on demand deposits; and merger restrictions.

Deposit insurance   The federal deposit insurance programme, which was introduced in 1934 in the wake of the collapse of more than 4000 banks in the previous three years of the Great Depression, was designed to stabilize the banking sector by reducing the incentive for depositors to participate in, or indeed, initiate, deposit runs.[4] Under the Federal Deposit Insurance Act of 1933, federal deposit insurance was made mandatory for national banks, state member banks and foreign banks engaged in retail branching, and some states also insisted upon FDIC insurance for their state-chartered non-member banks. Since enactment of the Financial Institutions, Recovery, Reform and Enforcement Act (FIRREA) in 1989, however, the FDIC has assumed responsibility for the administration of deposit insurance for virtually the whole of the US deposit-taking sector (see Hall, 1990, p. 493).

The current level of insurance cover enjoyed by depositors in the US is $100,000, the level to which it was raised (from $4,000) in 1980 under DIDMCA. Depositors holding accounts at the domestic offices of an insured institution receive complete protection up to this level.[5] Although the coverage is applied on a per customer per bank basis, the more wealthy can effectively extend the level of protection received either by holding a number of accounts under different names in a single institution (for example, under the 'trust fund' system) or by spreading their deposits, in $100,000 tranches, around a number of insured institutions. If the latter route is chosen, a burgeoning deposit brokerage system can be employed to effect the desired result at minimum cost. 'Large' depositors may also gain additional protection by virtue of the fact that, in the event of a failure, they will only be asked to repay an amount equal to their *net* indebtedness to that institution; that is, their deposits may be set against loans.

Apart from the *de jure* protection received, depositors enjoy additional benefits by virtue of the 'failure resolution' policies adopted by the FDIC (see below). This has meant that *de facto* coverage for depositors, at least in 'large' institutions, has become unlimited.[6]

As for the premium structure under federal arrangements, premiums have to date been levied twice-yearly on a flat rate basis as a percentage of assessable deposits. In the early days this percentage was set at 0.083° (that is, 8.3° basis points) but the current assessment rate for commercial banks is 0.23 per cent (that is, 23 basis points).[7]

It should also be noted that contributors to the Bank Insurance Fund are entitled to rebates if the fund exceeds a certain size (currently 1.25 per cent of insured deposits), although the surge in claims has precluded such payouts in recent years.

Entry requirements   Before legally engaging in banking operations in the US a local institution must first obtain a charter. Whether it is applying for a state or federal charter a similar set of criteria have to be satisfied. These relate to the general character and capabilities of the proposed management, the adequacy of the proposed capital structure, the bank's future earnings prospects and the 'convenience and needs' of the community in which the bank intends to operate.

Those US banking organizations seeking to operate overseas have to satisfy the requirements set out in the Federal Reserve Board's Regulation K (or, in the case of state non-member banks, the requirements imposed by the

FDIC), which include, *inter alia*, securing the Board's prior approval. The enabling legal powers are contained in the Federal Reserve Act of 1913, the Bank Holding Company Act of 1956 and state laws for member banks, bank holding companies and state-chartered non-member banks respectively.

Finally, the US operations of foreign banks are regulated on a 'national treatment' basis (Key, 1990) under the International Banking Act of 1978.[8] Similar entry requirements to those imposed on domestic concerns apply, although their US subsidiaries are treated as bank holding companies by the Federal Reserve Board and their US agencies and branches as affiliates of the bank.

Functional separation   The regulations relating to functional separation seek to split banking from securities business and other 'non-banking' activities.[9] The most famous piece of federal legislation in this area is the so-called Glass Steagall Act of 1933 which was enacted to ensure (at least partial) physical separation of investment and commercial banking activities. The Act relates, in fact, to sections 16, 20, 21 and 32 of the Banking Act of 1933 which, along with the National Bank Act of 1864, the Federal Reserve Act of 1913, the McFadden Act of 1927, the Bank Holding Company Act of 1956 and state laws, forms the primary legislation governing US banks' domestic securities activities (see Chapter 9 for full details).[10] Recent developments, however, have resulted in a significant erosion in the business between banking and securities business in the US, a situation complicated by the treatment of foreign institutions' US operations.[11] (Because these issues are covered in detail in Chapter 9 they are not developed further here.)

The general separation of banking from non-banking activities is secured by the Banking Act of 1933 and the Bank Holding Company Act of 1956 which limit the ability of commercial banks and bank holding companies respectively to engage in non-banking activities.[12] The latter piece of legislation is implemented via the Federal Reserve Bank's Regulation Y (and Regulation K for overseas securities activities). Similar prohibitions,[13] including that on the direct ownership of equities, apply to both US banks and bank holding companies, with parallel restrictions being applied to the US non-banking activities of foreign banks under the Federal Reserve Board's Regulation Y and Regulation K (which give effect to the International Banking Act of 1978).

The banks' ability to engage in insurance business is largely determined by state law as there is little federal legislation in this area. (The Garn-St Germain Act of 1982, however, under Title VI, amends the Bank Holding Company Act of 1956 by preventing bank holding companies from providing insurance as principals, agents or brokers, insurance activities being regarded as *not* closely related to banking.) Few opportunities to date, however, have arisen for banks to diversify in this fashion.[14]

Branching restrictions   The McFadden Act of 1927, which prohibits inter-state branching by national banks (section 9 of the Federal Reserve Act of 1913 applies the same rules to state-chartered member banks), and the Douglas Amendment (that is, Section 3(d)) to the Bank Holding Company Act of 1956 seriously restrict *inter*-state branch banking in the US for US commercial banks and bank holding companies respectively. The latter piece of legislation, for example, prohibits bank holding companies from acquiring banks operating in states other than those in which their banking subsidiaries operate *unless* expressly permitted by state law. This *caveat*, however, has been exploited by many states which have passed permissive legislation to facilitate inter-state branch banking on a reciprocal basis – the phenomenon of 'regional compacts'. Other loopholes have allowed bank holding companies in effect to establish nationwide branch banking networks by: (i) acquiring ailing savings and loan associations in different states; (ii) acquiring ailing banks from different states under authorization by the FDIC; (iii) establishing Edge Act corporation subsidiaries, which are chartered by the Board of Governors of the FRS under section 25(c) of the Federal Reserve Act of 1913 for the purpose of engaging in international or foreign banking or other international or foreign operations and which escape the more prohibitive legislation; and (iv) operating across state lines through the medium of 'non-bank' (that is, limited service) banks, which are not covered by the law. Moreover, because the geographic restrictions placed on bank branches by the McFadden Act do not apply to non-bank subsidiaries, inter-state banking by both national and state banks has proceeded through the establishment of bank-related subsidiaries and affiliates in other states. The fact remains, however, that restrictive federal (and state) legislation, initially designed to protect small state banks and limit concentrations, has forced most US[15] banking organizations to engage in nationwide banking through subsidiaries, thereby reducing their opportunities for potential gain from economies of scale and scope and cost-saving synergies especially those associated with compliance with capital requirements. Advances in information technology, on the other hand, have served to reduce the necessity for establishing a physical presence in other states for those with nationwide banking ambitions.

Intra-state branching is also affected by federal and state legislation. The latter, for example, which impinges on both banks and bank holding companies, may result in 'unit banking' (that is, banks being allowed to operate one full-service office) in some states and limited or statewide branching in others. Again, however, the bank holding company route may be used to extend opportunities (that is, in those states which do not allow statewide branching) if the laws imposed on banks are more restrictive than those imposed on bank holding companies.

The McFadden Act, by making federally chartered banks subject to state laws on branching, reinforces the state-imposed restriction, confining national banks to the branching freedoms enjoyed by their state-chartered counterparts.

Finally, banks must at present obtain regulatory approval for the opening of more branches. Similar criteria to those applied at the chartering stage are used in the assessment of such applications.

Merger restrictions   The Bank Merger Acts of 1960 and 1966 require that banks seeking to merge receive the prior approval of one of the three federal banking agencies. The agency with primary jurisdiction must, in turn, sound out the views of the other two agencies. Additionally, under US antitrust legislation, all bank mergers are subject to review by the Department of Justice, which has 30 days within which to give its verdict on whether or not the proposed merger would result in a reduction in competition or increase monopolistic tendencies in the financial sector. If the Department of Justice raises doubts about the merits of the proposed merger, it is up to the courts to determine whether in fact the antitrust laws would be breached.

In determining whether or not to approve mergers, the federal agencies take into account both banking and competition factors (Kidwell and Peterson, 1981, p. 225). Under the former, the agency is obliged to examine the financial condition of the banks, investigate the management of the acquiring bank and assess the 'needs and convenience' of the community. Under the last heading, proposals will be rejected if they are thought likely to create a monopoly or result in a substantial reduction in competition. The litmus test used to determine whether this would be the outcome is the so-called 'potential competition doctrine' under which a proposal will be rejected if it can be shown that one of the parties to the merger is a potential entrant into either the other's market area or into a common market area. Application of this test has generally resulted in mergers between small banks being favoured at the expense of mergers between larger banks, although mergers between small and large banks have occurred where the FDIC has set aside the competition criteria in instances where a bank is believed to be in imminent danger of being unable to meet its contractual obligations. More recently, however, pressure to cut costs has led to a spate of mergers between large banks (for example, the money centre banks Manufacturers Hanover and Chemical Bank announced their intention to merge in July 1991, followed shortly afterwards by BankAmerica and Security

Pacific), with the apparent blessing of regulatory authorities who also feel consolidation is necessary.

Bank ownership controls   Apart from the requirements applicable at the chartering stage, all planned changes in the control of FDIC-insured banks (including bank holding companies which control FDIC-insured banks) have to receive the prior approval of a federal banking agency under the Change in Bank Control Act of 1978. In this way, the 'fitness and properness' of prospective controllers can be assured, and the general public interest protected by allowing the regulatory agencies to disapprove those acquisitions[16] which would exacerbate monopolistic tendencies in the US banking sector or otherwise substantially reduce competition in circumstances where such deleterious efforts would not be clearly outweighed by any benefits accruing to the 'convenience and needs' of the community to be served.

Other   Of the other regulations listed above which are employed for 'safety and soundness' reasons, both capital requirements and lending restrictions are considered below (under the heading 'Other Prudential Safeguards'), leaving only prohibition on the payment of interest on demand deposits (of corporations) for discussion at this stage. As noted earlier, the prohibition, which initially applied to the demand deposits of the personal sector also, was introduced under the Banking Act of 1933 and implemented via the Federal Reserve Board's Regulation Q. It was designed to prevent 'destructive' interest rate competition. In accordance with the DIDMCA, however, the personal sector and non-profit-making organizations were exempted from the provisions because of the inequities and inefficiencies previously created, leaving only the transactions balances of corporations and government units subject to the legislation.

Regulations employed for 'consumer protection' reasons
Both federal and state regulations are used to protect the interests of consumers. The latter, typically, include usury provisions which limit interest (and other) charges for certain types of loan[17] and restrict the remedies available to creditors in the event of loan defaults. In addition, some states have passed their own versions of the Equal Credit Opportunity Act (see below) and other consumer protection legislation which reinforce much of the federal legislation.

The consumer protection legislation passed at the federal level embraces, *inter alia*, the Consumer Credit Protection Act (sometimes called the 'Truth in Lending Act') of 1969, the Equal Credit Opportunity Act of 1974, the Fair Credit Billing Act of 1974, the Real Estate Settlement Procedures Act of 1974, the Home Mortgage Disclosure Act of 1975, the Federal Trade Commission Improvement Act of 1975, the Electronic Funds Transfer Act of 1980, the Expedited Funds Availability Act of 1988, the Community Reinvestment Act of 1977, and the Fair Housing Act of 1968. As the focus of this text is primarily on the 'systemic interest' of regulation, however, this legislation is not analysed further; interested readers should consult Kidwell and Peterson (1981, pp. 226–31), and American Bankers Association (1989, pp. 100–165).

Miscellaneous regulations

The remaining set of regulations, which embrace *inter alia* the Bank Survey Act of 1970 (as amended) and a range of reporting requirements designed to facilitate the work of government departments (most especially the Inland Revenue Service), are also beyond the scope of this book but can be examined by consulting American Bankers Association (1989, pp. 167–83).

Other prudential 'safeguards'

The examination process Most commercial banks in the US are now supposed to be examined at least once a year (those regarded as being particularly 'risky' are examined more often) by a regulatory agency, with a federal examination taking place either every year or every other year. 'Well-capitalised', 'well-managed' banks with assets of no more than $100 million may, however, be examined every 18 months. The purpose of the examination is to prevent bank failures arising from poor management or fraud, with the bulk of the procedures being concerned with the former objective. State banking and federal agencies liaise to reduce the scope for supervisory overlap and underlap.

Bank examiners rely upon the submission of quarterly 'Reports of Condition' (the so-called 'Call Reports' which have to be filed by all FDIC-insured institutions), off-site, computer-based monitoring, and unannounced on-site examinations to discharge their supervisory obligations. The on-site examinations, including those of overseas branches and, local laws permitting, subsidiaries, are generally used to: check the records and the bank's physical possession of the cash and marketable securities shown in the books; examine the securities portfolio to check whether the securities claimed are on hand; establish a market valuation for the bonds held; evaluate the creditworthiness of the bank's loan portfolio (much of the examiners' time is spent on this task); check lending operations for compliance with the relevant laws and regulations (for example, large exposure limits); assess management capability and performance; check more generally the internal controls established to govern the way the bank is operated; check more generally for compliance with their internal controls and laws and regulations.

At the federal level, considerable effort is devoted to eliminating the possibility of supervisory overlap or underlap. The three agencies operate according to very distinctive systems, in spite of the establishment of the Federal Financial Institutions Examination Council (FFIEC) in 1980, which sought to ensure that uniform examination policies were adopted by all the federal agencies and to secure co-ordination between them (see below). There is general agreement that the Federal Reserve Board (FRB) examines only state member banks (although it has the right to examine all member banks) and bank holding companies (further agreement with the OCC and the FDIC has to be reached because many bank holding companies own both state and national banks); the OCC examines only national banks; and the FDIC examines only non-member FDIC-insured banks. Outside this juris- dictional split, it is generally the case that co-ordination between the federal agencies is better the bigger the bank and/or the greater its perceived prob- lems. It is also widely believed that the toughness of the agencies' examina- tions can be ranked, in descending order of severity, as: OCC; FRB; FDIC. This means that, within the scope available for regulatory arbitrage, the differential application of prudential regulations, through the examination process, has created incentives for a bank to have a state rather than a federal charter and to stay outside rather than inside the FRS.[18] (The new supervi- sory standards which all federal banking agencies are obliged to adopt during 1993 by the FDICIA – see below – may however impinge on the latter decision. For full details, see Gail and Norton, 1992, pp. 16–18.)

(a) *The FRB's approach*:   The FRB, which is primarily concerned with the examination of state member banks and bank holding companies, pays particular interest to the largest 50 bank holding companies (those with assets greater than $10 billion) which control around 60 per cent of total US banking assets. 'Full scope' examinations taken place annually for all the former and for certain[19] of the latter. Its on-site approach can be summarized using the acronym 'CAMEL' – 'capital', 'asset quality', 'management', 'earnings' and 'liquidity' – for which a composite rating for each institution is derived. As capital adequacy is now assessed on a uniform basis by all regulators, and because it is covered below and also more extensively in Chapter 8, only the non-capital elements of assessment are examined further here.

In its assessment of asset quality, the FRB pays particular attention to the loan portfolio. In determining its quality, it will select a sample of up to 80 per cent of all loans and focus on the borrower's ability to repay,[20] the repayment history of interest and principal, the guaranties taken (if any), the original underwriting standards and loan review standards.

Loans are classified as 'satisfactory', 'substandard', 'doubtful' or 'loss'. Satisfactory loans are those which are deemed to meet the standards suggested by prudent banking practice; substandard loans are those likely to be associated with some loss; doubtful loans are those for which there is a higher probability of loss occurring, although the likely losses cannot be determined precisely; and loss loans are those which are thought to be uncollectable and which the bank is required to write off.

Ratio analysis is also used in the evaluation exercise to provide early warning signs of trouble. For example, close attention would be paid to banks with ratios of total classified assets[21] to primary capital[22] in excess of 20 per cent, and to those with weighted classified assets[23] to primary capital ratios approaching 100 per cent. The ratios of non-performing assets[24] to primary capital are also carefully scrutinized.

The assessment of management, which also covers internal policies, operations and procedures, is highly subjective and, in large degree, represents a reflection of how a bank has scored within the other aspects of the 'CAMEL' exercise. Unlike in the UK, there are no statutory guidelines to assist the regulators in such assessment exercises. Despite this, management is generally deemed unsatisfactory if it fails to identify serious problem cases and/or does not accept the remedial advice given by the regulator. In the latter scenario, the end result may be a forced removal from power of the management.

In assessing the quality of a bank's earnings the regulators look at trends in earnings in relation to total assets and total equity. Peer group assessment is important in this context. Earnings are also compared with cash flow to see whether they are likely to prove sufficient to cover contractual obligations. Finally, the proportion of total earnings derived from continuing operations, as opposed to non-recurring operations (for example, the sale of fixed assets), is focused on: the higher the proportion, the better.

In its assessment of liquidity adequacy, which is conducted on a worldwide consolidated basis, the FRB does not impose minimum or average requirements.[25] Rather, it focuses upon the sufficiency (in relation to short-term liabilities) of cash and readily realizable asset holdings, the diversity of (potential) borrowing sources, the wholesale/retail deposit split, the extent to which assets and liabilities are matched by maturity,[26] and the adequacy[27] of internal controls.

(b)   *The OCC's approach*:   In its supervision of national banks, the bulk of which are owned by bank holding companies, the OCC, more than the other federal regulators, focuses on particular parts of the balance sheet and relies more heavily on off-site monitoring. The frequency of its examinations are no longer calendar-driven, its resources being apportioned according to a hierarchy of priorities which ranks as top priority banks thought likely to bring about systemic breakdown, the huge multinational/national banks as the second priority, and so on down to the regional/community banks which are accorded lowest priority.

The CAMEL acronym can also be used to describe the OCC's supervisory approach. Capital adequacy assessment is carried out in much the same way as the FRB assesses state member banks, and the assessment of asset quality is conducted in similar fashion. The examination of earnings and assessment of liquidity adequacy, too, are performed in more or less the same manner, leaving the assessment of management as perhaps the main distinguishing feature of the OCC's approach.

In the past, the OCC's rating of management was closely linked to its assessment of capital adequacy and asset quality; satisfactory rulings on the first two fronts ultimately led to a satisfactory rating of management. The focus today, however, is more on the assessment of managerial skill, because it is this above all else which is believed to be the major determinant of performance.

(c)   *The FDIC's approach*:   In looking at the supervisory approach adopted by the FDIC (which is responsible for supervising around some 8000 mainly small banks that account for less than 12 per cent of US banking assets), perhaps the most distinctive feature is the comparatively low priority accorded to assessment of management. Accordingly, the acronym 'CAEL' better describes its actions than the acronym 'CAMEL' that is applicable to the procedures adopted by the FRB and the OCC. A distinct lack of resources means that the FDIC is forced to target what it perceives as the major 'problem' institutions. Moreover, because there was until recently no minimum examination frequency rule, some banks were not examined for a number of years (although off-site monitoring was usually conducted in such cases).

(d)   *The supervision of foreign banks' US operations*:   As noted at various points in the text, a general policy of 'national treatment' applies in respect of the US operations of overseas banks. This, however, will change if the FRB's proposals for supervising foreign banks under the Foreign Bank Supervision Enforcement Act of 1991 are adopted (see below and note 50). This piece of legislation was passed by Congress last November to close the loopholes exploited by the Bank of Credit and Commerce International (BCCI) in its illegal acquisition of four US banks during the 1980s and generally to tighten supervision of foreign banks. Often referred to as the 'BCCI provisions' of the Banking Reform Act of 1991, they would provide the FRB with the power to: (i) review the establishment of any branch, agency or commercial lending company by a foreign bank – permission cannot be given unless the FRB is satisfied that the bank's worldwide activities are adequately supervized by its home authorities; (ii) close foreign bank offices for a violation of the law or for unsafe or unsound banking practices; (iii) supervize representative offices as well as full branches or subsidiaries; (iv) block any purchase of more than 5 per cent (the previous limit was 10 per cent) of the shares of a US bank by a foreign bank, even if the latter only operates a branch or agency; and (v) insist that all loans secured on 25 per cent or more of a US bank's shares are reported to it. Furthermore, foreign banks wishing to take federally insured deposits through their US operations would be required to set up separately capitalized subsidiaries for the purpose.

The FRB's proposals for implementing this legislation were published in April 1992. If implemented in their current form, the increased supervisory burden and the costs arising with subsidiarization (lending capacity, for example, would in future be determined by the capital of the subsidiary and not by that of the whole bank) may well cause foreign banks to reconsider their US banking strategies. At the very least, they are likely to reassess the relative merits of conducting their US banking operations through a commercial banking concern rather than through a securities or insurance form of operation.

Capital adequacy assessment In addition to the risk-based approach to capital adequacy assessment (discussed in Chapter 8),[28] which applies to all US banks and bank holding companies on a consolidated basis (see Exhibit 5.4 for the ratios recently posted by the latter), a leverage ratio requirement is imposed on all banking organizations.[29]

The FRB first implemented the requirement in the summer of 1990 to replace the minimum 'primary' and 'total capital' to total assets ratios previously employed under Regulation Y. Under the new requirement, member banking organizations have to observe a minimum ratio of Tier 1[30] capital to total assets of 3 per cent. Moreover, only those with a CAMEL rating of 1 (the highest) will be permitted to operate at the minimum level of 3 per cent; all other institutions must maintain an additional cushion of at least 100 to 200 basis points (that is, an additional 1 to 2 percentage points of capital). The OCC subsequently adopted a similar approach, as did the FDIC, that requires banks without the best rating to adhere to ratios of at least 4 per cent.

Since the successful passage of the Banking Reform Bill through the House of Representatives in November 1991 regulators now have more powers to penalise under-capitalized banks. Federal regulators, for example,

Exhibit 5.4   Risk-based capital ratios posted by the major US bank holding companies, 1989–92

Bank holding company	Capital ratios (%)							
	End- '89		End- '90		End- '91		End-Sept.'92	
	RAR	Tier 1 ratio	RAR	Tier 1 ratio	RAR	Tier 1 ratio	RAR	Tier 1 ratio
Bankamerica Corp.	9.09	5.61	9.30	5.96	10.83	7.25	10.88	6.50
Bankers Trust New York	8.26	4.48	10.03	5.43	10.90	6.10	12.55	6.95
Chase Manhattan Corp.	8.87	4.44	8.33	4.32	9.74	5.32	10.80	6.50
Chemical Banking Corp.	8.74	4.65	9.40	5.16	9.13	5.13	11.20	7.00
Citicorp	8.08	4.04	6.52	3.26	7.46	3.73	8.50	4.25
J. P. Morgan & Co.	10.10	5.90	10.00	6.30	10.72	6.95	11.40	7.50
Nationsbank Corp.	–	–	9.58	5.79	10.30	6.38	11.68	7.54
Security Pacific Corp.	8.60	6.10	7.45	4.13	8.09	4.08	–	–

Source: IBCA Inc., New York, 1992.

can now assume control of critically under-capitalized banks (although the exact circumstances in which such powers can be exercised have yet to be clarified); and under-capitalized banks are now prohibited from distributing dividends, paying unusually high interest rates or seeking brokered deposits. The responsibilities of regulators have also been formalized, with regulators now mandated to intervene promptly if banks' holdings of capital fall below specified levels (see below).

Accounting, auditing and reporting requirements   All federally insured banking institutions are required to file a 'Consolidated Report of Condition and Income' (the so-called 'Call Report') on a quarterly basis in a format specified by the FFIEC that covers assets, liabilities, deposits and deposit structure, loan exceptions and so on. This is the single most important report filed by banking organizations (bank holding companies must file similar reports on a quarterly basis) from the perspective of federal bank examiners (for a discussion of the remaining panoply of reporting requirements faced by banks, see American Bankers Association, 1989, pp. 57–64). Annual accounts must also be drawn up in accordance with Generally Accepted Accounting Principles (GAAP) and audited by an authorized firm of accountants. (For a discussion of the changes in reporting and audit requirements mandated by the FDICIA, see below, and Gail and Norton, 1992, pp. 33–6.)

In recent years, a great deal of attention has been devoted (especially by the FRB and the FFIEC) to securing consistency between federal regulatory reporting requirements and GAAP. This has resulted in the Call Report, for example, incorporating various Statements of the Financial Accounting Standards Board (FASB), although much remains to be done if the two parties – federal bank examiners and the accountancy profession – are to be brought closer together on a wider range of policy issues.

The assessment of liquidity adequacy   (See the bank examination process above.)

Lending restrictions   US commercial banks are constrained in the amount they can lend to one borrower and to bank affiliates, in the terms on which they can lend to affiliates and to 'insiders', and in their exposures to highly leveraged transactions and the securities market.

(a)   *Limits on loans to one borrower*:   Under the National Banking Act and state bank charters all depository institutions are required to observe 'loans-to-one borrower' limits. The current OCC statutory limit is 15 per cent of capital and surplus (25 per cent if 10 per cent is fully collateralized). 'One borrower' is defined to include any related parties and family members, and a 'loan' is defined to involve a variety of transactions including written loan commitments. No limits, however, apply to sectoral or country exposures, although the 15 per cent/25 per cent limits do apply to loans made to foreign governments and their agencies.

(b)   *Transactions with affiliates*:   In accordance with sections 23A and 23B of the Federal Reserve Act of 1913 (as amended in 1987) and section 18(j) of the Federal Deposit Insurance Act of 1966 all member banks and FDIC-insured institutions respectively face restrictions on transactions with affiliates. Under 23A, a bank may not directly or indirectly loan or extend credit to an affiliate (as defined in the Act) a sum in excess of 10 per cent of capital and surplus; and the total of such loans for a bank may not exceed 20 per cent of capital and surplus. And section 23B requires that loans and other transactions (that is, sales, leases, fee services and so on) with affiliates be conducted on identical terms as transactions with the general public.

(c)   *Loans to 'insiders'*:   In accordance with Title VIII of the Financial Institutions Regulatory and Interest Rate Control Act of 1978, all commercial banks are prohibited from extending credit to their executive officers, directors, principal shareholders and related interests, except on the terms specified in the Act. These restrictions (implemented under Regulation O by the FRB) create, among other things, a lending limit equal to the 'loans-to-one-borrower' limit and confine the terms on which such loans are made to those applicable to persons not covered by the regulation. The FRB also requires advance notification of any such loans exceeding the higher of $25,000 or 5 per cent of capital and unimpaired surplus. (Recodified restrictions came into force in 1992 under the FDICIA – see below. For full details, see Gail and Norton, 1992, pp. 22–7.)

(d)   *Highly-leveraged transactions*:   In 1989 the FRB issued new examination guidelines for highly-leveraged transactions (HLTs), which replaced those issued in 1984. The new guidelines were issued in the light of the dramatic upsurge in usage of such transactions since the middle of the 1980s and because of concerns relating to their impact on bank asset portfolios and their overall risk exposure.

The guidelines define HLTs to include leveraged buyouts (LBOs) and similar transactions used to finance corporate restructuring, including mergers and acquisitions funded by debt that results in high leverage. High leverage was initially defined as a ratio of total debt to total assets of 75 per cent or more but, following agreement between the federal bank regulatory authorities in October 1989, complementary definitions include transactions which: (i) at least double the subject company's liabilities and result in a leverage ratio in excess of 50 per cent; or (ii) are designated as an HLT by a syndication agent.

Apart from defining HLTs (the definition, together with associated reporting requirements, was discontinued in July 1992), the guidelines specify the procedures to be followed by bank management and examiners in assessing the effect of such transactions on the overall condition of the organization. In general, banking organizations are expected to

> evaluate the adequacy and stability of the borrower's current and prospective cash flow under varying economic scenarios through the following actions:
>
> • Setting reasonable 'in-house' limits on a consolidated holding company basis regarding exposure to individual borrowers, total exposure to all HLT borrowers, and industry concentrations resulting from HLTs;
> • Establishing procedures for credit analysis, approval, and review that take into account the high levels of debt involved in these transactions;
> • Maintaining internal systems, controls, reporting procedures, and limits;
> • Establishing pricing policies and practices that take account in a prudent manner of the trade-off between risk and return;
> • Avoiding any compromise of sound banking practices in an effort to broaden market share or to realize substantial fees. (Federal Reserve Board, 1989, p. 175)

Examiners are also held responsible for reviewing the organization's operations to ensure that the above policies and procedures are put into effect.

The action of 1989 was followed in April 1990 by the FRB's initiation of a series of special examinations of banks with large portfolios of leveraged buyout loans. The FRB were concerned at the possible deterioration in the quality of these loans in the light of a substantial increase in default rates and the possible inadequacy of the risk premiums.

(e) *Exposure to the securities market*: Apart from the limits placed on direct exposure by the prohibition on equity holdings and the limitations on engaging in securities operations (see Chapter 9), commercial banks face limits on indirect exposures incurred through loans made for the purpose of financing the purchase or carrying of securities. So-called 'margin requirements' are applied by the FRB under Regulation U (last amended in 1987) which prohibit commercial banks from extending any credit secured directly or indirectly by margin stock in an amount that exceeds the maximum loan value of the collateral securing the credit. Additionally, allowable loans in excess of $100,000 must be reported to the FRB.

Measures to limit exchange rate risk Although no limits or guidelines are set by the regulatory agencies, individual bank positions are monitored via a detailed reporting system which involves the submission of both weekly and monthly data covering exposures in a range of currencies. The latter data set must also incorporate a breakdown of (net) foreign currency positions by maturity. (For a discussion of how exchange rate risk might be accommodated within risk-based capital requirements, see Leahy, 1991.)

Measures to limit country risk A twice-yearly reporting system facilitates the measurement of a bank's country risk on a worldwide consolidated basis. Although no country exposure limits are applied, an Inter-Agency Country Exposure Review Committee (IACERC) meets three times a year to determine the level of 'allocated transfer risk reserves' which have to be held against country exposures. Moreover, loans to foreign governments and their agencies (which are grouped together according to the source of funds for repayment) are subject to the loans-to-one-borrower limits. The prime aim of bank examiners, however, remains the checking of the adequacy of each bank's in-house system for evaluating credit risk and establishing country exposure limits.

In its deliberations, the IACERC seeks to classify countries as 'strong', 'moderately strong' or 'weak'. Key ratios used in the past in this assessment process comprised, *inter alia*: (i) the latest annual current account balance as a percentage of total exports of goods and services in that year; (ii) the cumulative current account deficit in the three most recent years as a percentage of average annual export earnings during those years; (iii) net interest payments on external debt in the most recent year as a percentage of average annual export receipts during the three most recent years; (iv) net interest payments as a percentage of international reserves in the most recent period; and (v) total debt service requirements as a percentage of exports of goods and services.

Finance industry 'support'   Apart from the traditional 'liquidity support'[31] available to member banks (and others maintaining reserves with the FRS) at the discount windows of their district federal reserve banks (to which should perhaps be added the effective daily overdrafts accorded commercial banks under the Fedwire system), 'solvency support' is available via the FDIC.

The FDIC provides such support in one of three ways: (i) by paying off insured depositors and liquidating the bank's assets (as receiver) after a declaration of insolvency by the chartering authority: the so-called 'payoff option' (receivership collections, as far as they allow, are used to reimburse uninsured creditors and the FDIC, for the payments made to insured depositors, and to pay the FDIC's expenses); (ii) by arranging, through a bidding process, for the acquisition of the failed bank by another institution, which then assumes the bank's liabilities – the so-called 'purchase and assumption' (P and A) option;[32] and (iii) by providing direct assistance to ailing institutions in the form of loans or the purchase of assets. (For details, see Horvitz, 1986.)

The 'payoff' approach to resolving insolvencies is the most straightforward but not the most popular because of the 'cost' (such as the loss of credit facilities) that a bank closure may impose on a local community. Moreover, the 'P and A' solution is usually the cheapest for the FDIC, an important consideration for the latter which is mandated under the Federal Deposit Insurance Act of 1966 to regard cost-minimization as the *primary* consideration in its deliberations on the resolution policies to adopt. (In the case of large bank failures, however, preservation of financial confidence may outweigh such considerations.) The disadvantage is that market discipline may be eroded as, under the 'P and A' approach, all creditors, insured and uninsured, are protected. To overcome this problem a 'modified payoff' approach was added to the range of options in 1984. Under this approach, which seeks to combine the beneficial aspects of both the 'payoff' and 'P and A' policies, the FDIC arranges for another bank to assume only the insured deposits of a failed bank. Uninsured depositors receive an immediate credit for the amount of their claims that the FDIC calculates will ultimately be recovered, with *ex post* settlement being used to handle any disparities arising between expectations and actual sums realized.

The FDIC's provision of direct assistance was initially restricted under section 13(c) of the Federal Deposit Insurance Act of 1966 to instances where the continued existence of a failing bank was 'essential to its community'. Since enactment of the Garn-St Germain Act in 1982, however, the FDIC is able to provide direct assistance to keep a bank open if that is the least costly option available. If such action is taken, the FDIC usually takes an equity stake so as to allow it to benefit from any subsequent recovery of the institution. This limits the benefits that stockholders derive from such remedial action. Existing management, too, usually suffers when direct assistance is provided because those held responsible for the problems are normally required to be dismissed.

Since the enactment of the Deposit Insurance Reform Act of 1991, the FDIC has been obliged to deal with failing banks in the cheapest possible way for the banks' insurance fund (BIF); and from 1995 it will be prohibited from reimbursing uninsured depositors (which should help to curb the application of the 'too-big-to-fail' doctrine – see above) except when the Secretary to the Treasury, on the advice of the FRB, deems that such action would pose grave risks to the economy.

The continuing reform debate

Despite Congress's recent enactment of a financial reform package (see below) a number of important supervisory issues remain unresolved. These will now be addressed.[33]

The Treasury's reform package

A convenient starting point for the discussion is provided by the US Treasury's blueprint for reform (US Treasury, 1991). The recommendations contained in that document were designed, *inter alia*, to: increase the protection afforded depositors; reduce the exposure to ailing financial institutions faced by taxpayers; improve the service received by consumers of financial services; generally benefit businesses and their employees; and strengthen the economy through a strengthening of domestic banks. The principal argument in its case for reform was that most of the banking laws, which dated back to the Great Depression of the 1930s, had become outdated, having being overtaken by technological revolution and other significant developments. As a result stresses in the banking system had been exacerbated, US banks being placed at a competitive disadvantage *vis-à-vis* foreign organizations, and consumers and the economy in general suffering. In short, whatever their merits in the past, few of the then existing regulations continued to operate in the public interest.

In putting together its reform package the Treasury established a number of guiding principles: (i) that deposit insurance should be retained for 'small' savers; (ii) that taxpayer exposure to the fall-out from the ailing financial services industry should be reduced by reforming the federal deposit insurance system and tightening supervision;[34] (iii) that banks should be made stronger and safer by assigning greater importance to the role of capital; (iv) that banks should be made more competitive through a modernization of the law, thereby allowing banks to engage in a broader range of financial services; and (v) that the banking system (and hence the economy) should be strengthened by improving the cost-effectiveness of regulation and supervision.

The more significant of the Treasury's proposals for reform can be conveniently grouped under the following headings: reform of the institutional framework governing banking regulation and supervision (this is termed 'structural reform' below); proposals for capital-based supervision; proposals for reducing the scope of deposit insurance and otherwise reforming federal deposit insurance arrangements; proposals to extend banks' powers; and proposals for revamping the approach adopted towards foreign organizations' US banking operations.

Structural reform   The Treasury proposed that the number of federal regulatory agencies be reduced from four – the Federal Reserve, the OCC, the FDIC and the Office of Thrift Supervision – to two, with the same body being responsible for supervising a bank holding company and its banking subsidiaries. It further recommended that the Federal Reserve should assume supervisory responsibility for all state-chartered banks and their holding companies, and that a new 'Federal Banking Agency', under the control of the Treasury, should supervise all national banks and their holding companies. For holding companies which own both state-chartered and national banks, supervisory responsibility would be determined according to the nature of the charter held by the largest banking subsidiary.

The Treasury's proposals would, of course, have meant emasculation of the OCC in respect of banking supervision, while the FDIC would have been left to concentrate on its insurance and failure resolution roles. The Federal Reserve would also have assumed a greater supervisory role, contrary to the wishes of those, such as the ABA, who argue for a separation of the supervision function from monetary policy.

The stated aims of the proposed reforms were: to reduce the duplication of (federal) supervisory effort;[35] to improve the consistency and efficiency of federal supervision; to make federal regulators more accountable; and finally, to separate the insurance and regulatory functions.

Capital-based supervision   Proposals on this front complement the implementation of risk-based capital adequacy assessment (in accordance with the

Basle Committee guidelines – see Chapter 8) and represent an attempt to refashion supervision in a way which encourages banks to hold more capital by establishing a system of penalties and rewards. Rules would also ensure that prompt corrective action would be taken to address problems as capital levels declined, and certainly well before a position of insolvency was reached.

The system of penalties and rewards revolved around a grouping of institutions according to their holdings of capital. Institutions would be divided into five groups labelled from Zone 1 to Zone 5. Zone 1 institutions are classified as those with capital significantly in excess of the required minima (that is, 8 per cent of weighted risk assets from the beginning of 1993 according to the risk-based requirement agreed in the G10 forum, and 3 per cent or more of total assets under the leverage requirements). Zone 2 institutions comprise those which satisfy the minimum requirements but whose holdings of capital do not significantly exceed them. The labels Zone 3 to Zone 5 are used to categorize those institutions not satisfying the relevant minimum capital requirements. Zone 3 institutions, for example, would be running capital levels below, but not significantly below, the minima; Zone 4 institutions would be running levels significantly below the agreed minima; and Zone 5 institutions, the most poorly capitalized of the lot, would be those operating with a Tier 1 leverage ratio of 1.5 per cent or lower.

The rewards accruing to well-capitalized banks would be reduced compliance costs, greater access to outside capital and greater freedom to diversify. For example, a financial service holding company (see below) would be permitted to engage (through subsidiaries) in the so-called 'non-financial activities' (interstate branching, insurance, full-service securities operations and so on), would benefit from simplified regulatory approval procedures and could be owned by a commercial or industrial company if the bulk of its federally insured bank subsidiaries (those accounting for at least 80 per cent of the aggregate total of the banking subsidiaries' assets) were classified as Zone 1 institutions while the remainder secured Zone 2 status.

Lower down the solvency tree, the penalties would come into play, as banks faced progressively stricter regulation and supervision. Zone 3 institutions, for example, could be asked to restrict their rates of growth, dividend payments or activities, to improve their capital ratios, to limit remuneration of executives, to divest associated companies or to dismiss officers and directors of the bank. Moreover, those financial service holding companies (and their commercial or industrial controllers) that own one or more institutions falling into the Zone 3 category could themselves be subjected to capital requirements and restrictions on the payment of dividends. Similar restrictions would apply to Zone 4 institutions, although they could also be precluded from paying any dividends; and institutions in the Zone 5 category would normally be closed down and sold off or otherwise placed in receivership, even if their capital positions were still positive.

The reform of federal deposit insurance   First and foremost, the Treasury recommended a reduction in the *scope* of deposit insurance in order to reduce potential taxpayer exposure and to reintroduce market discipline. Thus, while 'small' depositors would continue to enjoy protection, unnecessary protection would be removed from 'large', sophisticated investors who had 'exploited' the system by holding a range of insured accounts – individual, joint, retirement and trustee – and using deposit brokers to maximize their insurance coverage. Accordingly, the Treasury proposed that federal deposit insurance coverage be limited for each individual, after a two-year transitional period, to $100,000 per institution plus a further $100,000 per institution for funds held in a retirement account. The FDIC was also asked to carry out a cost-benefit analysis of a system that provided only $100,000 of protection per person[36] and to report its findings within 18 months. The loopholes existing in the shape of brokered disposits[37] and pension plan 'pass-through' coverage[38] would also be closed. Finally, the FDIC would under no circumstances be allowed to bail out non-deposit creditors, and would only be permitted to protect uninsured deposits other than in exceptional circumstances, (that is, when the Treasury or the Federal Reserve deemed that the risks posed for financial stability warranted it, such as those which might arise from large interbank exposures or damage to the payments system) if it could show that this would represent the least costly resolution approach. In such instances, a 'final settlement payment' to uninsured depositors would be made. The changes suggested in FDIC operating procedures need not be implemented, however, for a further three years.

Apart from reducing the scope of the federal deposit insurance net, the Treasury was also keen to secure improved market discipline by changing the basis on which the 'premiums' paid by depository institutions are calculated. Accordingly, it recommended a switch from flat-rate premiums, which subsidize high-risk, poorly run institutions at the expense of well-run banks and the taxpayer, to risk-based premiums (accounting for credit and interest rate risk) linked to levels of capital (combining the Tier 1 and Tier 2 components developed by the Basle Committee – see Chapter 8): those with higher ratios of capital-to-risk weighted assets than required would pay lower premiums. Again, however, it was recommended that the change be phased in over a two-year period.

Finally, as a matter of urgency, the Treasury recommended a recapitalization of the banking industry's insurance fund (BIF), with the funds being extracted from the banking industry itself and not from the taxpayer. And the

FDIC was mandated to explore further the possibility of involving the private sector more closely in the deposit insurance process.[39]

Non-bank powers The justification for the Treasury's proposals for expanded bank powers is that outdated laws, such as the Glass–Steagall and McFadden Acts, have contributed to declining bank profitability, increased the number of bank failures and impeded the banks' ability to respond to rapidly changing market conditions. In its far-reaching proposals, the Treasury duly recommended that: (i) US bank holding companies be allowed to operate nationwide with current restrictions on interstate branch banking (by any banking organization) being phased out over a three-year period;[40] (ii) the barriers between investment and commercial banking be removed; (iii) well-capitalized US banks be allowed to engage in a wide range of activities – banking, insurance, securities operations, mutual funds and so on – as long as the new activities are conducted in separately capitalized subsidiaries subject to an adequate structure of 'firewalls'[41] and the bank alone has access to federal deposit insurance; (iv) other financial service companies 'with mutual synergies with banking' be allowed to invest in banks, thereby providing the latter with a much-needed source of capital; (v) a new financial service holding company structure be established to allow for the common ownership of affiliates engaged in banking, securities business, mutual fund operation and insurance; (vi) subject to tight regulation, commercial and industrial companies be allowed to own financial service holding companies.[42]

As can be seen, taken together the proposals represent a radical plan for restructuring the US financial services industry, involving the repeal of the McFadden Act and the bulk of the Glass–Steagall Act and significant amendment to the Bank Holding Company Act of 1956 (which effects, at least partially, the separation of banking from commerce).

Treatment of foreign intermediaries Under the Treasury's proposals, foreign banks wishing to engage in the 'new financial activities' in the US (including underwriting and dealing in securities other than US government obligations)[43] would be required to establish a financial holding company (which may be the bank itself) and offer such services through separately capitalized subsidiaries. Moreover, all existing branch and agency banking operations would have to be brought together in a separately insured banking subsidiary.

An assessment Although the reform package prescribed by the Treasury contained a range of mainly sensible suggestions for improving the soundness of the US banking system and the cost-effectiveness of regulation and supervision, it is not beyond criticism (for a more detailed critique, see Keeton, 1991). Even if the package had been approved by Congress, it would still have been a case of too little too late. For example, only a modest scaling back of the scope of federal deposit insurance was called for – although, longer-term, further reduction might have resulted, depending on the outcome of the FDIC's study – leaving the financial system and taxpayers still exposed to the consequences of moral hazard. (The determined attempt to end the more blatant abuse of the deposit insurance system, by closing some of the loopholes used to extend coverage, and the introduction of variable-rate premiums linked to an *ex ante* measure of risk (that is, the risk-adjusted capital ratio), would however represent considerable advances on the existing system.) Moreover, the let-out clause inserted in the revised operating procedures for the FDIC leads one to question the Treasury's renunciation of the 'too-big-to-fail' doctrine: only history will show if uninsured depositors enjoy less protection in the future than in the past. And on top of all this, it should be remembered that most of the reforms were to have been phased in over a number of years even though early action is necessary to deal with the damage and malaise identified by the Treasury to be currently afflicting the US financial services industry. Despite their obvious concerns for the potential disruption that the recommended changes would bring, time may not be on the side of the administration.

Finally, on specifics, the proposals for structural reform may be criticized for not going far enough[44] (two federal regulatory bodies would have survived) and for unnecessarily adding to the real resource burden associated with federal regulation and supervision by calling for the establishment of an entirely new federal agency and siting it in the Department of the Treasury, an agency hitherto not directly involved in banking supervision. The plans to force a change in the way foreign banks conduct their US operations are also open to criticism on the grounds that: (i) enforced subsidiarization of their US banking operations would result in an unacceptable increase in compliance costs (especially in respect of capital requirements) and could result in a reduction in the supply of credit in US banking markets at a time when capacity constraints may already be contributing to a generalized credit crunch; (ii) the changes might cause foreign banks to scale back their US operations or even withdraw from the US totally; (iii) the proposals run counter to the national treatment principle espoused by the authorities and risk provoking retaliation, especially from EC countries; and (iv) by impairing the operational flexibility of foreign banks in US markets, the proposals, if implemented, risk destabilizing this segment of the US financial services sector.

Congress's reaction

Whatever the merits of the Treasury's reform package (much of the detail remained to be fleshed out) and its individual components, the debate was rendered largely academic by Congress's rejection of most of the proposals late in 1991. Out of the window went the Treasury's plans for repealing the McFadden (and the Douglas Amendment) and Glass–Steagall Acts, along with its proposals for allowing capital to be injected into the US banking industry via the ownership of banks by industrial and commercial companies. A combination of heavy lobbying by small banks, insurance companies and securities firms, and a marked reluctance on the part of Congress to contemplate anything that smacked of risk-taking, however small the risk, killed off these proposals.

Not all of value was rejected, however. Congress's own slimmed-down reform package, which materialized in the shape of the Federal Deposit Insurance Corporation Improvement Act (FDICIA) in November 1991 (effective from 19 December 1991), did involve sanctioning the recapitalization of the banking industry's deposit insurance fund (BIF);[45] brokered deposits would henceforth usually be denied to all except well-capitalized depository institutions; and the FDIC was mandated to devise a system of risk-based deposit insurance premiums for introduction by 1 January 1994.[46] Moreover, changes in supervisory procedures along the lines suggested by the Treasury – 'rule-based' and 'capital-based'[47] – were agreed, along with the proposals concerned with the establishment of new operating procedures for the FDIC. Accordingly, banks must now be examined by a federal agency at least once a year unless they have assets of under $100 million and are deemed to be well-capitalized and well-managed, in which case they need only be examined every 18 months; regulators must intervene promptly and act in accordance with pre-specified rules, as set out in section 131 of the FDICIA (for further details, see Gail and Norton, 1992, Part I), if banks' holdings of capital fall below specified levels (the drawback of such an approach is that weak but potentially viable banks are not given a chance to redeem themselves); and the FDIC must deal with failed banks in a fashion which is least-costly for BIF and, from 1995, will be prohibited from offering compensation to uninsured depositors unless the Treasury, on the advice of the FRB, decides otherwise in the interests of promoting financial stability. Unfortunately, however, foreign banks engaged in retail banking (that is, taking deposits in amounts up to $100,000) will be required to operate through separately capitalized insured subsidiaries if they want to accept or maintain such deposits[48] unless the federal authorities are successful in getting this decision overturned.[49,50]

Outstanding issues
Apart from the need for monetary reform,[51] a number of issues clearly need resolving (see Sellon, 1988, for one view on what needs to be done) if the cost-effectiveness of banking regulation and supervision is to be improved in the US. The arguments in favour (for example, as put by the US Treasury) of allowing banks wider powers are highly persuasive, suggesting that repeal of the Glass–Steagall Act, the McFadden Act and the Douglas Amendment to the Bank Holding Company Act of 1956 is highly desirable even if politically unattractive.[52] Similarly, the desirability of some rationalization[53] in the institutional structure governing the federal regulation and supervision of commercial banks is beyond dispute if the problems associated with minimizing overlap and underlap are to be avoided. More contentiously, the present insurance coverage afforded by federal deposit insurance should be cut back,[54] and the FDIC's discretion to provide protection to uninsured depositors narrowed with immediate effect as part of a scaling-back of the 'too-big-to-fail' doctrine (see Kaufmann, 1990, for a deeper discussion of the issues involved). The decision to restrict supervisory forbearance and hence allow for earlier closure of ailing institutions according to pre-specified rules may, however, return to haunt banking supervisors because judicious application of judgement, which can result in a better outcome for taxpayers and the economy, is now severely circumscribed.

Despite the urgent need for a recapitalization of the US banking industry, which is still labouring under the might of non-performing loans (many of which are property-related) and suffering from intense competition from foreign banks and domestic non-bank financial intermediaries, the jury is still out on the issue of whether or not to remove the barriers separating banking from commerce, the conventional wisdom still (just) holding sway (see Corrigan, 1987 and 1991; and Keeton, 1991, for justification of the *status quo*). There is less dispute, however, over the need to effect a reduction in general compliance costs for the banking sector (see American Bankers Association, 1989, especially chs II and IV, for a detailed analysis); to make greater use of market value accounting in regulatory policies (especially in determining the point of intervention); to restrict the Fed's use of the 'lender of last resort' facility to liquidity rather than solvency support,[55] as far as practicable (see Todd, 1988; and Goodfriend and King, 1987); and to ensure that a policy of 'lead regulation' is effectively used where more than one agency is involved in the supervision of a banking organization or banking group. Moreover, Congress should be wary of supporting measures which conflict with the administration's general principle of giving national treatment (see Key, 1990) to foreign organizations conducting financial operations (which now account for some 45 per cent of the US industrial and commercial loan market – McCauley and Seth, 1992) on US soil, not least because of the longer-term damage this might do to the US economy (La Ware, 1992).[56]

Notes

1. The thrift industry is not covered in this text. For recent developments in this area, see Hall (1990).
2. Others involved are: the Department of Justice, which is concerned with the application of US Antitrust Laws and is required to review all proposed bank mergers to check for anticompetitive and monopolistic tendencies; the Federal Trade Commission, which attempts to protect consumers of financial services from unfair trading practices, in accordance with the Federal Trade Commission Improvement Act of 1975; and the Securities and Exchange Commission, which is concerned with certain aspects of banks' involvement in securities operations (for example, it regulates the 'section 20' subsidiaries of banks (see pp. 222–4), involving the imposition of capital requirements and its 'broker-dealer' requirements).
3. The vast majority of state banking authorities insist upon FDIC approval for deposit insurance before granting charters.
4   Supervision, under the FDIC, was also introduced in a bid to avoid the likelihood of collapse from mismanagement.
5. Since 1982, the 'full faith and credit' of the federal government has backed the insurance agencies' guarantees; and, apart from raising premium income in the normal fashion (see the text), the agencies (now only the FDIC) have had access to emergency lines of credit at the Treasury.
6. This is a result of the adoption of a so-called 'too-big-to-fail' doctrine. An example of this was the FDIC's decision in 1984 to guarantee *all* the deposits (plus other debts) of Continental Illinois, an episode repeated in respect of the depositors of the First Republic Bank of Texas in 1988.
7. The FDIC is empowered, under FIRREA, to set deposit premiums at whatever level it chooses, subject to a maximum assessment rate of 0.325 per cent and a maximum year-on-year increase of 0.075 per cent. For the latest FDIC intentions, see note 46.
8. Prior to the passage of this Act there was no federal (only state) oversight of the operations of foreign banks' US branches and agencies; only the activities of their US subsidiaries were covered.
9. Until recently, the authorities have sought (for example, through the Bank Holding Company Act of 1956 and attempts to halt the spread of non-bank banks) to separate 'banking' from commerce, although the decision to allow commercial enterprises to buy into the savings and loan associations industry represented a major breach of this principle. The Treasury's request that a similar development be allowed in respect of commercial banks – in order to secure a badly needed recapitalization of the sector – was, however, rejected by Congress in 1991 (see p. 77).
10. Their overseas activities are governed by the Federal Reserve Act of 1913 and the Bank Holding Company Act of 1986, as implemented by the Federal Reserve Board in accordance with Regulation K (see Chapter 9).
11. As noted earlier, they are regulated under the International Banking Act of 1978 in accordance with the Federal Reserve Board's Regulation K and Regulation Y.
12 Prior to the introduction of the Bank Holding Company Act of 1956 banks could evade the limitation imposed by the Banking Act of 1933 by setting up bank holding companies (that is, a holding company owning 25 per cent or more of the voting stock of one or more banks) which were authorized to engage in such activities. The exclusion of one bank holding companies from the Act, however, created a further loophole which was not closed until 1970.
13. Though not identical. Bank holding companies, for example, have been allowed under Regulation Y to establish subsidiaries engaged in activities which are closely related to banking yet such opportunities are denied to banks. Such activities embrace computer

services, credit card operations, discount stockbroking and finance company operations, among others. To be closely-related to banking, an activity must satisfy at least one of the following criteria:

(i)   a significant number of banks have undertaken it for a number of years;
(ii)   it involves taking deposits or lending;
(iii)   it is complementary to banking services;
(iv)   it is something in which banks have considerable expertise (such as data processing).

The full list of such activities sanctioned for bank holding companies is presented in Table 9.1, although it should be noted that additional authorizations can be secured by directly submitting applications for approval to the Federal Reserve Board. If the proposed activities may reasonably be expected to produce net public benefits they are likely to be approved.

14.   Under a loophole in Delaware state law, however, local banks (for example, Citicorp and Bankers Trust) have been allowed since 1990 to sell insurance products on a national basis from subsidiaries in that state – up to 25 per cent of total capital, surplus and profit can be invested in insurance operations. A Federal Reserve Board order barring them from underwriting and selling insurance nationwide was overturned by an appeals court in Manhattan in June 1991, a decision confirmed by the Supreme Court in January 1992.

15.   Under the International Banking Act of 1978 (the IBA), *foreign* banks lost the competitive advantage *vis-à-vis* domestic banking concerns which they had enjoyed because of the exemption of their branches and agencies from federal regulation; this allowed them, for example, to establish full service branches in more than one state, where permitted by state law. (Under the IBA, a foreign bank with a US branch or subsidiary was required to designate one of the states in which it operated as its home state, which could only be changed once. Deposit-taking powers of new branches or agencies established outside this home state then became limited to those permissible for an 'Edge Act' corporation; that is, they had to be related to international activities.) Existing multi-state operations, however, were 'grandfathered', and new competitive opportunities were created by permitting foreign majority ownership of 'Edge Act' corporations for the first time and abolishing the prohibition against foreign citizens serving as directors of national banks.

16.   That is, acquisitions by any person or corporation or combinations thereof of 25 per cent or more of the voting power of any depository institution plus, if no one owns more, individual acquisitions of 10 per cent or more of the voting power.

17.   Although the provisions of Title V of the DIDMCA, which phased out certain interest rate ceilings during the period 1980–3, override state usury provisions on certain types of loan, states were given until 1 April 1983 to reinstate usury ceilings if they thought it desirable. Some duly chose to do so, although in practice they are always set above market rates.

18.   Other factors, of course, impact on this decision, however, notably the borrowing facilities available at one's local federal reserve bank. (Under DICMCA, all banks, member or non-member, became subject to the same deposit reserve requirements thereby removing a previous incentive for banks to remain outside the FRS where such requirements were generally less onerous.)

19.   That is, those whose consolidated assets exceed $1 billion or which receive a 'BOPEC' ranking of three or above (the ranking runs from 1 to 5). (The acronym 'BOPEC' relates to the 'bank', 'other subsidiaries' (especially non-bank subsidiaries), the 'parent', 'earnings' and 'capital'.) Anything ranked 4 or above receives 'limited scope' inspection during the intervening period on a six-month frequency basis.

20.   In assessing a borrower's ability to repay, the FRB will look closely at collateral-to-loan-value ratios, especially when examining real-estate lending. The FRB requires

frequent reappraisal of the discount rates used to calculate the present value of the anticipated cash flow (taking a three- to four-year period view for real-estate lending) to reflect market changes, with the banks being required to write down any losses created as a result of the reappraisal.

21. That is, the sum of the value of loans classified as 'substandard', 'doubtful' and 'loss'.

22. That is, shareholders' equity plus reserves, broadly speaking.

23. That is, 20 per cent of the value of 'substandard' loans plus 50 per cent of the value of 'doubtful' loans plus 100 per cent of 'loss' loans.

24. That is, the sum of 'non-accrual' loans (loans which are at least 90 days overdue and which no longer accrue interest) and 'other real-estate owned' items (real estate which has been foreclosed upon). 'Performing non-performing loans' are another category of 'non-performing assets' comprising those loans which, at the moment, present a problem but which, regulators believe, in the long-term may pose problems because of the borrower's doubtful ability to repay. Such loans are classified as 'substandard' and put on a non-accrual basis.

25. Unintentionally, reserve requirements do, however, serve this purpose.

26. There is a presumption that banks are maturity-matched up to around the 60-day mark, although no guidelines apply as in the UK.

27. Designed, for example, to alert management to significant maturity-mismatching beyond the 60-day maturity threshold, and to ensure that a bank is always able to meet its contractural obligations, on both sides of the balance sheet, as they fall due.

28. The final assessment of an organization's capital adequacy takes factors other than the risk-based calculus into account. Such factors include the quality and level of earnings, investment and loan portfolio concentrations, loan and investment policies, and managerial capabilities. Account will also be taken of the organization's exposure to interest rate risk, liquidity risk, funding risk, market risk and asset quality.

29. The FRB justified this in a press release dated 19 January 1989 as follows: 'Retention of an overall leverage constraint is important since, in the absence of such a constraint and without a comprehensive measure for interest rate risk the assignment of a significant volume of assets to the zero percent risk category under the risk-based capital framework could allow a banking organization to assume an unwarranted degree of leveraging and risk-taking.'

30. As defined by federal regulators in accordance with the Basle Committee's rules for defining capital (see Chapter 8).

31. Four kinds of assistance are available under the FRB's Regulation A: (i) 'short-term adjustment credit', which may be provided to allow institutions to satisfy temporary requirements for funds or otherwise to allow them to cushion more persistent fund outflows, pending an orderly adjustment of the borrower's assets and liabilities; (ii) 'extended seasonal credit', which is available for longer periods on a seasonal basis to smaller institutions which lack access to national money markets; (iii) 'other extended credit', which is designed to be given to banks experiencing difficulties arising from exceptional circumstances (such as a generalized liquidity crisis), or practices peculiar to that institution in instances where such assistance is deemed to be in the public interest and is not available from other sources; and (iv) 'emergency credit' may be provided to other parties, such as individuals, partnerships, non-financial corporations and, since 1991, securities companies, in exceptional circumstances if it is believed that a failure to provide such credit would adversely affect the economy. Interest charges under the first two credit facilities are generally levied at the basic discount rate although a variable surcharge may be levied against persistent borrowers, while rates above the basic discount rate are typically charged on credit provided under the last two facilities. Collateral is also usually taken, subject to the Federal Reserve Bank's discretion.

32. If the acquirer is concerned about some of the bank's assets it can bid on a 'clean bank' basis; that is, the acquirer assumes all the liabilities of the federal bank but none of the assets, receiving instead cash from the FDIC equal to the liabilities minus the premium

that the successful bidder offers. The FDIC is then left to dispose of the assets, some of which are usually bought by the acquiring institutions.

33. For an overview, see Hall (1990a).
34. The bail-out of the savings and loan associations industry is still fresh in the minds of politicians and taxpayers alike. (For a discussion of how the problem of the US thrift industry was tackled, see Hall, 1990b).
35. Numerous calls have been made in the past for a rationalization of the federal regulatory structures, the most recent of which featured in the report of President Bush's 'Task Force' (Office of the Presidency, 1984).
36. This was the limit initially favoured by the Treasury but subsequently dropped following opposition from the FDIC and small banks.
37. That is, deposits placed by brokers, mainly on behalf of wealthy individuals, with a variety of banks in amounts up to $100,000. This is the most efficient means for wealthy depositors to maximize insurance coverage as such deposits are fully insured because coverage passes through to each of the deposit broker's customers no matter how large the broker's total investment in a bank. This, however, results in banks gaining access to large pools of funds at below market rates and the funds being placed without any thought being given to the riskiness of the borrowing institutions.
38. 'Pass-through' coverage arises when a fiduciary, acting on behalf of a client, deposits funds for a large number of beneficiaries, with $100,000 of deposit insurance cover passing through to each of the beneficiaries.
39. One avenue of approach that might be worth exploring is to use the private sector to provide reinsurance, in the process providing a price-indicator which the FDIC could employ in its pricing of deposit insurance. Deposit insurance, however, would remain primarily in government hands.
40. The Treasury study notes that although 33 states permit nationwide banking and another 13 regional banking, all such operations (except a few conducted by state-chartered, non-member banks) have to be conducted through subsidiaries, which is a costly and inefficient means of provision as compared with branching operations. The Treasury calculated that full interstate branching would save the banking industry $10 billion a year.
41. This is the *de facto* approach adopted by the Federal Reserve Board towards the erosion of Glass–Steagall, in which it has been instrumental (see Chapter 9).
42. The only powers taken away from banks under the Treasury proposals would be those currently possessed by FDIC-insured state chartered banks which allow them to engage in activities denied to national banks; under the Treasury's proposals, new federal deposit insurance qualifications would rule out such opportunities.
43. Those already authorized to conduct such operations would be required to seek new authorization three years after enactment of the bill.
44. Some, however, would refute this criticism on the grounds that competition in regulation is eminently desirable in the belief that 'good' regulation will drive out the 'bad'. (The danger, of course, is that the reverse may happen as a result of the 'competition in laxity' which may occur as regulators seek to pursue or expand their customer base.)
45. To be achieved by borrowing from the Treasury (BIF's line of credit at the Treasury was to be increased from $5 billion to $30 billion) and from the capital market (BIF would be allowed to borrow working capital up to a sum equivalent to 90 per cent of the value of its assets). The net effect of such measures would be to allow BIF to borrow up to $70 billion, with repayments being financed from the insurance premiums paid by the banks over the next 15 years. (The danger of rapid increases in premiums – see note 46 – however, is that more banks fail and the supply of credit is further restricted as even the well-capitalized banks are forced to curb their lending.)
46. In May 1992 the FDIC proposed that the level of premiums paid by insured banks should be increased from 23 cents per $100 of 'assessable deposits' to an average of 28 cents, with well-capitalized banks paying 25 cents and the least well-capitalized 31 cents per $100 of assessable deposits. The FDIC also classified banks into one of three categories based on their capital-to-assets ratios, restricting the taking of brokered deposits and the deposit rates paid by those in the lower two categories.

47. Five categories of bank were distinguished: well capitalized; adequately capitalized; under-capitalized; significantly under-capitalized; and critically under-capitalized. For further details, see Gail and Norton (1992, pp. 4–15).
48. Legislation putting this into effect appears in the shape of a new subsection (c) to section 6 of the International Banking Act of 1978.
49. The federal banking regulatory agencies have stated that foreign banks, for the time being, will not be held to be in violation of this requirement if they are complying with the 'old' rules (which allowed, for example, their insured state branches to accept deposits of under $100,000 from business entities, government units or other specified depositors) and are taking retail deposits either through an insured subsidiary bank or a 'grandfathered' branch. In the meantime, they are seeking the removal of the new requirement from the agreed package of reforms, at least until the FRB and the Treasury have completed their own examinations into the merits of subsidiarization (the latter's report must be submitted to Congress by the 26 November 1992).
50. The remaining provisions of Congress's reform package that relate to foreign banks' operations in the US are subsumed within the Foreign Bank Supervision Enhancement Act of 1991. Dubbed the 'BCCI Provisions' because they represent, in part, the FRB's attempt to block the supervisory loopholes so successfully exploited by BCCI in its illegal acquisition of a number of US banks, they required the FRB to:

(i)   formally approve the establishment of any *state* branch, agency or representative office by a foreign bank and its acquisition of ownership or control of a US commercial lending company (effective consolidated supervision by the home authority would be one precondition of approval);

(ii) formally approve the establishment of an initial *federal* branch or agency by a foreign bank;

(iii) determine that activities which are undertaken by state-licensed branches or agencies of foreign banks and which are not permissible for federal branches are consistent with sound banking practice;

(iv) assume primary authority to conduct examinations at least once every 12 months of any foreign bank branch, agency, representative office, commercial lending or bank subsidiary, or other US office or affiliate, co-ordinating such examinations with the OCC, the FDIC and relevant state supervisors where necessary;

(v)   close down any state branch, agency, representative office or commercial lending subsidiary of a foreign bank if it finds that either the foreign bank is not subject to comprehensive supervision or regulation on a consolidated basis by the relevant home authority or that there is 'reasonable cause to believe' that the foreign bank or affiliate has committed a violation of law or engaged in an unsafe or unsound banking practice in the US and, as a result, continued operation would not be consistent with the public interest or the purposes of the IBA, BHCA or FDIA;

(vi) take a wider range of factors into account than hitherto (for example, whether the applicant can provide adequate assurances that all information requested by the FRB will be provided; whether the applicant is subject to effective consolidated supervision by the home authority; the competence, experience and integrity of the officers, directors and principal shareholders of the applicant) when considering whether or not to approve applications from overseas companies subject to the BHCA to acquire control of a US bank;

(vii) formally approve any intended acquisitions by foreign banks subject to the BHCA of between 5 and 25 per cent of any class of voting shares of a US bank;

(viii) tighten up on reporting requirements relating to loans secured by 25 per cent or more of the outstanding voting stock of an insured depository institution by extending their coverage (to include, for example, extensions of credit made by *any* financial institution or its affiliates – this brings in foreign banks maintaining branches, agencies or commercial lending subsidiaries in the US – and extensions of credit made to 'any person or groups of persons').

The law is also amended to allow for the imposition by the regulatory agencies of civil penalties for violation of the IBA or for inaccurate or late reporting. Criminal penalties (including imprisonment for up to five years) may also be imposed on persons who, with the 'intent to deceive, to gain financially, or to cause financial gain or loss', knowingly violate the IBA.

51. It is far from clear that the two remaining monetary controls – prescribed reserve requirements and the prohibition on the payment of interest on corporate demand deposits – are necessary for the successful conduct of US monetary policy (see Goodfriend and King, 1987) which, given the distortions they create, suggest a need for their joint abolition. Their continued existence is probably due to the limited lobbying by the banks' trade association, the American Bankers Association, for their removal and the Treasury's concern at the loss of seignorage (despite the recent cuts in reserve requirements) that would result, and at the issues raised for the payment of interest on required reserves by any move to end the prohibition on the payment of interest on corporate demand deposits.

52. The arguments for and against repeal of the Glass–Steagall Act are considered in Chapter 9. For a study which questions whether the potential benefits arising from repeal of the McFadden Act and the Douglas Amendment would be realized, see Rose (1990).

53. Some, however, still hold the view that competition in regulation is desirable from a public policy perspective, as noted earlier.

54. Personal preference is for coverage of 90 per cent of $100,000 of 'assessable deposits' per depositor per institution.

55. In fact, under FDICIA, the Federal Reserve's freedom to lend money to a troubled institution will be restricted from the end of 1993.

56. Congress is still debating the introduction of a Fair Trade in Financial Services Act which would involve identification of, and the possible levying of sanctions against, foreign banks whose home countries discriminate against US banks. In their enthusiasm for the application of the national treatment reciprocity principle, however, the authorities should be aware of the shortcomings in their own application of such a principle. For example, although neither the McFadden nor the Glass–Steagall Acts discriminate directly against EC-based banks, the measures adopted to circumvent the restrictions (such as the policies pursued by state authorities to allow regional interstate banking) can result in EC-based banks being indirectly discriminated against.

References

American Bankers Association (ABA) (1989), *The Burden of Bank Regulation* (Washington, D.C.: American Bankers Association).

Board of Governors of the Federal Reserve System (1985), *Regulation K: International Banking Operations* (Washington, D.C.: FRS).

Board of Governors of the Federal Reserve System (1987), *Regulation D: Reserve Requirements of Depository Institutions* (Washington, D.C.: FRS).

Board of Governors of the Federal Reserve System (1988), *Regulation D: Reserve Requirements of Depository Institutions* (Washington, D.C.: FRS).

Board of Governors of the Federal Reserve System (1989a), *Regulation Y: Bank Holding Companies and Change in Bank Control* (Washington, D.C.: FRS).

Board of Governors of the Federal Reserve System (1989b), *76th Annual Report* (Washington, D.C.: FRS).

Corrigan, E. G. (1987), 'A framework for reform of the financial system', statement made before the US Senate Committee on Banking, Housing and Urban Affairs on 18 June 1987, reprinted in the *Federal Reserve Bank of New York Quarterly Review*, Summer, pp. 1–8.

Corrigan, E. G. (1991), 'The banking–commerce controversy revisited', *Federal Reserve Bank of New York Quarterly Review*, Spring, pp. 1–13.

Cox, A. H. (1966), 'Regulation of interest on bank deposits', *Michigan Business Studies*, vol. 17, no. 4.

Federal Reserve Bank of Chicago (1987), 'Leveling the playing field: a review of the DIDMCA of 1980 and the Garn-St Germain Act of 1982', *Readings in Economics and Finance*.

Federal Reserve Board (1989), 'Banking Supervision and Regulation', *76th Annual Report*, Washington: Federal Reserve Board, pp. 167–85.

Gail, D. B. and Norton J. J. (1992), 'The US banking reform legislation of 1991: more regulatory micro-management and supervision' (Dallas, Texas: SMU School of Law) mimeo.

Goodfriend, M. and King, R. G. (1987), *Financial Deregulation, Monetary Policy and Central Banking*, (Rochester, N.Y.: University of Rochester) mimeo.

Hall, M. J. B. (1990a), 'Banking reforms in the United States: the background to the current debate', *Journal of International Banking Law*, vol. 5, no. 9, pp. 389–94.

Hall, M. J. B. (1990b), 'Banking reforms in the USA: Part 1', *Journal of International Banking Law*, vol. 5, no. 12, pp. 489–98.

Horvitz, P. M. (1986), 'Alternative ways to resolve insolvencies', in G.J. Benston *et al.* (eds), *Perspectives on Safe and Sound Banking: Past, Present and Future* (Cambridge, Mass.: MIT Press).

Kaufman, G. G. (1990), 'Are some banks too large to fail?: myth and reality', *Contemporary Policy Issues*, October , pp. 1–14.

Keeton, W. R. (1991), 'The Treasury plan for banking reform', *Federal Reserve Bank of Kansas City Economic Review*, May/June, pp. 5–24.

Key, S. J. (1990), 'Is national treatment still viable?: US Policy in theory and practice', *Journal of International Banking Law*, vol. 5, no. 9, pp. 365–81.

Kidwell, D. S. and Peterson, R. L. (1981), *Financial Institutions, Markets and Money*, (Hinsdale, Ill.: Dryden Press).

La Ware, J. P. (1992), 'Statement made before the Subcommittee on Financial Institutions Supervision, Regulation and Insurance and the Subcommittee on International Development, Finance, Trade and Monetary Policy of the Committee on Banking, Finance and Urban Affairs on November 20 1991', reprinted in the *Federal Reserve Bulletin*, January, pp. 31–5.

Leahy, M. (1991), 'Determining foreign exchange risk and bank capital requirements', *International Finance Discussion Paper* no. 400 of the Board of Governors of the Federal Reserve System, Washington, D.C., June.

McCauley, R. N. and Seth, R. (1992), 'Foreign bank credit to US corporations: the implications of offshore loans', *Federal Reserve Bank of New York Quarterly Review*, vol. 17, Spring, pp. 52–65.

Office of the Presidency (1984), *Blueprint for Reform: the Report of the Task Group on Regulation of Financial Business* [Task Force Report], Washington, D.C., July.

Rose, P. S. (1990), 'The consequences of interstate banking deregulation for competition, the structure of service markets, and the performance of interstate financial service firms', (College Station, Tx.: Texas A & M University).

Sellon, G. H. (1988), 'Restructuring the financial system: summary of the bank's 1987 symposium', *Federal Reserve Bank of Kansas City Economic Review*, January, pp. 17–28.

Todd, W. F. (1988), 'Lessons of the past and prospects for the future in lender of last resort theory', paper presented at the *Conference on Bank Structure and Competition* organized by the Federal Reserve Bank of Chicago, Chicago, Illinois, May.

US Treasury (1991), *Modernising the Financial System: Recommendations for Safer, More Competitive Banks* [the Brady Report] (Washington, D.C.: US Treasury).

6   Bank regulation and supervision in Japan

Historical background

The postwar Japanese financial system was characterized by a rigid compartmentalization of financial institutions (and an associated separation of financial activities), underdeveloped financial markets and blanket regulation, reinforced by extensive 'administrative guidance' (that is, moral suasion), of all financial intermediaries.

Functional separation

The various financial intermediaries operating in Japan may be classified as shown in Exhibit 6.1. In principle, banking business is separated from securities business, deposit banking from trust business and, within the commercial banking sector, long-term from short-term finance. Further *de facto* separation, often secured through 'administrative guidance', results in additional functional segmentation in the form of the isolation of insurance business from banking and securities business, and foreign exchange business from deposit-taking (all depository institutions except the Bank of Tokyo have to obtain authorization from the Ministry of Finance (MOF), in accordance with the Foreign Exchange and Foreign Trade Control Law, before engaging in foreign currency operations). And further functional segmentation within the banking sector arises because of the founding charters of the various specialist banks. For example, the *sogo* banks, *shinkin* banks (including the *Zenshinren* Bank) and the *Shokochukin* Bank all specialize in the provision of finance to small- and medium-sized companies; and the *Norinchukin* Bank specializes in meeting the financial needs of the agricultural, forestry and fisheries industries.

As noted in Chapter 3, the separation of long-term from short-term finance within the private banking sector is achieved by law and the use of administrative guidance. The former results in the operation of two types of long-term credit institutions: long-term credit banks and trust banks, which specialize in the provision of long-term loans to industry and whose sources of funds are severely restricted (leading to a heavy reliance of the long-term credit banks on debentures and of the trust banks on loan trust accounts). The latter is used to limit the maturity composition of ordinary banks' borrowed funds (the longest maturity permitted for time deposits under these arrangements – no *legal* controls on the maturity composition of either deposits or loans exist – is two years)[1] and to limit the issue of financial debentures by institutions other than long-term credit banks.[2]

Exhibit 6.1   The Japanese financial system

The banking sector[a]

Non-bank deposit-taking intermediaries
    Private   credit co-operatives (including the National Federation of Credit
                    Co-operatives)
                    agricultural co-operatives (and their credit federations)
                    fishery co-operatives (and their credit federations)

    Public   the Post Office (postal savings)

Non-depository institutions
    Private   insurance companies: life assurance companies
                                    non-life insurance companies
                                  various mutual aid (*kyosai*) co-operatives
                    securities investment trust management companies
                    securities finance companies
                    consumer credit institutions
                    venture capital firms
                    private housing finance companies
                    securities companies
                    money market dealers
    Public   Trust Fund Bureau, Special Account for Post Office Life
                    Insurance and Postal Annuity, Industrial Investment Special
                    Account
                    Overseas Economic Co-operation Fund
                    People's Finance Corporation
                    Small Business Finance Corporation
                    Small Business Credit Insurance Corporation
                    Environmental Sanitation Business Finance Corporation
                    Agriculture, Forestry and Fishery Finance Corporation
                    Housing Loan Corporation
                    Finance Corporation of Local Public Enterprises
                    Hokkaido and Tohoku Development Corporation
                    Okinawa Development Finance Corporation
                    Government-related funding bodies

Note
[a]   See Exhibit 3.1 for a further breakdown.

Source: Derived from Federation of Bankers Associations of Japan, 1989, Figure 1.1, pp. 18–19.

The separation of banking from trust business, initially because of conflict of interest concerns but, after the Second World War, as a means of enforcing the separation of short- from long-term finance, was also secured by the joint use of legal provisions and administrative guidance. Under the Law Concerning Concurrent Operation of Savings Bank Business or Trust Business by Ordinary Banks of 1943 ordinary banks and long-term credit banks were permitted to engage in trust business, under licence from the MOF, in accordance with the Trust Business Law of 1922.[3] Administrative guidance (first adopted in 1958) has been used, however, to confine trust business to long-term financial institutions and, under the Loan Trust Law of 1952, non-trust banks engaging in trust operations are prohibited from obtaining long-term funds through the offering of loan trusts. The decision taken in 1985 to allow foreign banks to undertake trust business in Japan does undermine the principle of separation though.

The final major form of functional segmentation – the separation of banking from securities business – was effected for the first time in statute with the enactment of the Securities and Exchange Law of 1948. Article 65 of this law prohibits banks, in principle, from engaging in securities business other than for their own investment purposes or in pursuance of trust contracts. The underwriting and trading of public bonds, however, was exempted from the provisions, although administrative guidance ensured that all such activities except the underwriting of government bonds remained prohibited until the 1980s.

As for the separation of banking from trust business, the principle of separation of banking and securities business in Japan has since been breached with the admission in 1985 of securities subsidiaries of foreign banks to the Japanese market place. And the mushrooming in the securities operations of Japanese banks' overseas subsidiaries (and, indeed, in the banking operations of Japanese securities companies' overseas subsidiaries) since the mid-1980s further calls into question the rationale for continued enforcement of the remaining separation in domestic markets (this and other related issues are addressed in more detail below).

Financial market structure
The present-day structure of Japan's financial markets is illustrated in Exhibit 6.2. At the end of the Second World War, however, the situation was very different. The chief structural characteristics were that of a 'hollow', underdeveloped market place with indirect finance (that is, bank intermediation) the dominant force.

As far as the *money market* was concerned, development centred around the inter-bank market which, at that time, comprised only a call market. Moreover, rates in this market were strictly controlled. Freely negotiated

Exhibit 6.2   The structure of Japan's financial markets[a]

The money market

Interbank markets: the call market (1902)
the bill market (commercial bills – May 1971)
the 'Tokyo dollar' call market (April 1972)

'Open'[b] markets: bond repurchase agreement (bond[c] *gensaki*) market (1949)[d]
the (negotiable) CD market (May 1979 for issuing; May 1980 for secondary market trading)
the (yen-denominated) bankers acceptance (BA) market (June 1985)
the 'treasury bill' (i.e. short-term government bond) market (February 1986)
the commercial paper (CP) market (November 1987)
the euroyen market[e]

The Tokyo Offshore Market (December 1986)

The capital market

Bond markets: the government bond market (postwar reopening – the primary market, 1949; the secondary market, 1966)
the market for other 'public' bonds
the market for corporate bonds: bank debenture issues
'other' (public subscription and private placement)

Equity markets[f]

Futures and   bond futures (October 1985)[g]
options markets: stock (index) futures (June 1987)[h]
financial futures and options (interest, currency, other) (June 1989)[i]
US Treasury bond futures (December 1989)[g]
government-bond futures options (May 1990)[g]
options on euroyen futures (July 1991)[i]

The foreign exchange markets (July 1952)

Notes

[a]   The dates when trading started are shown in brackets.
[b]   That is, in which, in principle, the non-financial sector may participate.
[c]   There is also *gensaki* trading in CDs. This started in July 1981.
[d]   The market did not fully mature until 1967, although it took until 1976 for the market to be legalized by the MOF.
[e]   Prior to the abolition of the limits on the conversion of foreign currency into yen in June 1984 a separate yen conversion (broadly defined, i.e. spot foreign exchange position plus inter-office euroyen accounts) market was distinguished.
[f]   Stock exchanges are located in Tokyo, Osaka, Nagoya, Kyoto, Hiroshima, Fukuoka, Niigata and Sapporo with Tokyo accounting for over 80 per cent of trading by volume and value.
[g]   These are traded on the Tokyo Stock Exchange (TSE).
[h]   The date when trading first started on the Osaka Securities Exchange. (Stock index futures trading began on the TSE in September 1988.)
[i]   Trading takes place on the Tokyo International Financial Futures Exchange, established in April 1989.

Sources: Federation of Bankers' Associations of Japan (FBAJ), 1989, ch. 6; FBAJ, 1992, p. 14; Japan Centre for International Finance, 1988, parts II, III and V; Suzuki, 1987, part II, ch. 4.

money market rates did not arrive on the scene until the fledgling bond *gensaki* (that is 'repo') market materialized in 1949; the lack of a secondary market in government bonds led securities companies, the major holders, to initiate sale-repurchase agreements with agricultural financial institutions. But even here the market did not become well-established until 1967. The deepening of the money market did not begin to occur until the mid-1970s, when the newly established markets began to blossom, although the 'deregulation and internationalization' measures adopted thereafter (see below) eventually led to rapid growth in most segments of the market.

In respect of the *capital market*, a similar picture emerges. The government bond market was not reopened until 1949, and secondary trading remained virtually non-existent, despite the reopening of trading on the Tokyo and Osaka Exchanges in 1966, partly because of the dearth of supply – public sector deficits were not significant until the mid-1970s – partly because of the marketing tactics adopted by the monetary authorities whereby the bonds (treasury bills, in the form of 'discount bonds', were not issued until 1986) taken up at issue by the underwriting syndicate (comprising mainly banks and securities companies) were bought back by the Bank of Japan after one year; and partly because the low yield paid on the bonds meant that pre-maturity sales would result in capital losses. By choice, the Bank of Japan also preferred to secure its monetary policy objectives through the use of 'direct' controls (see below) rather than open market operations, so little pressure emerged for change from this source until the efficacy and efficiency of such a system began to be called into question in the mid-1970s. This, as noted earlier, was also the time when the emergence of sizeable public sector deficits began to put a strain on the chosen method for getting the associated government bond issues absorbed in the market place. Once again, deregulation and internationalization measures (see below) did not result in the emergence of a broad and active secondary market in government bonds until the mid-1980s.

The postwar corporate debenture market was also subdued, partly because of the restrictive issuing practices and controls involving, *inter alia*, demanding eligibility standards for prospective issuers, limitations on the size of issues, collateral requirements (under the so-called 'collateral rule'), anticompetitive underwriting practices and restrictions on the private placement of bonds. Despite later modifications to issuing practices and relaxation of the allied restrictions (see below), the market for straight corporate bonds (as opposed to 'convertibles', which benefited from the rising stock market) remained depressed during the 1970s and '80s, partly because of the attractions of the overseas market (restrictions on the issuing of foreign bonds were lifted in November 1975) with bullish views on the yen predominating. Further reforms will be necessary if the market is to realize its full potential.

A final reason for the hollowness of Japan's postwar capital market was its isolation from the rest of the world, a position secured by close regulation of all financial market participants and extensive foreign exchange controls, which were not substantially relaxed until 1980. As regards non-resident activity in the Japanese capital market, *Samurai* bond issues (yen-denominated bonds issued in Japan by non-residents) did not make an appearance until 1970, with *Shogun* bond issues (foreign-currency-denominated issues by non-residents) first putting in an appearance in 1972. And non-resident eurobond issues arrived even later, in 1977, with the market stagnating until 1984.

Regulatory structure

In addition to the functional separation achieved by the use of law and administrative guidance, all financial intermediaries to a greater or lesser extent were burdened by a plethora of regulations affecting most aspects of their operations. As far as private depository institutions were concerned such restrictions impinged, *inter alia*, on: their sources and uses of funds; the terms on which they could borrow and lend (that is, restrictions on yield, maturity and minimum denomination had to be observed along with collateral requirements); the activities in which they could engage; their branching and merger activities; and their investment decisions in respect of holdings of other companies' stock under the Antimonopoly Law of 1947. (See Suzuki, 1987, pp. 239–304 for a discussion of how private, non-depository financial intermediaries were affected.) In addition, the requirements of monetary policy necessitated the imposition of yet further restrictions in the form of reserve deposit requirements, credit ceilings on borrowing from the Bank of Japan, and lending (that is, 'window) 'guidance', both qualitative and quantitative. (These requirements are discussed further below). Once again, a mixture of legal requirements (such as Banking Law and cabinet and ministerial ordinances which are used to enforce it) and moral suasion (in the guise of MOF circulars and administrative notices) were used to secure the authorities' objectives.

Apart from the prohibitions applied under the foreign exchange, securities and trust laws which have already been noted, the scope of (ordinary) private banks' domestic activities is determined by Banking Law, as interpreted by the Banking Bureau at the MOF. Under the current Banking Law of 1981, basic (that is, 'typical') banking business is defined as the taking of deposits or instalment savings, the lending of funds or discounting of bills, and funds transfer (Article 10: clause 1). In addition, ordinary banks are permitted to engage in 'ancillary' and 'peripheral' business (in the latter case, only through associated companies, which may also undertake some ancillary business, such as factoring, the provision of credit guarantees, and credit card and mortgage certificate business, and act as agents for the banks), and in 'permissible' securities (Article 11) and trust (Article 12) business.

Ancillary business is defined in Article 10: clause 2 and comprises the following:

(i)   the guarantee of liabilities and acceptance of bills;

(ii)   the purchase and sale of securities and dealing in major index securities futures, in securities options and in foreign securities futures (but only for investment purposes or on receipt of a written request from a customer);

(iii)   the lending of securities;

(iv)   the underwriting of government bonds, local government bonds, and government-guaranteed bonds (but not for subsequent sale) and placement of bonds underwritten;

(v)   the acquisition and ceding of monetary claims (for example, negotiable Certificates of Deposit (CDs) and other items designated by MOF ordinances; as of end-1989 this included commercial paper, housing mortgage bonds, and beneficiary certificates for housing loan trusts;

(vi)   the provision of subscription agency services for local government bonds, corporate bonds and other securities;

(vii)   the provision of agency services for banks and other entities engaged in financial business;

(viii) the handling of money transactions on behalf of national and local government bodies and corporations;

(ix)   the safekeeping of securities, precious metals and other items;

(x)   the changing of money (that is, of domestic currency into different denominations);

(xi)   dealing in financial futures on a custodial basis.

The list is designed to reflect those business activities which are related to banking business and of a similar nature to it. Those activities on the list are expected to be used to generate income and, in volume terms, should not exceed banking business.

The permissible *peripheral* business activities are stipulated in circulars issued by the Director General of the Banking Bureau of the MOF. The list currently includes venture capital, management consulting and advisory services, computer work, leasing, housing finance and loans. Prohibited activities include real-estate business involving the general public, the sale of goods or commodities, travel agency business and insurance brokerage.

Apart from the rules governing the range of ordinary banks' permissible peripheral business activities, there are also rules concerning the size of the equity stake that the parent bank may take in the associated company and the physical separation of the company's office from that of the parent bank. Accordingly, parental shareholdings must not exceed 5 per cent and the company's office is not allowed to be located in the same building as the parent bank's office.

The range of permissible *securities* activities listed in Article 11 comprises various activities associated with the undertaking of business in government and other forms of bond. This includes both underwriting and the offering of bonds for subscription or sale. Notwithstanding this, however, banks must still obtain permission from the MOF to engage in such securities activities, in accordance with Article 65 of the Securities and Exchange Law (see Chapter 9). Apart from these activities, further activities in the securities field are sanctioned under Article 10 of the Banking Law under the heading of permissible ancillary business, as noted above.

Finally, banks are allowed to engage in *trust business* under the Law Concerning Concurrent Operation of Trust Business by Ordinary Banks of 1981 (previously, the Law Concerning Concurrent Operation of Savings Bank Business or Trust Business), in accordance with the Trust Business Law of 1922. They may also participate in mortgage debenture trust business, bond registration business and the lottery business in accordance with the Mortgage Debentures Trust Law, the Law for Registration of Corporate Debentures and the Law for Establishment of Certificates with Prizes respectively.

Having established the allowable scope of banks' activities, it is also worthwhile to highlight the controls and restrictions imposed on banks' borrowing and lending terms in the early postwar period. The relevant piece of legislation at this time was the Temporary Interest Rate Adjustment Law (TIRAL) which superseded the deposit rate accords operated by the regional banking associations (see Suzuki, 1987, pp. 40–1) in 1947. Under the TIRAL, which was designed to eliminate destructive interest-rate competition and to contribute towards the achievement of price stability, the Policy Board of the Bank of Japan, on the advice of the MOF, would set upper limits on interest rates for all *private* financial institutions, abolishing or changing them as deemed necessary. As far as deposit rates were concerned, ten types of deposit were initially distinguished although this was reduced to four in 1970: current deposits (which yield no interest); term deposits; deposits for tax payment; and 'other' deposits. Even after this date, though, guidelines were still used by the Bank of Japan to control the rates paid on the other types of deposit (including savings accounts) previously distinguished (see Suzuki, 1987, p. 149). Since the mid-1970s, however, the number of TIRAL-exempt (as determined by the MOF) deposit or deposit-like instruments (such as money market certificates) has increased to include CDs, non-resident yen deposits of foreign governments, foreign central banks and international institutions, and foreign currency-denominated deposits, and rates have been gradually liberalized on TIRAL-affected instruments (see below).

As for the *lending rates* of private financial institutions, the TIRAL prescribed maximum interest rates for loans of under one year to maturity and over Y1 million made by commercial banks, trust banks, insurance companies and the *Norinchukin* Bank (the loan rates charged by *sogo* banks, *shinkin* banks and credit co-operatives are circumscribed by their founding laws). This set the upper limits for short-term lending rates for these institutions, although the *de facto* loan rate ceilings, and the floors, were established according to agreed market practice. Despite the abolition of such anticompetitive market practices in 1975, increased *de facto* flexibility in the setting of loan rates did not materialize until the mid-1980s (see below).

Although the private financial institutions' long-term loan rates (that is, of a maturity greater than one year) were not subject to the TIRAL nor determined according to formalized market arrangements they were nevertheless subject to implicit rules agreed between interested parties, including the official authorities. Accordingly, the pre-1980 *de facto* floors for long-term loan rates were represented by the 'long-term prime rates' (that is, the rates charged to the highest-quality corporate customers) of the long-term credit banks and trust banks. Each institution would set its own prime lending rate at an agreed margin above these rates and changes would be synchronized and be of identical amounts. This system survived intact until the early 1980s since when the long-term prime rates of the long-term credit banks and trust banks have ceased to set the floor for the long-term loan rates of other private banks, and greater flexibility has been introduced into the determination of the latter. Moreover, 'effective' loan rates (nominal rates adjusted for the effects of compensating balances, which are deposited with the lender by the borrower as part of a long-term customer relationship) have converged on nominal loan rates as competitive pressures have forced down the level of compensating balances required either to meet contractual obligations (as in the case of *buzumi* or *ryodate* deposits) or to satisfy customary business relationships.

Another source of influence over lending terms derived from the market practice of operating on the basis of collateralized transactions. As for most types of financial transaction in Japan, the provision of collateral was required in all lending transactions, with market practice being standardized in 1962. The internationalization of the money and capital markets (see below) in recent years, however, has brought about a reduction in the incidence and significance of collateral requirements with uncollateralized transactions, for example, now routinely taking place in the interbank market (see Suzuki, 1987, p.16).

The final forms of control which impinged upon the private banks' borrowing and lending terms were the restrictions placed on the maturity and minimum size of denomination for certain types of deposit and deposit-like instruments. Maturity controls, for example, applied to time deposits (initially, they had to be of three months, six months, one year or two years initial term), 'maturity-designated' time deposits (for a period of one year or more and under three years), CDs (initially, for terms of over three months and under six months, although today the terms can vary from one month to one year) and money market certificates (MMCs) (initially, they could only be issued with maturities of between one and six months but today maturities can range from one month to three years, matching those of time deposits). Similarly, minimum sizes of deposit were prescribed for time deposits (Y100), 'maturity-designated' time deposits (Y100, with a maximum of Y3 million applying), CDs (initially, Y500 million but today, Y50 million) and MMCs (initially Y50 million but today, Y1 million). And, finally, to qualify for the payment of 'freely-determined' interest rates, large-scale time deposits had, at least initially, to be in excess of Y1 billion, although this figure has since come down to Y3 million, with the abolition of the restriction promised for 1993.

Pressures for change

Internal pressures
In the aftermath of the first oil-price shock of 1973, the Japanese economy underwent important structural change which radically transformed the domestic financial scene. This duly led to internal demands for deregulation at home which would not only improve the efficiency of domestic markets but also end their isolation from the rest of the world.

The structural change alluded to above, which was brought about largely by the impact of higher oil prices on inflation and economic growth – both were adversely affected – resulted in significant changes in the financial positions of the different sectors of the economy. Specifically, the public sector deficit increased along with the personal sector surplus, while the corporate sector's deficit began to decline. The impact of these changes in the sectoral flow of funds on the financial system was dramatic.

The deterioration in public sector finances,[4] caused by the slowdown in economic activity and a loosening of the fiscal reins, created pressures both for reform of the primary market for government bonds and for expansion of the secondary market. The operating practices in the primary market were put under strain because of the sheer increase in the volume of bonds which the underwriting syndicate (comprising mainly banks but also other financial institutions) was being asked to absorb (see p.127, for further details on the operation of the syndicate). Resale in the market place was prohibited until 1977 and, in any case, would have resulted in capital losses being incurred because of the low yields paid on the bonds. As the syndicate members were obliged to hold the bonds for a minimum period of one year after which, in general, the Bank of Japan would purchase them, the burgeoning budget deficits posed funding problems for the banks (being over-lent, they would have to turn to the Bank of Japan for further advances) and threatened to reduce their profitability by virtue of the enforced increase in the proportion of their investment portfolio held in low-yielding form. Thus, although the operating practices in the primary market had served the purposes of the government well in the past, by minimizing debt-servicing costs, it began to realize that the post-1974 situation would require modification to existing market procedures. In particular, the funding (that is, cash reserve) burden on the banks, as the main syndicate members, would have to be alleviated by making issues direct to the general public (and non-bank financial intermediaries)[5] and/or by allowing banks to sell on to the general public. Both measures would help to reduce the adverse impact on bank profitability which would otherwise result, a goal which would also be served by paying market-related interest rates on the bonds. Indeed, without this the desired secondary market expansion would not occur as insufficient incentives would be provided to prospective purchasers to guarantee the required non-bank take-up of government stock. We can see, then, that the authorities' desire to finance the burgeoning budget deficits in a non-monetary fashion (control of the money supply came to the fore in 1974) and to protect the banking system from the adverse consequences that would otherwise result led to a diversification in the types and methods of bond flotation, and this in turn stimulated the development of the secondary market. The concomitant freeing-up of long term yields acted in turn to promote expansion in the short-term open markets and to increase pressure on the authorities to relax, if not abolish, interest rate controls. While the latter, reinforced by extensive administrative guidance, had served the real economy well in the past (for example, by promoting economic growth through industrialization and by stabilizing the financial system), albeit at the expense of a loss of efficiency, a new dawn had arrived. Somewhat belatedly perhaps but nevertheless quite unashamedly, officialdom began to champion the cause of efficient markets and institutions and of equity in regulation, and competition was actively promoted. Moreover, the internationalization of the Japanese financial system was adopted as a clear policy objective.

The needs and demands of the corporate and private sectors were also important in shaping the reform debate. The slowdown in economic activity and general uncertainty following the first oil-price shock caused industry to curtail investment dramatically. This, in turn, substantially reduced their demand for bank credit, a situation in keeping with their desire to reduce dependence on the banking sector for external funding. Indeed, it was this desire which led the corporations to demand greater access to the money and capital markets. This in turn would necessitate a widening and deepening of domestic markets and the dismantling of barriers denying entry to overseas markets. Such demands for wider access to alternative sources of funds went hand in hand with a search for higher real returns as corporate financial management gained in sophistication (the so-called *zaiteck* phenomenon). All these demands duly increased the pressure on the government to deregulate domestic markets and interest rates and to internationalize the Japanese financial system.

The personal sector, too, added its weight to demands for reform. Their chief concern was the acceleration in inflation following the oil-price hike and the explosion in monetary growth during 1972 and 1973, which had sharply reduced real rates of return on savings and cut real income growth. This duly led them to seek investment outlets offering higher real returns, especially in the light of the absence of any government-financed retirement scheme. Lower product/service charges and greater choice would also have been welcomed. In terms of political muscle, however, it is probably fair to say that the consumer lobby carried little weight at that time.

This was certainly not the case with the banks and other financial institutions, however. The banking lobby in particular was in full swing following the fall-off in corporate loan demand and the loss of depositors to institutions (such as the post office) and instruments offering higher real returns. Naturally enough, such a state of affairs led them to demand liberalization of their deposit (and lending) rates, removal of maturity restrictions on their deposits and the power to offer new instruments on which they could pay competitive rates. They also sought the ability to diversify their customer base, which would require, *inter alia*, removal of constraints on domestic activities for some and on foreign activities for all, and additional freedoms to allow them to improve risk management. For the banks, the latter freedom was particularly important because of the maturity mismatch forced upon them by the rigid separation of short-term from long-term finance (at least in respect of borrowing operations). But new hedging and funding opportunities would have been welcomed by all indigenous intermediaries operating in Japan at that time, along with the opportunity to operate overseas in order to diversify-away portfolio risk and to maximize risk-adjusted portfolio returns.

By the late 1970s, as a result of a full appreciation of the new economic realities and under growing pressure from all sections of society at home (the pressure from overseas is considered below), the Japanese government had clearly accepted the need for wide-scale deregulation and internationalization. From this time, as is explained below, the process of reform accelerated, a policy by then in keeping with the monetary authorities' wishes. For despite the risk of destabilizing the financial system, particularly in the adjustment phase, the funding problems created by the burgeoning budget deficits, the monetary management problems caused by a more liquid corporate sector and the growth of unregulated non-bank financial intermediaries, together with the need to deepen the foreign exchange market, all necessitated reform.[6] And, on top of these pressures, demands from overseas were reaching a crescendo.

External pressures
Apart from the 1973–4 oil-price shock which, because of Japan's almost total reliance on imported fuel, did so much to transform the domestic economy and end the isolation of Japan's financial system from the developed world's capital markets, external pressure for reform materialized as overseas governmental demands for the liberalization and internationalization of the Japanese financial system and for reciprocity in the treatment of overseas financial intermediaries.

The US government was the standard-bearer on both fronts, campaigning vociferously on behalf of the world economy and its own financial institutions, although EC governments – notably West Germany and the United Kingdom[7] – were active on the second front. Leaving aside the issue of reciprocity for the time being, the gist of the US government's argument was that the use of the yen as a reserve currency and in trade and international finance was not commensurate with Japan's position in the global economy (that is, as an important trading nation with huge balance of payments surpluses, and as a large net capital exporter). The hope, of course, of the US government was that, by forcing a speedier deregulation of domestic markets on the Japanese government and forcing them to open up their financial system to the outside world, the value of the yen would appreciate, thereby reducing some of their trading surpluses (particularly in manufacturing) with the rest of the world. Unfortunately for the US, the strength of capital flows won the day as far as the yen was concerned, with large net outflows going to the US, in part because of the higher interest rates available there.

The demands for reform arising essentially from trade friction[8] were formalized in bilateral meetings between the governments of the US and Japan within the forum of the Joint Japan–US *Ad Hoc* Group on Yen–Dollar Exchange Rate, Financial and Capital Market Issues (henceforth termed the 'Joint Group'), which comprised representatives from the Ministry of Finance of Japan and the US Department of the Treasury. The first evidence of the progress made in these discussions materialized with the publication of the Joint Group's first report in May 1984. This report set out the agreement reached on how Japan should deregulate its financial system and internationalize the yen. The discussion was compartmentalized into the measures required to deregulate Japan's money and capital markets, the requirements needed to ensure 'national treatment reciprocity' for overseas financial intermediaries (that is, the treatment of foreign institutions as domestic intermediaries in respect of their activities in Japan) and the measures to be taken to ensure internationalization of the yen through expansion of the euroyen market. On the first front, the Japanese agreed to remove interest rate ceilings on 'large' time deposits within three years; on the second, they agreed to allow foreign banks into the trust banking industry; and, on the last, they agreed to relax controls on euroyen lending, eliminate the 'real demand' rule in forward exchange transactions and remove the limits on the banks' oversold spot foreign exchange positions (see Suzuki, 1987, pp. 130–1).

The rationale underlying the Japanese government's general approach to financial deregulation and internationalization of the yen was spelt out in a MOF report which accompanied the publication of the Joint Group report in May 1984. This report, entitled *Present Status and Prospects for the Deregulation of Finance and Internationalization of the Yen*, was followed by a further report, *The Internationalization of the Yen*, which was published in March 1985 and set out the various steps necessary to secure such an objective. And in June 1987 yet another MOF report, *Current Plans for the Liberalization and Internationalization of Japanese Financial and Capital Markets*, was published, setting out the Ministry's latest plans for reform. These comprised: further deregulation of interest rates; expansion of the short-term money market; consolidation and expansion of the futures market; consolidation of the capital market; more freedom and flexibility for financial intermediaries in the conduct of their business; international coordination on the supervision of banks and assessment of their capital adequacy; examination of the issues relating to the interpenetration of business by financial intermediaries; and improving the access of foreign financial intermediaries to the securities market.

The reform measures instituted and the drafting of blueprints for reform went some way to placating antagonistic foreign governments in the second half of the 1980s; yet discord remained. This was largely due to the pace, rather than substance, of reform, with concomitant implications for the reciprocity problem. Thus, for example, although foreign banks were admitted to the trust banking industry in 1985, the speed with which foreign firms were being admitted to the Tokyo Stock Exchange ensured consternation on both sides of the Atlantic. Moreover, the US Treasury's national treatment studies served only to highlight the competitive disadvantages faced by foreign firms trying to break into the Japanese market place.[9] While acknowledging the formidable cultural and customary barriers facing foreign institutions' attempting to establish market share, the US government was keen to ensure that success would not be stymied by regulatory inequities. Accordingly, pressure was brought to bear to remove or reduce tangible barriers to entry and to reduce regulatory disparities by, for example, pushing for a fully developed interbank market (without it, foreign banks, because of their lack of a branch network and hence access to low-cost, retail deposits, would be disadvantaged) and for greater access for foreign banks to the Bank of Japan's discount window.

Despite the moves made by the Japanese government to accommodate the demands of foreign governments (the Joint Group was dissolved in April 1988), not everybody in the latter camp has been satisfied. In the US, this dissatisfaction manifested itself in the Riegle–Garn bill which threatened retaliation if national treatment reciprocity and effective market access were not perceived to have been given to US institutions operating abroad. Although aborted in October 1990, and in spite of the Federal Reserve's continued opposition to its implementation, the strength of feeling in Congress at the adoption of what is perceived to be deliberate delaying tactics by the Japanese government remains sufficiently strong to ensure that the resurrection of the Bill and its subsequent enaction cannot be ruled out. And the vigilance of EC governments and commissioners, especially after the completion of the Single Market in financial services in 1992, will continue to ensure that pressure from this side of the globe for national treatment reciprocity (including effective market access) is not relaxed in the near future.

The programme of financial deregulation in Japan

Internationalization of the yen
The various post-1978 liberalizing measures which contributed to the internationalization of the yen are presented, in chronological order of appearance, in Exhibit 6.3. As can be seen, the measures comprise three groups: (i) those associated with the liberalization of the euroyen market (including the establishment of a Tokyo Offshore Market); (ii) those associated with the liberalization of the yen-denominated[10] foreign bond market in Japan; and (iii) those associated with a deepening and internationalization of the foreign exchange market.

Liberalization, in fact, predated these initiatives, a major turning-point arriving in February 1973 with the floating of the yen. This was followed by some piecemeal relaxation of exchange controls (for example, in April 1978 non-corporate residents were allowed to hold foreign currency deposits with Japanese banks up to a limit of Y3 million) and then, in March 1979, foreign

Exhibit 6.3 Internationalization of the yen: the programme of deregulation post-1978

Liberalization measure	Date effective
Foreign governments and international organizations authorized to issue euroyen bonds.	1 March 1979
Liberalization of exchange controls under an amendment to the Foreign Exchange and Foreign Trade Control Law of 1947	1 December 1980
Ban on short-term euroyen lending to non-residents lifted	1 June 1983
'Real demand' rule abolished	1 April 1984
Guidelines on issue of euroyen bonds by residents relaxed	1 April 1984
Standard for issuing *Shibosai* bonds relaxed	1 April 1984
Rules concerning the issue of *Samurai* bonds relaxed	1 April 1984
Ban on issue of external bonds with long-term forward exchange contracts lifted	1 April 1984
Ban on issue of dollar-denominated yen-linked bonds lifted	1 April 1984
Non-prudential limits on overseas yen lending from Japan abolished	1 April 1984
Ban on short-term euroyen lending to Japanese residents lifted	1 June 1984
Restrictions on conversion of foreign currency into yen abolished	1 June 1984
Investment in Japanese real estate by non-residents liberalized	1 July 1984
Rules concerning issuing of *Samurai* bonds relaxed	1 July 1984
Issuing of euroyen bonds by foreign private corporations, state and local governments and government agencies authorized	1 December 1984

Liberalization measure	Date effective
Rules concerning non-resident euroyen bond issues relaxed	1 December 1984
Lead management of euroyen bond issues liberalized	1 December 1984
Standard for issuing of *Samurai* bonds by private companies relaxed	1 December 1984
Issuing of euroyen CDs (up to six months maturity) authorized	1 December 1984
Medium-term and long-term euroyen lending to non-residents sanctioned	1 April 1985
Regulations preventing currency swaps lifted	1 April 1985
Standard for issue of *Samurai* bonds by private companies relaxed	1 April 1985
Standard for eligible private sector issuers of non-resident euroyen bonds relaxed	1 April 1985
20 per cent withholding tax payable by non-residents on Japanese euroyen bonds abolished	1 April 1985
'Dual currency' euroyen bond issues sanctioned	1 June 1985
Criteria for resident euroyen convertible debenture issues relaxed	1 July 1985
Criteria for resident euroyen bond (straight and with warrants) issues relaxed	1 October 1985
Abolition of the 'no return rule' for *Samurai* bond issuers	1 February 1986
Floating rate euroyen notes and currency conversion euroyen bond issues sanctioned	1 April 1986
Standard for issue of *Samurai* bonds by private companies relaxed	1 April 1986
Rating system introduced for issuers of *Shibosai* bonds	1 April 1986
Standard for eligible private sector issuers of non-resident euroyen bonds changed	1 April 1986

Liberalization measure	Date effective
The period during which 'flow-back' of resident euroyen bond issues into Japan is barred cut from 180 to 90 days	1 April 1986
Foreign banks authorized to issue euroyen bonds	1 June 1986
Relaxation of the 'one-third rule' for *Shibosai* bond issuers	1 November 1986
Operations on the Tokyo Offshore Market commenced	1 December 1986
Restrictions on the issue of euroyen bonds with a four-year maturity lifted	1 June 1987
Criteria for resident euroyen bond issues relaxed	1 July 1987
The euroyen CP market was established	November 1987
Medium-term and long-term euroyen lending to residents sanctioned	May 1989
Four year minimum maturity threshold for non-Japanese issues of euroyen bonds relaxed (to three years)	June 1989
Liberalization of rules relating to residents' overseas deposits	July 1989
Relaxation of restriction on overseas deposit accounts	July 1990
Samurai bond market opened up to issuers with an investment grade credit rating	1 July 1992
Criteria for resident euroyen bond (convertible, straight and with warrants) issues relaxed	1 July 1992

Sources: JCIF, 1988, pp. 37–60; Osugi, 1990, pp. 10–17; Suzuki, 1987, pp. 124–7; FBAJ, 1992, p. 12.

governments and qualifying[11] international organizations were added to the list of overseas bodies – previously comprising only the International Financial Institutions – eligible to issue euroyen bonds. The amendment to the Foreign Exchange and Foreign Trade Control Law of 1947 in December

1980, however, set the scene for a dramatic acceleration in the pace of the yen's internationalization in the early to middle part of the 1980s.

Under the exchange control amendment, the philosophy underlying control was turned on its head. That is, in principle, cross-border transactions were made completely free unless specifically disallowed, although there is a proviso allowing for their reintroduction under broadly defined emergency conditions. This policy change both recognized and further encouraged the rapid growth of cross-border flows of funds. Prior to the amendment, such cross-border flows manifested themselves largely in the growth of 'impact loans' to Japanese residents (that is, foreign currency loans made by foreign banks resident in Japan which were not tied to any particular use).[12] After December 1980, however, the scale and diversity of cross-border flows expanded enormously as a result of the growth in yen-denominated loans by Japanese residents to non-residents,[13] in resident holdings of foreign currency[14] and in non-resident issues of yen-denominated bonds in Japan.[15] Japanese companies were also given more freedom to borrow abroad.

Despite the amendment and further subsequent easing in the exchange control regulations (see Exhibit 6.3) the position reached at the end of 1990 was still such that Japanese residents could not open portfolio investment accounts overseas nor avoid channelling funds for overseas investment through authorized financial companies in Japan. While these arrangements allow the MOF to oversee all such transactions, they do nevertheless undermine the spirit of the new approach adopted towards the use of exchange controls.

Liberalization of the euroyen market   The euroyen markets are those on which yen-denominated financial assets are traded outside Japan. The biggest euroyen market is based in London, other important centres being located in Singapore, Hong Kong and New York. Trading is conducted through the medium of eurocurrency instruments (euroyen deposits, euroyen CDs, euroyen CP and euroyen loans) and euroyen bonds. The Japanese banks have the largest share in euroyen transactions; the remainder are accounted for by foreign banks, foreign monetary authorities and other non-financial institutions.

The markets flourished in the early 1980s because of the relative advantages they enjoyed *vis-à-vis* domestic markets. For example, euroyen transactions have always been free from domestic controls in the shape of interest rate controls and legal reserve requirements and from the practices that prevail in domestic markets, such as the collateral requirements. But gradual relaxation of restrictions on euroyen trading and the abolition of the withholding tax on interest income received by non-resident holders of euroyen bonds served to accelerate the rate of growth towards the middle of the decade. This deregulation can be traced in Exhibit 6.3.

As far as the *non-resident issue of euroyen bonds* is concerned, the first major development occurred in March 1979, when foreign governments and international organizations with a good previous trade record in issuing yen-denominated foreign bonds in Japan were added to the list of institutions eligible to make such issues. Since the inauguration of the market in 1977 and prior to March 1979 the only eligible issuers had been the International Financial Institutions (the European Investment Bank made the first issue). The range of eligible issuers was further expanded in December 1984 when foreign private corporations, state and local governments and government agencies were added to the list. At the same time, the guidelines relating to non-resident euroyen bond issues were relaxed, in line with the May 1984 Joint Group report, together with the standard determining the eligibility of the issuer. For public sector issuers, those with a credit rating of 'A' or above from Standard & Poors or Moody's were eligible; for private sector issuers, a minimum of an 'A' rating from either of the two aforementioned credit rating agencies plus fulfilment of the *Samurai* market criteria (see below) was required. The standard for private sector issuers (or guarantors) was further relaxed in April 1985, to a minimum credit rating of 'A'. And finally, one year later, the criteria for determining the eligibility of private sector issuers were further changed (relaxed?) by making eligibility depend solely on achieving a minimum credit rating from any one of five rating agencies: two foreign[16] (Standard & Poors and Moody's) and three domestic (the Nippon Investors Service, the Japan Credit Rating Agency and the Japan Bond Research Institute).[17] Accordingly, non-resident private-sector firms (or their guarantors) with a minimum credit rating of 'A' were unconditionally eligible to make euroyen bond issues, just like non-resident public sector bodies.

The only other deregulatory move of note on this front, apart from the diversification in products sanctioned,[18] was the sanctioning of foreign bank issues of euroyen bonds[19] in June 1986, permission for which had previously been withheld because of the implied infringement of the principle of separation of long-term from short-term finance.

Turning to *resident issues of euroyen bonds*, the first deregulatory move was the relaxation in April 1984 of the guidelines governing their issue. Accordingly, collateral and disclosure requirements were modified although this failed to elicit any issues. The exemption from withholding tax on interest income granted to non-resident holders of Japanese euroyen bond issues in April 1985 under the Special Taxation Measures Law, however, duly stimulated demand.

Further measures to stimulate supply were forthcoming in July 1985 when the criteria of issue for resident euroyen convertible debentures were relaxed. This was followed in October 1985 with a relaxation of the criteria for resident euroyen bond issues in the form of straight corporate bonds and bonds with warrants. Then in February 1987 the criteria determining the eligibility of prospective resident issuers of euroyen bonds were further relaxed by introducing the credit rating system that applied in the domestic (unsecured) corporate bond market. The new system took effect from 1 July 1987 and meant that all Japanese companies rated 'AA' and above and those rated 'A' with net assets of over Y55 billion could unconditionally issue straight euroyen bonds by public offering in the euromarkets. Additionally, those Japanese companies with net assets in excess of Y150 billion and to which the warrant of straight bonds is applicable, could unconditionally issue straight euroyen bonds by public offering. For all other prospective resident euroyen bond issuers, size-related requirements had first to be satisfied (see JCIF, 1988, p. 82, for details). Finally, with effect from 1 July 1992, the criteria for resident euroyen bond issues were further relaxed. Henceforth, the minimum rating requirement for a company to issue yen-denominated convertible bonds was 'BBB'; and Japanese companies with a credit rating of 'A' or better became eligible to issue straight and with-warrants euroyen bonds. Net-asset requirements were also eased for other prospective issuers.

Apart from the relaxation of the criteria of issue, liberalization also occurred through the sanctioning of a more diverse set of products and through a relaxation in the restriction limiting 'flow-back'[20] into Japan. On the former front, the issuance of dual currency bonds was recognized in June 1985, with the recognition of floating-rate note issues and currency conversion bond issues following in April 1986. And on the latter front, the minimum period of time from the date of issue during which flow-back is prohibited was cut from 180 days to 90 days in April 1986.

Switching attention towards the trade in *eurocurrency instruments*, it can be seen from Exhibit 6.3 that measures were also taken on this front to stimulate activity. For example: the ban on short-term euroyen (bank) lending to non-residents was lifted in June 1983; the non-prudential limits on overseas yen lending were abolished in April 1984; the ban on short-term euroyen lending to Japanese residents was lifted in June 1984; the issue (by non-resident banks including banking affiliates of Japanese financial institutions and foreign branches of Japanese banks) of euroyen CDs (with a maturity of up to six months) was authorized in December 1984; medium- and long-term euroyen lending to non-residents was authorized in April 1985; and the euroyen CP market was established in 1987 (issues confined to non-residents). Restrictions on medium-term and long-term euroyen lending to Japanese residents remained (at least until May 1989) however, because of fears that liberalization would put unsustainable pressure on Japan's domestic long-term prime rate, thereby complicating monetary and exchange rate management.

Following this liberalization a relatively free market in yen-denominated eurocurrency instruments developed.[21] Euroyen deposits made by non-residents were completely free of control, although, in respect of residents' transactions, some controls did apply. Thus, while interbank transactions were free in principle, administrative guidance prohibited medium- or long-term euroyen borrowing by domestic branches. Moreover, foreign deposits by non-bank residents were also prohibited in principle (that is, they required prior approval). As far as euroyen lending was concerned, loans to non-residents were free of controls for those institutions not required to provide notification, although voluntary restraint was expected to be exercised in respect of medium- and long-term loans to foreign branches of domestic corporations. As regards euroyen lending to Japanese residents (impact loans), however, only the short-term loans were regulation-free; the medium- and long-term loans were subject to advice concerning voluntary restraint until May 1989. Similarly, while yen remittances from domestic to foreign offices were completely liberalized, only the short-term ones moving in the other direction were so treated, the others being subject to advice concerning voluntary restraint. Finally, as regards euroyen CD issues, they were free of controls for those institutions not required to provide notification so long as they had an original maturity of less than six months. Sales to residents, however, were prohibited.

The third general area of liberalization which was used to stimulate activity in the euroyen market was the establishment in December 1986 of a *Tokyo Offshore Market*.[22] By functioning as the centre for the world's transactions in yen, the offshore market should promote both the expansion in euroyen transactions and the internationalization of the yen.

The difference between the offshore market and the euroyen market is that only the latter is open to residents, thereby achieving isolation of the former from domestic banks. Thus, within the offshore market, authorized foreign exchange banks mediate between non-residents through transactions in any currency. Securities trading, however, is not authorized for fear of breaching the principle of separation of domestic and offshore markets.

To date, the market's growth has been unspectacular (outstanding claims stood at around $400 billion by the end of 1988). This is because of the market's comparative lack of appeal *vis-à-vis* the offshore centres of London, New York, Singapore and Hong Kong. For although transactions are free of interest rate controls, reserve ratio requirements, deposit insurance requirements and withholding taxes, as in other offshore centres, the participants' inability to trade securities (only loans and deposits are authorized) and liability to corporate and local taxes and stamp duty, among other things, render participation relatively unattractive. (Economist Publications, 1986, ch. 2; for a more detailed analysis, see Hanzawa, 1991).

Liberalization of the market in foreign yen-denominated bonds   Yen-denominated foreign bonds may be divided into two distinct categories: those issued by public offering (*Samurai* bonds) and those issued by private placement (*Shibosai* bonds). The reform of each market will be considered in turn.

As can be seen from Exhibit 6.3, the first amendment to the issuance rules established in February 1981[23] for the *Samurai* bond market was carried out in April 1984. The range of eligible issuers was expanded – henceforth, it would include those with an 'AA' credit rating (the old minimum rating requirement was 'AAA') in respect of first-time public offerings of international organization bonds and public bonds – and the maximum amount per issue stipulated for international organizations was increased.[24]

Further relaxation in the rules of issuance occurred later in the year. In July eligibility for the first-time public offering of international organization bonds and public bonds was extended to embrace those with a minimum credit rating of 'A'; the per-unit issue amount was further increased and ceilings for the finest issues were also scrapped; and issuing plans were made more elastic, from adjustments every quarter to every month. And then in December, the standard determining the eligibility of private sector issuers was changed yet again, the standard used in the domestic market for unsecured straight corporate bonds being applied. Yet further revisions of this standard were carried out in April 1985 and April 1986 to match the revisions made to the standard applying to Japanese companies in the domestic straight corporate bond market. Accordingly, after April 1986 all overseas companies (or guarantors) with a credit rating[25] of 'A' or above ('BBB' if their issues carried a government guarantee) were unconditionally eligible to issue *Samurai* bonds in Japan.[26] The eligibility standards applying to new issuers[27] in both the public and private *Samurai* bond markets thereby became harmonized, depending on a uniform rating system. And finally, with effect from July 1992, access to the *Samurai* bond market was extended to all foreign borrowers or organizations with an investment grade credit rating.

Apart from the relaxation of issuance rules, liberalization of the *Samurai* bond market also took place through official recognition of a more diversified set of financial products. Thus, for example, dual currency bond issues were authorized in November 1985.

In the *Shibosai* bond market, a standard determining the eligibility of issuers did not surface until July 1983. This was duly relaxed in April 1984, and then in April 1986 a formal rating system was introduced. Under this system, issuers (confined to international organizations, states, provincial governments and other government agencies) are restricted in the amount that they can raise according to their credit rating: the higher it is, the higher the permitted ceiling on issue amount. All issues, however, are subject to the same maturity restriction – a minimum of five years.

As well as the relaxation in the standard determining the eligibility of issuers, liberalization also manifested itself in other areas. For example, in February 1986 the so-called 'no return rule' was abolished. This rule had been used to prohibit issuers of *Samurai* bonds in Japan from also making *Shibosai* issues. The rule was dropped following protests from former *Samurai* bond issuers who were keen to tap the *Shibosai* market.

Another example was the relaxation of the 'one-third rule' for *Shibosai* bond issuers in November 1986. Under this rule, the amount of funds raised from *Shibosai* issues could not exceed one-third of the amount raised from *Sumarai* bond issues. Again, following protests the rule was relaxed by allowing *Samurai* bond issuers to include their foreign-currency-denominated bond issues within the calculations, thereby reducing the severity of the restriction.

Although these changes, together with the liberalization of the *Samurai* bond market discussed above, certainly expanded the capacity of the yen-denominated foreign bond market in Japan, it became relatively unattractive to issuers compared with the euroyen-bond market once deregulation of the latter market had begun in earnest. Accordingly, the market began to decline in 1986 both by number and volume of issuance, although the popularity of *Shibosai* issues in the first half of 1986, following the relaxation of issuing guidelines, ensured that this segment of the market actually grew during the calendar year. Future growth, however, could not be relied upon and by the end of the first quarter of 1987 the share of euroyen bonds in international bond issues had risen to 14 per cent (from 1 per cent in 1984).

Internationalization and deepening of the foreign exchange market The final group of measures covered in Exhibit 6.3 relates to the government's attempt to internationalize and deepen Japan's foreign exchange market in order to promote and sustain the internationalization of the yen.

The first post-exchange-control-liberalization measure of note was the abolition of the 'real (or actual) demand' rule in April 1984. The control was designed to prevent exchange rate volatility due to speculation by ensuring that there always existed an actual underlying transaction whenever an authorized foreign exchange bank engaged in a forward exchange transaction.

The need to expand risk-hedging opportunities for economic agents in the wake of the dramatic expansion in foreign transactions, however, spelt the end for this restriction.

The abolition of the yen conversion limits in June 1984 was the other significant development. Designed to prevent exchange rate instability arising from a sudden influx of short-term capital, it involved the establishment of ceilings on the amount of yen which banks could secure through conversions of foreign currency.[28] Following the Joint Group's recommendation that it be scrapped as part of the effort to internationalize the foreign exchange market, the authorities duly obliged.

The only other measures taken related to the types of foreign exchange transaction sanctioned. In July 1984, for example, 'direct' (by-passing the foreign exchange brokers) foreign exchange dealing between banks was permitted except for yen/dollar transactions; and in February 1985 even this exclusion was removed. (For more recent developments, see Nakaishi, 1991.)

Liberalization of interest rates

Deposit rate deregulation   In accordance with the so-called 'Action Program', the MOF began deregulating deposit interest rates in October 1985. The initial move involved allowing banks to pay whatever rates they liked on *time deposits* of an initial term to maturity of between three months and two years which had a minimum denomination of Y1 billion. The minimum deposit amount for the qualifying time deposits on which freely determined rates could be paid was then gradually reduced during the ensuing 18-month period (see Exhibit 6.4), with the cut-off point being down to Y100 million by April 1987. Then, in October 1987, *all* 'large' (over Y100 million) time deposits with a minimum initial term to maturity of one month were freed from interest rate controls.

These moves, however, still left 'small' time deposits and all demand deposits subject to regulation,[29] although rates in the bond *gensaki* market (see below) and the CD market remained free from control (as they had been since the markets' inception), together with the rates applying in the interbank market (which were liberalized in 1979).[30] But the October 1989 lowering of the qualifying threshold for the payment of freely determined rates on time deposits to Y10 million (further reduced to Y3 million in 1991) reconfirmed the authorities' regulatory zeal, which is planned to culminate in the complete liberalization of interest rates on time deposits by the end of June 1993 at the latest, and on other kinds of deposit by the end of June 1994. The ban on the payment of interest on current accounts will remain, however.

Apart from the deregulation of interest rates on 'large' time deposits, the Japanese authorities also sought to increase the range of interest-rate-con-

Exhibit 6.4   Liberalization of time deposit rates in Japan

Date introduced	Liberalization measure
October 1985	Time deposits in excess of Y1 billion and with initial term of between 3 months and 2 years were freed of interest rate controls
April 1986	The minimum-sized time deposit of the above type freed from interest rate controls was reduced to Y500 million
September 1986	The minimum size of time deposit of the above type on which interest rate controls ceased to apply was changed again, to Y300 million
April 1987	The qualifying level for the payment of 'freely-determined' interest rates was reduced, yet again, to Y100 million for time deposits of the above type
October 1987	The interest rates on *all* 'large' (i.e. over Y100 million) deposits with a minimum initial term of one month were liberalized
October 1989	The qualifying threshold for the payment of 'freely-determined' rates on time deposits was cut to Y10 million
November 1991	The qualifying threshold for the payment of 'freely-determined' rates on time deposits was cut to Y3 million
June 1993 (at the latest)	All time deposit rates to be liberalized

trol-free deposit-type instruments available in the market place. Indeed, the sanctioning of issues of non-negotiable money market certificates (MMCs) (in essence, time deposits) in March 1985 was the first official step taken to liberalize 'large' deposit rates since the agreement reached in 1984 by the Joint Group on how Japanese financial markets were to be deregulated and internationalized. At the beginning, however, restrictions were applied on the minimum denomination, the initial term and the maximum interest rate payable. Moreover, banks were limited in the amount of funds they could take through this medium. Gradually, however, these restrictions were re-

Exhibit 6.5   Relaxation of controls on money market certificates

Date new control applied	Minimum denomination (Ym)	Initial term	Interest rate ceiling	Funding limit[a]
			Nature of controls	
March 1985		1–6 mths		75% of net worth
			CD rate minus	150% of net worth
October 1985	50			
April 1986		1–12 mths	0.75%	200% of net worth
September 1986	30	"		250% of net worth
April 1987	20	"	CD rate minus 0.75% for maturities up to 1 year; CD rate minus 0.5% for maturities of over 1 year	300% of net worth
October 1987	10	"		No limit
June 1989	3	6 mths–1 yr		
October 1989		3 mths–3 yrs		
April 1990	1	"		
November 1990			Ceiling removed	
April 1991	0.5			
June 1992	Minimum requirement abolished			

Note
a   Applied to Japanese banks.

Source: Japan Centre for International Finance, 1988, Table 2-15, p. 33 (as adapted and updated).

laxed (see Exhibit 6.5), with the result that by October 1987 the banks' funding limits had been removed, the minimum denomination was down to Y10 million and the initial term could run from one month to one year. Interest ceilings remained in place until November 1990, however, although the minimum size of deposits qualifying for the liberalized rate was reduced further in subsequent years, falling to Y1 million in April 1990 and to

Y500,000 during 1991. The minimum denomination constraint, moreover, was abolished during 1992, paving the way for full liberalization of interest rates on small lot deposits by end-June 1993.

Such deregulatory moves meant that by the end of September 1990 the share of city bank deposits taken on a deregulated interest rate basis had risen to 65 per cent of total deposits as compared with 16 per cent at the end of March 1986. And for credit unions, the growth was even more remarkable: from 2 per cent to 44 per cent during the same period. The figures explain why, even without the deregulation of non-time deposits, the funding costs of Japanese deposit-taking intermediaries have risen so dramatically in recent years.

Two factors which significantly affected the pace of deposit rate liberalization were the attitude of the Ministry of Posts and Telecommunications and the nature of the fiscal system which provided individuals with a limited range of opportunities for tax-free saving. Moreover, as is explained below, both these factors were interrelated.

Under the fiscal system prevailing until April 1988, an individual saver could obtain exemption from tax of up to Y14 million of savings. These exemptions applied to 'small-lot' deposits with the banking system under the so-called *maruyu* system (up to a maximum of Y3 million of deposits), to deposits with the Postal Savings Service managed by the Ministry of Posts and Telecommunications (MPT) (up to a maximum of Y3 million of deposits, the same as the limit imposed on such holdings), to investment in government bonds under the so-called *marutoko* system (again, up to a maximum of Y3 million of investments), and to 'property accumulation savings' (up to a maximum of Y5 million). Such tax exemptions were very much seen by investors as a *quid pro quo* for the suppressed deposit and investment yields which they were forced to accept and, as a result, any liberalization scheme was always likely to be preceded by tax reform (that is, a reduction or removal of tax relief) if post-tax yields were not to increase too dramatically. Tax reform of this nature, however, was more widely supported by the banking industry than the MPT as, despite the apparent competitive neutrality achieved under the above arrangements, widescale abuse of the Y3 million limit on individual deposit holdings with the Postal Savings Service ensured that *de facto* the banks were at a competitive disadvantage.

In the event, the system of tax exemptions was revised in April 1988, the first two exemptions listed above being removed from all except the aged (65 plus), widows and the physically handicapped. The exemption on investment in government bonds was retained, however, as was the last-mentioned exemption, with pension contributions qualifying alongside housing investment for the first time.

To soften the blow for the Postal Savings Service which, at that time, accounted for about one-third of all personal savings in Japan and constituted the largest financial institution in the world, new freedoms were extended to it. These embraced the ability to sell government bonds over the counter (up to a maximum of Y5 million per customer), to extend loans to customers using such bonds as collateral (loans on the security of 'time', 'collection' or *Teigaku* (see below) deposits were sanctioned in 1973), and to manage directly a proportion of the funds invested with it.

The last-mentioned freedom is significant because prior to May 1987 the Postal Savings Bureau had to hand over all its receipts to the Trust Fund Bureau at the MOF which, in turn, used the proceeds for infrastructural investment. Under the agreement which accompanied the tax reform, the MOF's Trust Fund Bureau would pay Y2000 billion into a Postal Savings Financial Deregulation Fund in fiscal 1987 against the funds deposited with it by the Postal Savings Bureau. Half of this was to be used to underwrite newly issued government bonds and half was to be available for self-management by the Postal Savings Bureau, although, at least initially, investment was to be restricted to government and municipal bonds, public corporate bonds, short-term deposits at financial institutions, 'principal guaranteed' money trusts and designated corporate and foreign bonds. The plan also called for further annual additions (increasing by Y500 billion each year) to the fund until 1991 at which time it was estimated that around 10 per cent (that is, Y15,000 billion) of the Postal Savings Bureau's funds would be under internal management.

The new investment freedom accorded the Postal Savings Bureau was certainly welcomed by the MPT which for a long time had argued that liberalization of its own investment yield should precede or, failing that, accompany 'deposit' rate liberalization. The above move, together with the payment of a market-related 'redeposit rate' by the Trust Fund Bureau in 1987 on the balances turned over to it for investment by the Postal Savings Bureau, was thus conducive to securing the MPT's support for full deposit-rate liberalization. Nevertheless, the latter's preferred solution was for gradual reform, with market-rate-linked 'deposit' products being introduced prior to full 'small-lot' interest rate liberalization. The approach adopted by the MPT inevitably slowed the pace of reform with the banks being reluctant to move without the Postal Savings Bureau's concurrent movement on the rates and terms applicable to its own deposit instruments.

Consideration of the latter conveniently leads into a discussion of the competitive balance prevailing at that time between the commercial banks and the Postal Savings Service. In 1987 the Postal Savings Service offered six kinds of deposit to the general public: ordinary deposits; collection ('instalment') deposits; *Teigaku* deposit certificates ('fixed amount' deposits); time ('fixed term') deposits; housing instalment deposits; and education instalment deposits (Postal Savings Bureau, 1987). Of these instruments, the 'fixed amount' deposits were by far the most significant, accounting for 90 per cent of all Postal Savings at the end of March 1985. They are unique to the Postal Savings Service and may be withdrawn without prior notice and without penalty after six months on deposit. Moreover, they can remain on deposit for up to ten years, with interest being compounded twice a year. Holdings of housing instalment deposits and educational instalment deposits entitle the holder to privileged-rate loans from the Housing Finance Corporation and People's Finance Corporation respectively.

Compared with its commercial bank competitors, the Postal Savings Bureau could thus offer (government-guaranteed) deposits of a longer term (ordinary private banks were restricted to maturities of up to two years at that time and long-term credit banks to maturities of five years maximum); and the yields on instruments of a comparable term were generally more competitive by virtue of the policy adopted on compounding of interest (banks only compound once a year) and their freedom from the restrictions imposed under the TIRAL (see below), reserve ratio requirements and deposit insurance requirements. On the other hand, the investment restrictions noted above reduced the Postal Savings Bureau's relative competitiveness, although the full gamut of prudential controls (see below) was also avoided.

The determination of deposit rates on postal savings was conducted in a different manner to that used in respect of private deposit rates. In place of the TIRAL regulations was a system involving the Cabinet, the MPT and the Postal Services Advisory Council, a body comprising a mix of academics, postal savings depositors, postal life insurance policyholders and postal annuities owners. In accordance with the Postal Savings Law, the interest rates on postal savings are determined by Cabinet on the basis of a report submitted by the Minister of Posts and Telecommunications who, in turn, consults the Postal Services Advisory Council. In this way, a two-tier system of deposit rates arises which, on occasions, can complicate monetary management of the economy. As a result, the MOF has been keen to ensure a degree of conformity in the private and postal deposit rate structures by securing a tripartite agreement between itself, the MPT and the Cabinet Secretariat. First established in 1981, this tripartite agreement remains in place today. Notwithstanding this, however, there have been occasions (such as in the winter of 1983) when the spirit if not the letter of the agreement has not been adhered to, with the MPT widely viewed as the offending party. With the Postal Savings Bureau operating as a non-profit-making body, such obstinacy can only but serve to accentuate the competitive imbalances already evident in the market-place in the run-up to full deposit rate liberalization.

Loan rate deregulation   Like their deposit interest rates, the *short-term* loan rates of private financial institutions are regulated in accordance with the Temporary Interest Rates Adjustment Law of 1947 (see below). Under this law, lending rate ceilings are established for all commercial banks, trust banks, insurance companies and the *Norinchukin* Bank. For the *sogo* banks, *shinkin* banks and credit co-operatives, the maximum loan rates are set in accordance with the relevant laws – that is, the *Sogo* Bank Law, the *Shinkin* Bank Law and the Law for Small Business Co-operatives – which empower the Minister of Finance to set the ceilings.

In principle, private financial institutions are free to determine their short-term (less than one year) lending rates within the legal ceilings but in practice their actual room for manoeuvre has been circumscribed by agreed market practice. In the case of the banks, for example, the actual maximum short-term loan rates charged were linked to the official discount rate in June 1958 in accordance with the agreed policy of the Federation of Bankers' Associations of Japan (FBAJ). And in March 1959, again under an FBAJ agreement, a standard rate (*hyojun kinri*) system was adopted whereby the standard rate (known as the 'short-term prime rate'), which applied to loans and discounts of bills of the highest creditworthiness, moved by exactly the same amount as the official discount rate. This, of course, set the *de facto* floor for short-term lending rates, with lending rates being set at levels between this and the agreed ceiling largely according to the perceived credit-worthiness of the borrower and the closeness of other business relationships with the bank.

These arrangements, however, were called into question in 1975. Under the Antitrust Laws they were clearly anticompetitive and were duly abolished in April of that year. After that the Governor of the BOJ requested that banks follow changes in the official discount rate, usually by the same absolute amount, and the banks, accordingly, moved both their prime rates and their actual loan rate ceilings in line with the discount rate, with certain banks leading the way under the so-called 'leading bank' system.

This arrangement survived until the mid-1980s but, with the rapid increase in the growth in the share of funds procured by banks through floating-rate deposit instruments after interest rate liberalization, pressure inevitably built up to link loan rates to a prime rate reflecting more closely the actual costs of raising funds. Such a new formula was formally adopted in January 1989, whereby the prime rate is determined by adding a certain 'spread' (or margin) to a base rate which represents a weighted average of various types of interest rates, regulated and deregulated. Thus, today, short-term prime rates are no longer closely linked to the discount rate, although legal ceilings still apply, but at levels which are not constraining. And the growing use of 'spread' banking will further sever the traditional linkage.

This will have knock-on effects for the long-term prime lending rate, traditionally determined by adding a certain spread to the five-year funding costs of long-term credit banks and trust banks.

The deepening of domestic financial markets

The money market   A substantial degree of deepening of the Japanese money market was achieved during the 1980s by liberalizing operations on existing markets, creating new markets and securing closer integration with overseas markets. These policies will now be addressed by analysing developments in the interbank and open markets in turn.

As noted earlier in this chapter, the *inter-bank market*, the bulk of transactions in which had to pass through one of the six money broking firms (the *tanshi*) until December 1990, comprises the call money market, the bill discount market and the 'Tokyo-dollar call' money market. The call money market is where financial institutions engage in the borrowing and lending of very short-term funds between themselves. Although in principle call transactions have to be conducted through call money market dealers, some take place directly between institutions. Traditionally, only those financial institutions which had accounts at the Bank of Japan were allowed to borrow in the call money market, all transactions took place on a secured basis (for details of acceptable collateral, see JCIF, 1988, p. 18), and rates were fixed under the 'quotation' system.[31]

The process of liberalization (see Exhibit 6.6) began in June 1978 when the Bank of Japan, under pressure from the city banks, introduced greater flexibility into the setting of call rates. It did this by offering guidance to the call dealers as to when and by how much rates should be changed, thereby introducing a greater element of flexibility into the quotation system. After liberalization, rate changes occurred every day to reflect even minor changes in demand and supply conditions and in expectations. This move was followed in October 1978 by the introduction of seven-day transactions (prior to this, transactions were for settlement on the same day ('same day' transactions), or on the following day ('unconditional' transactions)) which were to be conducted on a 'free-rate' basis. And the process of rate-liberalization culminated in the scrapping of the rate quotation system in April 1979, after which, in theory at least, all transactions were to be conducted on a free-rate basis.

Apart from these rate-liberalization measures, the authorities also sought to promote the development of the call market by expanding the range of transactions that can take place in the market and the number of eligible participants.

Exhibit 6.6   *Liberalization of the Japanese money market: the programme of financial deregulation in the interbank market*

Date action taken	Developments in the call money market	Developments in the bill discount market
June 1978	Rate quotations made flexible	Deregulation of resale and of rates on bills of more than one month's outstanding maturity
October 1978	Introduction of free-rate 7-day calls	
November 1978		Introduction of free-rate 1-month bills; rates on 'over-3-months ends' bills and 'over-4-months ends' bills liberalized
April 1979	Rate quotation system scrapped and all rates liberalized. Unconditional calls were changed into virtual 'next-day' calls (the former variety ceasing to exist). Introduction of 2–6 day calls	
October 1979		Rate quotation for 'over-2-months-ends' bills scrapped: all rates liberalized
October 1980		Settlement terms changed from the 'over-month-end' way of computation to one computed by the number of months after the day of response
November 1980	'Straddling' (i.e., the listing of both borrowing and lending as outstanding at the same time) by lenders (e.g., regional banks, trust banks, etc.) recognized. The four major securities companies authorized to borrow call money	'Straddling' of bills bought by lenders and call money recognized
April 1981	City banks allowed to make call loans	

Date action taken	Developments in the call money market	Developments in the bill discount market
December 1981	Eight more securities companies allowed to borrow call money. Borrowing limits for 'large' securities companies increased	
April 1982		Dealing by money market dealers authorized
February 1983	Two more securities companies allowed to borrow call money	
March 1985		City banks allowed to purchase bills
May 1985		Securities houses allowed to invest in the bill market
June 1985		Introduction of 5–6 month bills
July 1985	Unsecured transactions in overnight calls and 7-day calls began	
August 1985	Introduction of 2–3-week calls	
September 1985	Unsecured transactions in 2–3-week calls allowed	
August 1986	Introduction of unsecured 'weekend' calls	
July 1987	Start of unsecured transactions in 2–6-day calls	
November 1988	Unsecured transactions in calls of up to 6 months allowed	Range of acceptable maturities expanded to include instruments with maturities down to 1 week. Abolition of quotation system
April 1989	Unsecured transactions in calls of up to 1 year allowed	Dealings in bills of up to one year to maturity allowed
November 1990	Abolition of quotation system and introduction of offer-bid system in unsecured call money market	

Sources: Adapted from JCIF, 1988, Table 2.6, pp. 14–16; Osugi, 1990, p. 40.

The first policy resulted in the introduction of two-to-six day calls in April 1979 and two-to-three week calls in August 1985, together with the introduction of unsecured trading ('intermediary calls').[32] Initially (July 1985) confined to overnight calls and seven-day calls, unsecured trading spread to two-to-three week calls in September 1985 and to two-to-six day calls in July 1987. Unsecured transactions in 'weekend' calls were also introduced in August 1986.

Expansion in the numbers eligible to participate in the market was achieved by first allowing city banks to make call loans (April 1981) and then by re-admitting securities companies – the four major ones in November 1980, followed by eight middle-ranking ones in December 1981 and a further two in January 1983 – to the call market as borrowers (they were excluded following the crisis in the securities industry in 1966).

Liberalization of the bill discount market can also be traced using Exhibit 6.6. As far as the deregulation of interest rates is concerned, the initial move was made in June 1978 when the rates were liberalized on bills with an outstanding maturity of over one month. This was followed by the liberalization of rates on 'over-three-months-ends' bills[33] and 'over-four-months-ends' bills in November 1978 and of rates on 'over-two-months-ends' bills in October 1979. As one-month[34] bills had been traded on a 'free-rate' basis since their introduction (in November 1978), this meant that by October 1979 all bill rates had been liberalized.

As well as the deregulation of interest rates, liberalization of the bill discount market was also concerned with expanding the range of transactions undertaken. Thus, the resale of bills of over one month's outstanding maturity was liberalized[35] (in June 1978) and the maturity of bills traded was diversified (five- and six-month bills were introduced in June 1985). The latter move was made to accommodate demands for longer-term trading and to facilitate interest rate arbitrage between the interbank and open markets by creating instruments of the same maturities as are available there (that is, in the CD, BA and euroyen markets). The range of bills eligible for discount in the market has also been enlarged through time[36] as has the ranks of eligible participants; money market dealers were admitted in April 1982 and city banks, as purchasers, in March 1985.

Deepening of the Tokyo-dollar call money market, the third constituent of the interbank market, has been achieved through deregulation of transactions in foreign currencies, removal of the restriction on the maturity of transactions (a limit of six months applied prior to December 1980) and a rapid expansion in the number of participants active in the market (authorized foreign exchange banks – domestic and resident foreign – and brokers are eligible).

The Tokyo dollar-call market, or the short-term foreign currency market in which financial institutions borrow and lend on an unsecured basis amongst themselves, was established in April 1972 to smooth out the short-term surpluses and deficits which arose in foreign currency. Since the December 1980 amendment to the Foreign Exchange and Foreign Trade Control Act, however, which deregulated foreign-currency-denominated transactions, the market has functioned as a convenient place in which to invest surplus foreign currency balances or raise short-term foreign currency loans, thereby deepening the local foreign exchange market. Although, as implied by the name, almost all transactions are denominated in US dollars there is, in fact, no restriction on the type of foreign currency which may be transacted.

Moving over to an assessment of developments in the *open money markets*, it is convenient to start by looking at the liberalization of the (negotiable) CD market. As can be seen from Exhibit 6.7, the first development following inauguration of the market in May 1979 was an increase in the ceiling placed on the amounts which (deposit-taking) financial institutions could raise from CD issues in April 1980, although it did not take effect until April 1981. The ceiling was raised from 25 per cent of net worth for Japanese banks (10 per cent of yen-denominated loan and securities accounts for foreign banks) to 50 per cent of net worth (20 per cent of yen-denominated loan and securities accounts for foreign banks). The ceiling on issuance was gradually extended through further increases in January 1983, January 1984, October 1985, April 1986, September 1986 and April 1987 (see Exhibit 6.7 for details), with the limit finally being removed in October 1987 (April 1987 for foreign bank issuers).

Apart from the gradual relaxation in issuance limits, the terms of issue were also deregulated. Thus, for example, the stipulation of May 1979 that the maturity of CDs must be over three months and under six months was relaxed in April 1985 when the minimum term was reduced to one month from three. In a similar vein, the maximum term was increased to one year in April 1986. Finally, in April 1988 issues with maturities of between two weeks and two years were sanctioned. Restrictions on the minimum unit size of issue were also relaxed. Set at Y500 million in May 1978, it came down to Y300 million in January 1984. It was cut again in April 1985 to Y100 million, reaching the current level of Y50 million in April 1987.

The only other major developments in the CD market were the admission of securities companies as traders, in June 1985 (prior to this date, trading had been confined to money market dealers, financial institutions and their affiliates) and the start of *gensaki* trading in CDs in 1980.

As for the bond *gensaki* market, the first major development following the market's inauguration in 1949 was the expansion of the ceiling on *gensaki* selling (that is, borrowing) by city banks from Y5 billion to Y20 billion,

Exhibit 6.7   Liberalization of the Japanese money market: the programme of financial deregulation in the open market

Date action taken	Developments in the CD market	Developments in the bond *gensaki* market	Other developments
October 1978		Ceiling on *gensaki* selling by city banks expanded (from Y5bn to Y20bn)	
May 1979	Negotiable CD (free-rate) market established. Minimum unit size of issue set at Y500m; ceiling on issuance (effective January to March 1980) set at 25% of net worth (10% of yen-denominated loan and securities accounts for foreign banks, which were also given a minimum issue limit of Y3bn); term of CDs to be over 3 months and under 6 months. Money market dealers started trading in CDs	Non-resident participation (through securities companies) allowed	
April 1980	Ceiling on issuance increased (effective April 1981 to January 1983) to 50% of net worth (20% of yen-denominated loan and securities accounts for foreign banks)	Ceiling on *gensaki* selling by city banks abolished	
April 1981		City banks authorized to buy *gensaki*	
February 1983	Ceiling on issuance expanded (effective January to March 1984) to 75% of net worth (30% of yen-denominated loan and securities accounts for foreign banks, with a minimum issue limit of Y5bn)		

Date action taken	Developments in the CD market	Developments in the bond *gensaki* market	Other developments
January 1984	Minimum unit of issue reduced from Y500m to Y300m. Ceiling on issuance increased (effective April to June 1985) to 100% of net worth[a] (50% of yen-denominated loan and securities accounts for foreign banks, with a minimum issue limit of Y8bn)		
April 1984			Domestic trade in CDs and CP issued abroad permitted
June 1984			Yen conversion limits scrapped
April 1985	Minimum unit of issue reduced from Y300m to Y100m. Minimum term of issues reduced from 3 months to 1 month		
June 1985	Securities companies allowed to trade in CD market		Yen-denominated bankers acceptance (yen-BA) market created
October 1985	Ceiling on issuance expanded to 150% of net worth plus 25% of uncommitted MMCs to take effect immediately (75% of yen-denominated loan and securities accounts for foreign banks, with a minimum issue limit of Y12bn)		
February 1986			First 'treasury bills' (TBs) (of 6 months maturity with a minimum denomination of Y100m) issued
			Securities companies authorized to operate in the secondary yen-BA market

Date action taken	Developments in the CD market	Developments in the bond *gensaki* market	Other developments
April 1986	Maximum term of issues increased to 1 year. Ceiling on issuance expanded, with immediate effect, to 200% of net worth plus 25% of un-committed MMCs (100% of yen-denominated loan and securities accounts for foreign banks, with a minimum issue limit of Y20bn)		
September 1986	Ceiling on issuance expanded, with immediate effect, to 250% of net worth		
April 1987	Ceiling on issuance expanded with immediate effect to 300% of net worth (but all limits scrapped for foreign banks). Minimum size of issue cut from Y100m to Y50m		
May 1987			Minimum denomination for BAs halved to Y50m; maximum maturity extended to 1 year (from 6 months)
August 1987			Minimum denomination for TBs halved to Y50m
October 1987	Ceiling on issuance scrapped (took effect immediately)		
November 1987			CP market established
April 1988	Issues with maturities of between 2 weeks and 2 years sanctioned		
September 1989			3-month TBs intro-duced
April 1990			Minimum denomination for TBs cut to Y10m

Date action taken	Developments in the CD market	Developments in the bond *gensaki* market	Other developments
April 1991			Minimum net asset requirement (Y33bn) for prospective issuers of CP abolished

Note:
a From July to September 1985 the ceiling on issuance was expanded, yet again, to include 25% of uncommitted MMCs.

Source: Adapted from JCIF, 1988, Table 2.6, pp. 14–16.

authorized in October 1978. This decision was made in the light of the growth of the market and the large-scale flotation of government bonds and was followed by the abolition of the ceiling in April 1990.

Under guidance issued by the MOF[37] all corporations are eligible to engage in transactions[38] in the bond *gensaki* market although, in practice, the participants have comprised securities companies, financial institutions (public and private) and other corporate entities. Non-resident participation was first authorized in May 1979 and city banks were authorized to act as buyers (that is, lenders) in April 1981. Non-financial corporations were traditionally the largest lenders, with securities companies being the largest borrowers. These decisions were taken in the light of the decline in lending activity which followed the establishment of the open market in CDs in May 1979 and the stultifying effect of the securities transactions tax which is levied on sellers. The liberalization of capital transactions under the 1980 amendment to the foreign exchange law led to further growth in the market share of non-residents.

Developments in the open market outside these two markets centred, in the main, on the creation and subsequent evolution of new money markets (see Exhibit 6.7). Thus a yen-denominated bankers acceptance (yen-BA) market was created in June 1985; treasury bills (TBs) were first issued in February 1986; and a commercial paper (CP) market was established in November 1987.

The creation of the yen-BA market was a direct outcome of the US–Japan 'Yen–Dollar' deliberations and was designed to broaden and deepen the short-term money market in Japan and to contribute towards the internationalization of the yen. Prior to June 1985 the yen-BA was virtually non-existent because of the development of the short-term money market around the interbank market and because of the very low level of yen-denominated trade financing.

The market is open to financial institutions and corporate entities, resident and non-resident, although for the time being at least the original sale of eligible[39] bills is limited to the authorized foreign exchange banks which underwrite the bills.[40] Those authorized to deal in the secondary market, however, comprise financial intermediaries, money market dealers, affiliates of financial institutions and (since April 1986) securities companies. To date, the market's development has been stymied by the imposition of stamp duty on sales (although this was reduced in October 1987) and cumbersome rules on secondary market trading. And the costs of borrowers and net-returns to lenders have not been sufficiently attractive to stimulate interest.

Treasury bill (TB) issues started in 1986 in the form of issues of six-months maturity discount bonds. TBs (or, more precisely, short-term government bonds) differ from other short-term (with a maturity of about 60 days) government securities such as Foreign Exchange Fund Bills in that they cannot be underwritten by the Bank of Japan[41] and are issued through a competitive price bidding system to institutional investors (individuals cannot buy them). Although the minimum unit size of issue has been progressively reduced in recent years, from Y100 million to Y50 million in April 1987 and then to Y10 million in April 1990, and the minimum term reduced to three months in September 1989, a fully fledged TB market, as the British and Americans know it, is still some way off.[42] This militates against further use of the yen as a reserve currency and the development of efficient money market operations in short-term government securities as the main instrument of monetary policy. In this manner, the internationalization of the yen and of Japanese financial markets is impeded.

The last open money market to be established in Japan was the commercial paper (CP) market in November 1987. The delay in its introduction stemmed, in part, from the banking industry's opposition on the grounds that it would violate the principle of collateral in markets, to the detriment of the investor and possibly the wider financial system, and retard the development of the bill markets (the induced disintermediation was not mentioned). The arguments in favour, such as lower cost and more flexible funding, espoused by the industrial sector, eventually won the day, however, and the market has proved very successful.[43]

A rating system was introduced in December 1988 to determine the eligibility of issuers. To qualify, firms had to have over Y33 billion in net assets and their debt had to be rated in the top two rating classes. The borrowers in the CP market are highly rated corporations while the lenders (that is, the purchasers) are institutional investors. Sales are handled by banks and securities companies (resident foreign and domestic) and issues are generally guaranteed. The minimum issue size is Y100 million and maturities range from two weeks to nine months.

The capital market The deepening of the capital market in Japan has been achieved through liberalization of the bond market, internationalization of the stock and bond markets and the introduction of futures markets for bond and other trades. Much remains to be done, however, if the private bond market (that is, the market in industrial bonds – *shasai* – issued by non-financial, private companies) is to realize its full potential.

As far as the liberalization of the public bond market is concerned, the reform programme is almost entirely associated with the development of the government bond market (see Exhibit 6.8). In terms of issuing (primary market) activities, the government has contributed to the deepening of the market by broadening the range of bond types on offer, by diversifying their maturities and by diversifying selling methods. Thus, for example, 'deficit bonds'[44] (alternatively termed 'special government bonds') that are issued each fiscal year to make up for any shortfall in the general account, were introduced in 1975 for the first time to complement the other two types of government bond available: construction bonds and refunding bonds. The former of these two are used to finance public works projects, in accordance with Article 4 of the Public Finance Law; and the latter, in accordance with the Law Concerning Special Account of Government Bonds Consolidation Fund, to redeem earlier bond issues. Government bonds may also be differentiated by the form in which the yield is offered; fixed rate coupon, floating rate and discount bonds are all available today.

Diversification by maturity began in earnest in the mid-1970s. As can be seen from Exhibit 6.8, five-year discount bonds supplemented the usual ten-year interest-bearing bond issues in 1977 and this was soon followed by the introduction of medium-term (two-, three- and four-year) interest-bearing bonds before the end of 1980. These medium-term bond issues were, in turn, followed by issues of very long-term bonds (with maturities of 15 years and upwards) in 1983, further filling in the spectrum of maturities.

Finally, in respect of marketing tactics, new methods of issue were experimented with towards the end of the 1970s. Thus, for example, medium-term government coupon bonds were sold through public auction rather than through indirect public subscription, where a syndicate for the subscription is formed to guarantee uptake of the full issue in the event of under-subscription by the general public, the method traditionally used to sell long-term government coupon bonds. Similarly, private placement gave way to public issue, initially by indirect public subscription but later by auction, in respect of the sale of very long-term bonds in 1986 and, in 1987, the first (partial) public auction of ten-year coupon bonds was carried out. The first full public auction occurred in 1989.

As for developments in the secondary government bond market, the impetus for change came from governmental recognition in the mid-1970s that

Exhibit 6.8   Liberalization of the public bond market: the programme of deregulation

Date effective	Liberalization measure
1975	Government issues of 'deficit bonds' begins
January 1977	Government issues of 5-year discount bonds begins
April 1977	The selling of 'deficit' bonds one year after issuance by the members of the underwriting syndicate recognized
October 1977	The selling of 'construction' bonds one year after issuance by the members of the underwriting syndicate recognized
June 1978	Government issues (by public auction) of 3-year interest-bearing bonds begins
June 1979	Government issues of 2-year interest-bearing bonds begins
May 1980	The selling of government bonds listed on the stock exchange seven to nine months after issuance by the members of the underwriting syndicate permitted
June 1980	Government issues of 4-year interest-bearing bonds begins
April 1981	Minimum period before syndicate members could sell government bonds listed on the stock market reduced to the beginning of the month following a three-month period after issue (i.e. about 100 days)
February 1983	Government issue of very long-term (i.e., with a maturity exceeding 10 years) interest-bearing bonds begins with the issue (by private placement) of 15-year floating rate bonds
April 1983	Banks and other financial institutions begin to engage in retail sale of newly issued, long-term interest-bearing government bonds
August 1983	Government issues (by private placement) 20-year fixed rate bonds
October 1983	Retail sale of newly-issued, medium-term and discount government bonds begun by banks and other financial institutions
June 1984	Banks permitted to deal in (existing) government bonds with a remaining term of under two years in the secondary market
October 1984	Three US banks allowed to start dealing in government bonds

Date effective	Liberalization measure
June 1985	In respect of bank product accounts, sales of government bonds listed on the stock exchange permitted at the beginning of the second month after issuance (i.e., after about 40 days). Restrictions on which government bonds banks could deal in lifted. More banks authorized to deal
October 1985	Bond futures market established in Tokyo
April 1986	In respect of bank product accounts, minimum holding period of government bonds listed on the stock exchange reduced, allowing sales at the beginning of the first month after issuance (i.e., after about 10 days). In respect of bank investment accounts, sales were permitted at the beginning of the second month after issuance (i.e. after about 40 days)
June 1986	More banks added to the list of authorized dealers in government bonds. Full dealing permitted to those authorized in June 1985
October 1986	20-year interest-bearing government bonds sold by public issue (using syndicate underwriting method)
December 1986	*Zenshinren* Bank allowed to engage in retail sales of government bonds
January 1987	Post offices allowed to engage in retail sales of government bonds (but does not take effect until April 1988)
April 1987	Agricultural co-operatives authorized to engage in retail sales of government bonds
June 1987	In respect of bank product accounts, all time restrictions on the sale of government bonds listed on the stock exchange scrapped. In respect of bank investment accounts, sales permitted at the beginning of the first month after issuance (i.e., after about 10 days). Life assurance companies authorized to engage in retail sales of government bonds (with effect from October 1987). Foreign banks, *sogo* banks and *shinkin* banks allowed to deal in government bonds
September 1987	Public auction system for sale of 20-year interest-bearing government bonds introduced.
October 1987	Part of a 10-year interest-bearing government bond issue sold by auction
April 1989	Auction system for the sale of long-term (i.e., with a maturity of 10 years) interest-bearing bonds introduced
June 1989	Futures and options trading (e.g., in interest, currency, etc.) begun on the Tokyo International Financial Futures Exchange

the likely scale of future budget deficits necessitated alleviation of the burden borne by the members of the underwriting syndicate and most especially the city banks (see below). Accordingly, measures were taken to promote the wider circulation of government bonds. This involved, at first, relaxation of the restrictions on the sale by syndicate members of bonds to the general public but then spread to authorization of banks' retail sale of newly issued bonds and eventually of their dealing in existing bonds.

The relaxation of the restrictions on the syndicate members' sale of government bonds is traced in Exhibit 6.8. As can be seen, liberalization started with deficit bonds, spread to construction bonds and then to bonds listed on the stock exchange. In respect of bank product accounts, all time restrictions on selling were eventually scrapped in June 1987 although, for bank investment accounts, the minimum period banks had to wait before selling remained at around ten days after June 1987.

The first retail sales of newly issued government bonds (*madohan*) by banks and other financial institutions were made in April 1983, in accordance with the guidelines established by the MOF in March 1982 within its document entitled *On the Securities Business of Banks and Others*. Retail sales of medium-term bonds followed in October 1983 after the issuance of new guidelines in May 1983 incorporated in a MOF document entitled *On the Securities Business of Financial Institutions*. Other institutions authorized later to engage in the retail sale of government bonds include the *Zenshinren* Bank (received authorization in December 1986), post offices (permission granted in January 1987 but it did not take effect until April 1988), agricultural co-operatives (authorized in April 1987) and life assurance companies (granted permission in June 1987, with effect from October 1987).

Bank dealing in existing public bonds began in June 1984 although, at least initially, only in bonds with a remaining term of under two years. This restriction was lifted in June 1985 for those banks authorized in June 1984 and in June 1986 for those authorized in June 1985. Those banks acquiring authorization at this stage comprised the city banks, the long-term credit banks, the trust banks, ten regional banks and the *Norinchukin* Bank. This list, however, was gradually extended to include foreign banks (three US banks received authorization in October 1984 and more were authorized in June 1987), more regional banks (a further 50 received authorization in June 1985), *sogo* banks (over 40 were authorized in June 1986 and more in June 1987) and *shinkin* banks (which received authorization in June 1987).

Apart from these liberalizing measures, the development of the government bond market has also been enhanced by the creation of a bond futures market in October 1985, the creation of a financial futures exchange in April 1989, on which both options and futures are traded, and the adoption of more flexibility in the setting of issue terms (they are now revised every month).

The incentive to set up futures markets came from recognition of the need to create additional hedging opportunities for securities holders (for further details, see Suzuki, 1987, p. 140) and of the danger that the development of the domestic capital market would be adversely affected if Japan did not move to match the international competition in the global financial market place. The authorization granted to certain foreign securities companies resident in Japan to act as participants in the (government) bond futures market, alongside the member companies of the Tokyo Stock Exchange, a number of domestic non-member securities companies and the other financial institutions[45] licensed to deal in public bonds, was a further testament to the authorities' desire to broaden, deepen and internationalize the domestic bond market.

As for the increased flexibility in issue terms (that is, yields to subscribers) evident in today's government bond market, it is clear that this is both a result and a cause of the market's consolidation. Increased flexibility was made possible (and necessitated) by relaxation of the restrictions on resale. In turn, it stimulated further demand, thereby broadening and deepening the market.

The final set of measures concerned with the internationalization and deepening of the Japanese capital market comprise those associated with the deregulation of the yen-denominated foreign bond market and the euroyen bond market, the internationalization of the yen and the authorization of foreign companies to operate in domestic financial markets. All these issues have already been covered in some depth but, in connection with the development of the local stock market, it is worth re-emphasizing the growth of the foreign presence in Japan.

The rise in foreign stock listings, the growth in the number of overseas companies with securities dealing licences and the admission of foreign companies to the Tokyo Stock Exchange, whether under foreign governmental pressure or not, are arguably as important for the development of the local stock market as was the admission of foreigners into trust banking, funds management and investment advisory activities for the development of those industries. Concerted efforts to improve transparency (over-the-counter transactions in listed stocks are prohibited in principle) and to eliminate malpractice, notwithstanding the scandals of the late 1980s and early '90s,[46] through, for example, the toughening of insider dealing legislation, should also eventually bear fruit once belief in the integrity of the market has been re-established.[47] The ability to engage in stock futures trading, first undertaken on the Osaka Securities Exchange in June 1987 (although stock index trading did not take place until 1988), is another positive feature contributing to the deepening of the local market.

The segment of the capital market with a less-than-auspicious track record is the local (straight) corporate bond market. Thus, while the volume and value of convertible (into stocks of the issuing company at a stated time in the future) and 'with-warrants' (providing holders with the right to purchase a given amount of stock at a fixed price at a stated date(s) in the future) bond issues soared during the latter half of the 1980s, in line with the local stock market, the market in straight corporate bonds languished.

Apart from the competitive advantage or disadvantage deriving from gy-rations of the stock market, the reasons behind the market's relatively poor performance have long been recognized: the inflexibility, compared with both the eurobond market and the domestic convertible debenture market,[48] of the criteria determining the eligibility of issuers, of the collateral require-ments,[49] of the terms of issue, and of issuing procedures. To date, however, reform of practices in the domestic primary market has been slow to materi-alize and of limited impact.

The reform that has been undertaken began with relaxation of the 'collat-eral rule' which required issuers of general industrial bonds[50] to put up collateral[51] to cover the payments of interest and principal. Initiated in January 1983, the process of deregulation involved relaxation of the criteria determining eligibility for issues of unsecured domestic bonds. The reforms implemented in April 1984, October 1985 and February 1987 meant that by the latter date the number of companies eligible to issue unsecured straight bonds by public offering had increased from two in March 1979 to 180.

Under the regime ruling in February 1987, all companies rated 'AA' and above (or their equivalents) by recognized rating agencies and those rated 'A' with net assets in excess of Y55 billion, could issue unsecured straight corporate debentures by public offering. Additionally, companies with net assets in excess of Y150 billion and which had been authorized to make 'with-warrant' issues were also eligible to issue unsecured straight corporate debentures by public offering. And finally, companies not satisfying these requirements but with net assets of at least Y55 billion were still eligible to make such issues if they met certain financial requirements (the require-ments were tougher for firms with net assets of under Y100 billion – for further details, see JCIF, 1988, p. 82). The switch from using minimum-net-worth criteria to credit ratings to determine the eligibility of issuers was carried a step further in July 1987 when a *bona fide* rating system was introduced for bond issuance.

Reforms designed to increase competition in the new issuing market and to increase flexibility in issuing conditions (that is, coupon, issue price, maturity issuing amount, issuing period and so on) centred on curtailment of the system of rotating underwriting mandates whereby the big four securities houses took it in turns to act as underwriters to bond issues, negotiating on the issuer's behalf the issuing conditions with the issuer's 'commissioned bank' (see below). From May 1987, issuing companies were encouraged to solicit competitive bids from a range of securities companies and to choose a lead manager on the basis of its evaluation of the companies' proposals in respect of issuing conditions. Subsequent to this, the actual issuing conditions would then be confirmed following discussions between the issuing company and the lead manager. The lead manager would then be held responsible for arranging a syndicate of managers and underwriters, determining the allocations within the syndicate, and helping to ensure the success of the issue by acting as a market-maker in both the primary and secondary markets.

The improvement in flexibility in issuing conditions secured through this route was complemented by the authorities' decision to relax the restrictions on the maturity of issues and to sanction floating rate note (FRN) issues. Accordingly, the traditional range of maturities – 6, 7, 10, 12 and 15 years – was extended to include shorter maturities (four years and less)[52] and FRN issues were sanctioned, all before the end of 1989.

Attempts were also made to boost the private placement (*shibosai*) market which prior to July 1987 suffered from restrictions on the size of issue (it could not exceed the minimum issuing amount of bonds sold by public offering – Y2 billion); the range of issuers (companies that had previously issued bonds by public offering were not eligible to make private placements under the so-called 'no return' rule); the range of purchasers (only institutional investors, totalling not more than 49 in number, could make purchases and, for issues of over Y1 billion, confirmation of investment purposes had to be filed with the head of the Securities Bureau of the MOF); and on resale (the extent of it was limited, and the Securities Bureau had to be informed of such occurrences). Following concerted pressure from the corporate sector the market was reformed with effect from July 1987 by abolishing the 'no-return' rule, raising the limits on individual issues to Y10 billion and liberalizing the resale of bonds for issues of over Y2 billion (banks, securities companies and, later, insurance companies were authorized to operate in this fashion).

The remaining reforms undertaken relate to attempts to simplify issuing procedures. Traditionally, issuers had to wait up to 30 days from the date of registration before they were allowed to proceed with their issues but this waiting time was reduced to 15 days in April 1987. Shelf registration, along the lines operating in the US market, duly followed in 1989. The costs associated with the perpetuation of the 'commissioned bank' arrangement, whereby issuers are legally required under Article 304 of the Commercial Code to commission a bank to arrange collateral and to deal with many aspects of bond placement, remain in place, however, as does the ceiling on corporate bond issues (which limits firms' borrowing to twice their net asset value). Both have been recommended for abolition by an advisory body to the Justice Ministry of Japan, although it remains to be seen if these and other developments manage to effect a resuscitation of the market in the foreseeable future. Signals emanating from the government in the spring of 1992, however, suggested that it is in favour of abolishing the 'commissioned-bank' system, allowing companies to issue bonds with maturities of one and two years, eliminating the limits on corporate bond issuance and broadening the range of companies allowed to raise funds through the domestic bond market. Notwithstanding this, an agreed timetable for reform has still not materialized.

Implications of financial liberalization for the conduct of monetary policy

Choice of instruments

With a transmission mechanism in mind of the type set out in Exhibit 6.9, one of the first decisions the monetary authorities must take concerns the appropriate mix of instruments to be used in an attempt to secure the end goals of policy (Hall, 1982, ch. 6). In the light of the condition of Japan's postwar economy and the lack of development in its money and capital markets it is hardly surprising that regulations featured prominently in the monetary authorities' armoury in the early postwar era. The overriding purpose of such regulations, supported by exchange controls, was to promote economic growth through the regeneration of private industry, the promotion of exports and the rebuilding of the public sector infrastructure. This was to be achieved through the channelling of low-cost savings to industry (especially the export sector) via the banking system. The low interest rate policy also contributed to growth indirectly by stabilizing the financial system (destructive interest rate competition was avoided) and promoting indirect finance at the expense of direct finance.

As identified in Exhibit 6.9, the controls and regulations employed at that time embraced exchange controls, interest rate controls, reserve requirements, 'window guidance' and price and quantity controls on central bank lending to private financial institutions.

The significance of *exchange controls* was that they reinforced the functional separation of finance (discussed on pp. 86–8) by isolating the Japanese financial system from the rest of the world. In particular, by denying (city) banks access to foreign sources of funds, the banks were made heavily dependent on the Bank of Japan, the only alternative source of short-term funds to the call money market. This greatly enhanced the effectiveness of monetary policy by increasing the leverage exerted by the Bank of Japan

Exhibit 6.9 The transmission mechanism of monetary policy in postwar Japan

Instruments of monetary policy	Operational objectives	Intermediate targets	End goals of policy
For example: (i) transactions in financial markets (ii) lending policy of the Bank of Japan • official discount rate policy • quantitative controls on loans to city banks (iii) reserve requirements (iv) 'window guidance' (i.e., quantitative controls on individual bank's lending) (v) interest rate controls (vi) exchange controls	For example: (i) interbank interest rates (i.e. call and bill rates) (ii) Bank reserves	For example: (i) growth in bank lending (esp. to the non-bank private sector) (ii) growth in monetary aggregates (iii) market interest rates	(i) Price stability (ii) Full employment (iii) External balance (iv) Maximum (real) economic growth

over the banking system both directly, through the determination of its lending policy (see below), and indirectly, because of its pervasive influence over activities in the call money market (see pp. 117–21). Accordingly, changes in bank reserves had a predictable impact on interbank rates.

Interest rate controls (discussed on pp. 110–17) also played a significant role by limiting the banks' flexibility in the setting of deposit (both demand and time) and loan rates, thereby increasing the predictability of monetary policy in terms of the likely effects of changes in the stance of policy on both intermediate and ultimate targets of policy. (For full details, see Suzuki, 1987, pp. 332–4.) Changes in interbank (that is, call) rates, for example, brought about by official transactions in the interbank market or by adjustments in central bank lending policy, had a highly predictable impact on the quantity of bank credit supplied to the non-bank private sector (the relevant intermediate target of policy at this time) because of the banks' limited ability to pass on the higher borrowing costs (assuming a monetary squeeze) to their customers.[53] Given the prevailing excess demand for bank credit, itself partly due to the suppression of loan rates, the resultant change in credit supply was effected largely through credit rationing, the speed with which this was effected being influenced by the Bank of Japan's 'window guidance'. This, in turn, had a fairly predictable impact on aggregate expenditure in the economy because of the dependence of the corporate sector on bank credit for satisfying its borrowing needs.

Reserve ratio requirements, involving the holding of non-interest-bearing deposits at the Bank of Japan by commercial financial institutions in proportion to their monthly average of deposit and other liabilities (see Suzuki, 1990, p. 325 for a discussion of this 'reserve progress ratio' system) were first applied in 1959 in accordance with the Law Concerning the Reserve Deposit Requirement System of 1958. Since that date the scheme has undergone a number of revisions, resulting in an extension of the range of institutions[54] and liability types[55] covered by the scheme, an increase in the maximum reserve ratio that could be levied (from 10 per cent to 20 per cent – 100 per cent for foreign currency-denominated liabilities and liabilities to non-residents), and the application of reserve ratio requirements to *increases* in liabilities. And finally, in July 1986 a progressive reserve ratio system was introduced under which a progressive scale of reserve ratios is applied (that is, reserve requirements are applied differentially to different tranches of deposits). The purpose of this last reform was to reduce the burden on rapidly expanding institutions as compared with the previous system.

Although frequent changes in reserve ratios were made until 1980 it is questionable how significant a contribution they made to the effectiveness of monetary policy during the high-growth period because of the very low levels at which they were set. Accordingly, active use of reserve require-

Exhibit 6.10   Reserve ratio requirements imposed on Japanese banks (effective from 16 October 1991)

On the outstanding of yen deposits of residents[a]

Banks[b]	time deposits[c]	on amounts above Y2.5 trillion	1.2
		on amounts above Y1.2 trillion to Y2.5 trillion	0.9
		on amounts above Y0.5 trillion to Y1.2 trillion	0.05
		on amounts above Y50 billion to Y0.5 trillion	0.05
	other deposits	on amounts above Y2.5 trillion	1.3
		on amounts above Y1.2 trillion to Y2.5 trillion	1.3
		on amounts above Y0.5 trillion to Y1.2 trillion	0.8
		on amounts above Y50 billion to Y0.5 trillion	0.1
The Norinchukin Bank	time deposits[c]		0.05
	other deposits		0.1

On the outstanding of foreign currency deposits of residents[d]	time deposits	0.2
	other deposits	0.25

On the outstanding of securities issuance of long-term credit banks and foreign exchange banks	0.1
On the outstanding of principal of money trusts (including loan trusts)	0.1
On the outstanding of foreign currency liabilities to non-residents[d]	0.15
On the outstanding of liabilities regarding yen accounts of non-residents[d]	0.15
On the outstanding of fund transfers from the special account for international financial transactions to domestic accounts	0.15

Notes
[a] Including instalment savings, but excluding the deposits regarding the special account for international financial transactions.
[b] Ordinary banks (including foreign banks in Japan), long-term credit banks, and foreign exchange banks. In addition, *sogo* banks and *shinkin* banks with deposits of more than Y160 billion are included.
[c] Including CDs.
[d] Only authorized foreign exchange banks are applicable. Excluding the liabilities regarding the special account for international financial transactions.

Source: Press release of the Bank of Japan, 1 October 1991.

ments as a policy tool was dropped in the early 1980s (Kasman and Rodrigues, 1991), notwithstanding the switch to a 'progressive' system in 1986. The reserve requirements currently applying (they were last changed in October 1991 when they were cut to reduce the burden imposed on institutions) are presented in Exhibit 6.10.

Window guidance refers to the Bank of Japan's guidance given to financial institutions (especially the city banks)[56] concerning the 'appropriate' course for the yen lending of their domestic offices in the period ahead. Such guidance has in the past taken the form of directives issued to keep credit growth on a monthly or, more usually, a quarterly basis within pre-specified limits, to restrain the growth in lending to trading companies and/or to restrain investment in securities. In recognition of the drawbacks associated with its persistent usage (it is inequitable, distortive and results in a misallocation of resources), it was designed to be used as a short-term supplementary instrument. But after 1982 it assumed an even more limited role as a result of the Bank of Japan's policy of accepting the lending plans of the individual banks (implying a relaxation in the forcefulness of any moral suasion exercised by the former). It was formally abolished in mid-1991.

The final area in which control is exercised in the name of monetary policy, namely in the policies adopted by the Bank of Japan towards its extension of credit to private financial institutions at the lending window, involves the establishment of both price and quantity controls. Price control is effected through the setting of the official discount rate, the rate charged by the Bank of Japan on loans[57] to eligible[58] financial institutions. Changes in the discount rate thus directly affect the borrowing costs of banks and others, thereby eliciting interest rate and portfolio adjustments which affect both the money supply and real economic activity.[59] Volume or quantity control is effected through the setting of credit ceilings (on a quarterly basis) on loans to city banks, a policy first introduced in 1962 with a view to reducing the city banks' dependence on Bank of Japan funding in the prevailing over-loaned situation.[60] The resultant impact on banks' reserve positions, like discount rate changes, elicits in turn the familiar interest rate and portfolio adjustments by both the banks and their customers, with consequences for the money supply and the real economy.

Such then was the nature of the regulatory framework used to support monetary policy in the early postwar period, with changes in the Bank of Japan's lending policy, particularly in respect of the setting of credit ceilings for city banks, and window guidance generally reckoned to have been the most important instruments, especially in the high-growth period from 1955 to 1970 (Katayama, 1985). But what of the Bank of Japan's transactions in financial markets at this time, limited as they were?

Apart from trading in bullion, which ceased in 1978, the Bank of Japan was also involved in transactions in both bills and government bonds.[61] Collateralized[62] loans at official discount rates were replaced by official operations in government and government-guaranteed bonds in November 1962, for example. And in 1972 bill rediscount operations were started to complement the sale of government bills and bills drawn on the Bank of Japan inaugurated in 1966 and 1971 respectively.

Bond transactions were initiated with a view to diversifying the range of monetary instruments at the central bank's disposal and originally they simply represented bilateral trades with financial institutions – ordinary banks, long-term credit banks, foreign exchange banks, *sogo* banks and the Federation of Credit Co-operatives – at fixed rates and on a repurchase agreement basis. The reopening of the bond market in 1966, however, witnessed a switch to the current trading practice of sales at market price without repurchase agreements. Later, the range of counterparties was extended to embrace securities companies (in 1966), the *Norinchukin* Bank (in 1967) and some *shinkin* banks (in 1978). Despite those and other developments,[63] designed to enhance operational flexibility, however, the bond transactions did not represent open market operations in the true sense of the word as non-banks were still excluded as counterparties.

The *rediscounting* of eligible bills (such as cover bills with less than three months initial maturity and acceptances) represented a further attempt to broaden the range of policy instruments. Although all client financial institutions were at first able to act as counterparties to the transactions, after 1975 the privilege was confined to the money market dealers.

As far as the official *bill sales* were concerned, the intention was to smooth the impact on the money markets of seasonal fluctuations in the supply and demand for funds. To this end, the Bank of Japan began selling government bills from its own portfolio to money market dealers on a repurchase basis in January 1966. While such operations ceased in November 1972 they were reactivated in May 1981, with resale to financial institutions (who could then sell on to corporate customers) being allowed. In this way open market operations proper began although the paucity of government bills militated against further development of the market.

The other type of bill sales undertaken by the Bank of Japan involved the sale of bills drawn on itself. The bills, of up to three months maturity, were usually sold to the short funds companies but occasionally direct sales to client financial institutions were made.

In summary, the pre-1975 monetary control regime was characterized by a heavy reliance on direct monetary controls. The segmentation of financial markets, at both the long and short ends, secured by interest rate controls and participation rules and supported by exchange controls, ruled out the option of conducting open-market operations on the grounds of ineffectiveness which, at any rate, would have proved impossible because of the dearth of eligible paper in the market place.[64]

As we saw earlier, however, the pace of financial liberalization quickened after the mid-1970s. The money and capital markets (both primary and secondary) were broadened and deepened, interest rates were liberalized, participation rules were relaxed and the yen was internationalized as the

Japanese government implemented measures to end the isolation of its financial system from the rest of the world. This process of change was, of course, conducive to a switch in emphasis on the part of the monetary authorities away from the use of direct controls and towards the wider use of securities (bond and bill) operations (Yoshitomi, 1985). Accordingly, as noted earlier, less reliance was placed on the use of regulations, such as interest rate controls, reserve requirements and window guidance, within the monetary policy process, as the Bank of Japan expanded both the scale and variety[65] of its market transactions (Shigehara, 1991). The full transition to an open-market operations-based regime is still some way off, however, mainly because of the lack of a fully developed Treasury bill market[66] but also because of the remaining restrictions on participation. Moreover, foreign firms still complain[67] that they operate at a competitive disadvantage *vis-à-vis* their Japanese counterparts because of the fragmented nature of the interbank market, the associated collateral requirements and the continuing restrictions imposed on access to the Bank of Japan's discount window.

Choice of intermediate target
Apart from affecting the choice of monetary instruments, financial liberalization also impinges on the choice of intermediate target (see Exhibit 6.9). 'Operational objectives' were not affected although the priority accorded to the growth objective amongst the end goals of policy was dropped around 1975 with emphasis switching to the control of inflation, which became regarded as a precondition for the maintenance of employment and growth in the medium term. The floating of the yen in 1973 obviously facilitated this move although, even after this time, concern with the exchange rate occasionally complicated monetary management (Suzuki, 1987, p. 317). The Japanese authorities, in line with most of their Western counterparts, duly switched attention away from controlling the growth in bank credit and towards the growth in monetary aggregates in the mid-1970s (see Bank of Japan, 1975): M2 initially assumed prime importance, although by 1979 M2 plus negotiable CDs had become the fêted aggregate. Whilst many Western central banks embarked upon monetary targeting (see Hall, 1982, pp. 13–33), however, the Japanese authorities adopted a more pragmatic approach, publishing quarterly forecasts (as opposed to targets) for annualized growth in the chosen aggregate after July 1978. Rigid adherence to such forecasts was not the authorities' main aim, although undoubtedly movements in the selected aggregate relative to the forecasts (that is, the desired movements) heavily influenced official policy at this time. More recently, with the switch in emphasis towards the use of open-market operations as a major instrument of policy, market interest rates have assumed greater importance as intermediate objectives of monetary policy.

The last-mentioned change in policy tack, involving a down-grading of the significance attributed to movements in broad money, deserves further analysis. A wealth of evidence from around the world (see Hall, 1987, ch. 3, for comparison of the UK and Australian experience) suggests that large-scale financial liberalization at the very least severely complicates the task of interpreting movements in broad money, in all likelihood rendering monetary targeting impossible. This explains the dropping of money supply targets (at least for broad money)[68] in the mid-1980s in Australia and the UK, for example. And even for those countries which soldiered on with monetary targets, the degree of success achieved in hitting targets has left much to be desired, calling into question the very rationale for monetary targeting (Hall, 1982, ch. 7).

The sources of the likely complications are not hard to identify. Any process of liberalization will undoubtedly favour those most adversely affected under the previous regime which, for a number of reasons, is likely to have been the banks. Accordingly, the process of reintermediation will usually follow financial liberalization although the pace, extent and duration of it often prove hard to predict. This reintermediation will, of course, fuel the growth in broad money.[69] Similarly, relaxation of the restraints imposed on the scope of business activities for various intermediaries will naturally lead to potentially significant changes in market shares of (domestic) intermediation, further complicating interpretation of movements in broad money aggregates. Finally, interest rate liberalization, whether in the form of deposit rate,[70] lending rate or bond rate liberalization, will also cause problems for monetary management by increasing the interest rate sensitivity of final expenditure because of the greater interest arbitrage opportunities. The magnitude of the increase and the speed with which it materializes will, again, prove hard to predict.

To these problems for interpretation, must be added the difficulties associated with the switch towards interest rate control of the *demand* for money and bank credit, which is an essential prerequisite for running a successful monetary targeting regime in a post-liberalization era. Once again, there is much evidence (for the UK experience, see Hall, 1983, chs 4 and 6) from around the globe pointing to the relatively low interest sensitivity of the demand for money[71] and bank credit,[72] with fairly lengthy and unpredictable lags existing between the moment in time when action is taken (for example, through open-market operations) and the point in time when the interest rate effects have run their full course. The implications of this for the conduct of policy are that large and sustained increases in interest rates may prove necessary if the growth in credit demand is to be restrained so as to be consistent with pre-announced targets for broad money growth; and there can be no presumption that interest rates alone will secure the necessary degree of tightening in the time-scale required by targeting policy. Accordingly, strict adherence to annual targets for the growth in broad monetary aggregates in a fully liberalized environment is likely to result in an increase in both the average level and variability of (nominal) interest interests (see also note 71), with 'overfunding' (that is, the nominal value of net sales of public sector securities being in excess of the size of the public sector deficit) all too often proving necessary if targets are to be hit consistently. Such outcomes, however, with their own attendant costs for the real economy, may be regarded by political administrations as representing too high a price to pay for the control of statistics of dubious significance.[73]

Other complications for monetary management
The remaining set of problems arising from liberalization centre on the implications of the internationalization of the yen (see pp. 100–104). In principle, a perfectly free (as opposed to a managed) float of the yen should have minimized the problems created by external transactions for monetary management but in practice certain concerns remained. These arose, at various times, because of the continuation of external imbalances in spite of the floating yen and the tendency for the exchange rate to overshoot its long-run equilibrium level; because of the potential control problems arising from the application of differential reserve requirements on domestic and Euroyen deposits; because of the Japanese banks' ability to evade the discipline imposed by window guidance through the extension of yen-denominated loans to Japanese residents via their foreign branches (Osugi, 1990, p. 68); and because of the problems created for defining money by the growth in Euroyen business (see Osugi, 1990, pp. 64–6; for further details, see Suzuki, 1987, pp. 341–4).

Implications of financial liberalization for prudential policy

The 'risks'
The financial liberalization programme was undertaken with a view to increasing efficiency (partly through an accommodation of technological advances) in the face of growing overseas pressures for the Japanese financial system to be internationalized and for foreign intermediaries to be given reciprocal rights of access to Japanese markets and, domestically, from the intermediaries' desire to meet the changing requirements of their customers. It has serious implications for the conduct of prudential policy.

At the macro level, the stability of both the banking and wider financial systems is threatened as a result of the exposure of individual intermediaries to new risks and to an increase in existing risks (see below); of the induced changes in market shares of intermediation services experienced by the different segments of the financial services industry; and of the greater variability in profits for the individual intermediaries induced by the intensification in competition faced both at home and overseas and, in the case of banks, by the deregulation of deposit rates.

At the micro level, and despite the benefits deriving from the wider diversification opportunities created which offer the prospect of a reduction in overall portfolio risk and/or higher risk-adjusted portfolio returns, risk management is at a premium. This is because of the emergence of new risks and an increase in existing risks. *Management risk*, for example, which refers to management's ability to handle satisfactorily the diversification embarked upon, will be a new phenomenon to many engaged in the financial services sector who have been brought up in, and hence become accustomed to, the traditions of the highly segmented nature of the Japanese financial system. Similarly, the ever-widening use of derivatives in risk management and the growth in off-balance-sheet business poses problems for management (as well as for the wider financial system), who may fail to grasp fully the risks assumed by virtue of their engagement in such activities. The more traditional banking risks may also pose problems. *Credit risk*, for example, is likely to increase in the face of the intensification in competition which all too frequently results in a lowering of creditworthiness assessment standards and a concomitant reduction in risk-adjusted returns on the loan portfolio. The relaxation of collateral requirements will accentuate this problem. *Interest rate risk* and *foreign exchange risk* are also likely to increase, as a result of the interest rate liberalization programme in the former case and the floating of the yen and the internationalization of Japanese intermediaries' activities in the latter case. *Liquidity risk*, too, may increase as the funding mix is changed to embrace the new borrowing opportunities; and *position risk* will also increase as a result of the authorities' willingness to tolerate greater variability in the yields on bonds and other securities. Whilst this is by no means an exhaustive survey of the new risk environment faced by Japanese financial intermediaries it nevertheless serves to indicate the seriousness of the situation.

The policy issues
Apart from the need to address these issues, the supervisory authorities must also deal with a further set of threats and demands. The threats comprise the damage to the integrity of the financial system (already damaged by the numerous, mainly securities-related, scandals which have surfaced during the last few years[74]) that would result from a failure to handle in an appropriate fashion the myriad conflicts of interest that result from the relaxation of controls on the scope of business activities that may be undertaken; and the damage to the economy that might result should excessive concentration in

the financial sector or overseas domination be the end results of the liberalization programme. The more pressing demands, in turn, relate mainly to concerns about competitive equity. These concerns are expressed both overseas – witness the demands for reciprocity and convergence in the regulation of internationally active intermediaries in the face of the trend towards the globalization of finance – and domestically, in the latter case largely because of the dismantling of the participation barriers which has yet further intensified competition in local markets.

Accordingly, and apart from the need to reduce systemic risk, the supervisory authorities have to deliver cost-effective solutions to the problems posed by conflicts of interest, increasing concentration and regulatory anomalies at both the domestic/international interface and the domestic industry/industry interface.

The solutions

Systemic risk   The chosen solutions of the supervisory authorities' (the Bank of Japan and the Ministry of Finance – see below for a delineation of their responsibilities) to handling the systemic risks created by financial liberalization comprise the following elements: (i) a controlled pace of deregulation (already covered on pp. 100–134); (ii) an expansion of the safety net, in the form of an increase in the level of protection given to depositors under the deposit insurance arrangements and enhanced powers for the Ministry of Finance (MOF) in facilitating bank mergers; (iii) the imposition of tougher capital requirements on banks; and (iv) enhanced supervision of financial intermediaries, especially banks.

Changes to the *deposit insurance arrangements*[75] were made fairly early in the liberalization programme. With effect from June 1986: the insurance coverage was increased from Y3 million to Y10 million; the premiums payable by the intermediaries were increased by 50 per cent (that is, from 0.008 per cent of deposits to 0.012 per cent for banks); the limit imposed on the Deposit Insurance Corporation's (DIC) emergency borrowing from the Bank of Japan was increased from Y50 billion to Y500 billion;[76] labour credit associations became subject to deposit insurance; and the range of aid-giving (and failure-preventing) methods available to the DIC was expanded, allowing the DIC to become involved before a declaration of insolvency is made.[77] These changes were introduced through amendments to the Deposit Insurance Law of April 1971 and the corresponding law covering agricultural co-operatives and fishery co-operatives, which resulted in the establishment of the Savings Insurance Corporation for Agricultural and Fishery Co-operatives (SICAFC) in September 1983.

Enhancement of the MOF's powers to *facilitate bank mergers* also resulted from the 1986 revision to the Deposit Insurance Law. This is because the law now allows the MOF to initiate merger proceedings even if the institution itself has not applied for assistance. This is authorized under the so-called 'emergency merger' provisions, which provide the MOF with such discretionary powers in situations where a breakdown in the credit system is threatened. To allay fears that it might act precipitately in this capacity, however, the MOF agreed to proposals that the Justice Ministry give prior approval to the activation of the emergency merger procedures and that MOF authorization of a merger should not be given in situations where at least 20 per cent of the shareholders of the troubled institution are opposed to the move.

An early decision to raise banks' *capital requirements* was taken in the spring of 1986. Following the failure of earlier MOF guidance to get banks to observe minimum net worth ratios of 10 per cent, explicit targets were set for raising capital ratios. Banks were asked to observe a minimum 4 per cent ratio of capital to total assets by 1990; and those with overseas branches were given a minimum target ratio of 6 per cent, to be achieved by the end of 1987 at the latest. For the latter set of institutions, 70 per cent of 'hidden reserves' in the form of unrealized gains on securities holdings were eligible for inclusion in the capital base.

Subsequent to this, the Japanese authorities, keen to be seen to be abiding by the spirit if not the letter of the UK–US accord on capital adequacy (see Hall, 1989, pp. 81–2, for further details), also asked the banks to provide them with regular reports on their risk asset ratios from September 1986 onwards; and more recently the Japanese banks have been forced to fall into line with the G10 agreement on capital adequacy assessment (see below).

Enhanced supervision of financial intermediaries has taken a number of guises. An early package of measures aimed at the banking sector was introduced in the spring of 1986 on the recommendation of the Financial System Research Council. Apart from the introduction of a new two-tier system of capital ratio requirements and the reform of deposit insurance arrangements noted above, the package comprised: the imposition of reporting requirements in respect of off-balance-sheet activities (designed to facilitate continuous assessment of off-balance-sheet exposures); the imposition of reporting requirements to cover the activities of overseas subsidiaries (designed to enhance the effectiveness of consolidated supervision); the imposition of requirements relating to the regular submission of data on funding from the money market and holdings of floating rate instruments (designed to assist in the assessment of liquidity adequacy and interest rate risk); the imposition of tougher loan exposure rules – although the limits on loan exposures to single borrowers were raised from 20 per cent of net worth for commercial banks, 30 per cent for long-term credit banks and trust banks, and 40 per cent for the specialized foreign exchange bank to 40 per cent, 45 per cent and 50 per cent respectively, with effect from May 1986 they covered both off-balance-sheet activities as well as loans to corporate customers' affiliates; the introduction of minimum risk asset ratio require-ments in respect of external (including off-balance-sheet, securities-related activities) operations[78] – risk-weighted external assets could not exceed 3.5 times net worth after September 1986 (reduced to 2.5 times net worth at the end of 1987); and the use of guideline liquidity ratios in the assessment of liquidity adequacy (to ensure that the risks associated with the possible drying up of euromarket sources of funds are accounted for). Inspection procedures were also strengthened, involving an increase in the frequency of inspections for banks' domestic operations and overseas branches (hence-forth, for the latter, to be made at three-yearly intervals rather than every eight years, as previously); an extension in the scope of supervision, to include, for example, the banks' activities in Hong Kong and Australia for the first time; computerization of monitoring; and an increase in emphasis given to the growth in shareholders' equity, asset quality, earnings, liquidity and managerial skill.

The large number of components of the package concerned with more intensive monitoring of the banks' overseas operations reflected the author-ities' increasing anxiety at the rapid expansion in such activities, which lay outside the traditional supervisory framework. The measures duly intro-duced complemented those already in existence, such as the extensive guid-ance given after 1983 on what constituted 'appropriate' levels of lending to non-industrialized countries (a limit of 40 per cent of net worth was eventu-ally applied to the aggregate of loans outstanding, excluding debt reschedul-ing) and the prudential limits on overseas yen lending introduced in 1984, and were later followed by yet further measures. These latter initiatives involved, *inter alia,* the provision of administrative guidance on the question of what levels of provisions against less-developed country (LDC) debt were appropriate, and the introduction of country lending limits and prudential limits on the net foreign asset positions of the trading banks.

Inspection procedures, too, were kept under constant review and towards the end of the 1980s a number of further policy adjustments were imple-mented. First, more importance was attached to the extent and form of capital enlargement, the management of profitability, risk and liquidity, the assessment of asset quality and the review of management and control systems. Secondly, the authorities determined to tailor their inspections more to the individual characteristics of institutions, taking due account of the risks they faced, in order to increase the flexibility of operations. Thirdly, an attempt was made to enhance the effectiveness of inspection by computerizing procedures as far as possible and by extending the scope of the inspection process to keep pace with the latest developments in international and domestic business, for example the growing use of derivative instruments. Finally, the authorities, in response to the globalization of finance trend and as a result of their acceptance of a policy of internationalization, sought to strengthen their liaison with overseas supervisory authorities with a view to fostering greater mutual understanding of each other's policies and facilitating the development of mutually acceptable reciprocity provisions to cover the entry and regulation of foreign firms in local markets.

Individual bank risk Many of the policies aimed at reducing or at least containing systemic risk also, of course, serve to reduce the probability of an individual bank failure. Higher capital requirements and improved supervision and inspection procedures will all contribute to achieving this goal, as will improved settlement systems and, through its impact on depositor confidence, the extension of the safety net.

Investor confidence Such measures, however, in themselves are not sufficient to instil confidence in investors in a deregulated environment, a prerequisite for preservation of the markets' integrity. This is because of their increased exposure to conflict of interest abuse following the relaxation or abolition of the participation barriers. Mindful of the efficiency losses associated with preventive measures, such as outright prohibition on the joint participation in certain undertakings, and the doubts surrounding the effectiveness of market-based solutions, based on the alleged restraints associated with the desire to preserve reputation, and self-regulation (for example, the use of Chinese Walls and rule books policed by compliance officers), the Japanese authorities quite rightly sought comfort from legal provisions. These can be used to deter fraud, for example, in the regulation of insider trading under the 1988 amendment to the Securities and Exchange Law, and to elicit adequate disclosure of relevant information (as provided for in the Commercial Law, the Securities and Exchange Law, and the Banking Law). External regulation and supervision were also enhanced. The mix of policies adopted in respect of the joint offering of banking and securities services is highlighted in detail below with a view to illustrating the authorities' attempts to reconcile the often conflicting requirements arising from considerations of equity, efficiency and effectiveness.

Concentration and foreign dominance Concerns about excessive concentration in the financial services sector can presumably be dealt with by invoking the Antimonopoly Law should such fears ever be realized. Similarly, should the spectre of foreign dominance ever appear on the horizon (a most unlikely event if present trends are anything to go by), domestic laws can be redrafted if necessary to ring-fence the cores of the domestic credit and settlement systems and any other parts of the financial system thought likely to be damaged by foreign dominance, such as the primary government bond market.

Competitive equity   The final issue to be addressed, namely the need to accommodate demands for competitive equity as far as is practicable, has been taken on board at both the national and international levels. Domestically, deregulation has proceeded at a pace and in a manner designed to satisfy industry demands for 'fairness' without the authorities being required to adjudicate on the fairness of the existing regulatory and supervisory frameworks for example, through reforms allowing mutual interpretation of different segments of the financial services industry. And at the international level, bilateral negotiations, such as those with the US government and the EC Commission acting on behalf of EC Member States, have been, and continue to be, pursued with a view to promulgating mutually acceptable proposals concerning the licensing and regulation of intermediaries' overseas operations.

The current regulatory and supervisory framework

Regulations employed for monetary policy purposes
As noted on pp. 134–40, the present conduct of monetary policy in Japan relies much less heavily on regulations than in the recent past. Indeed, since the formal abolition of BOJ window guidance in the middle of 1991, one can characterize the conduct of policy as the use of open market operations, for example, in short-term government bills and CDs and in the bond *gensaki* and CP markets, alongside the more traditional transactions in the government bond and interbank markets to secure the desired levels and structure of (short-term) market interest rates thought compatible with the ultimate goals of macroeconomic policy such as price stability and full employment (see Exhibit 6.9; and Kasman and Rodrigues, 1991). The only regulations still used to support monetary policy (apart from an administered discount rate and prescribed reserve requirements) comprise the interest rate controls still applied to 'small-lot' time and non-time deposits, but even these are due for abolition by end-June 1993 and end-June 1994 at the latest respectively. After the latter date, only the prohibition on the payment of interest on current accounts will remain on the statute book, and even this is under attack as being an unnecessary impediment to market developments.

Prudential regulation and supervision

The two-tier system of supervision Banking supervision in Japan is conducted by two separate institutions: the Ministry of Finance (MOF) and the Bank of Japan (BOJ). The MOF, however, is the primary supervisory authority for banks (and, indeed, for other financial firms). Its Banking Bureau is responsible for the supervision of banks and their overseas affiliates and, through its Insurance Department, for the supervision of insurance companies and oversight of the deposit insurance programme; while its International Finance Bureau has responsibility for overseeing the supervision of the foreign activities of Japanese financial firms.

The MOF's supervisory powers derive from Banking Law and other pieces of primary legislation. Under the Banking Law 1981, for example, the MOF is held responsible for the licensing (Article 4) and inspection (Article 25) of banks. It is also empowered to demand the provision of interim and final business reports twice a year (Article 19) and to demand the provision of *ad hoc* reports as and when deemed desirable from any bank or a subsidiary company (Article 24). Finally, the MOF is required to *approve* a miscellaneous set of banking matters covering such issues as the establishment or closing down of branches or other business offices (including agencies), changes in their location or type, and reductions in the level of capital held below a pre-specified minimum.

In contrast with the MOF, the BOJ's supervisory role lies mainly in bank examinations (reporting requirements are also imposed on certain financial institutions) and is based on contractual agreements struck between itself and financial institutions at the time they opened current accounts with it (consistent with Articles 42 to 44 of the Bank of Japan Law). Institutions holding such current accounts are city banks, regional banks, trust banks, long-term credit banks, *sogo* banks, *shinkin* banks, foreign banks, money market dealers and some securities companies, including their overseas branches and affiliates and some wholly-owned domestic subsidiaries[79]. They are liable to on-site examinations by the BOJ which take place, in principle, every two (in practice, maybe every five)[80] years. For the leading banks, simultaneous examination of the head office and overseas offices has taken place since January 1990; for the others, overseas offices are examined four times a year. Through these examinations, which are aimed at maintaining the safety and soundness of the financial system through, *inter alia*, assessment of an institution's risk management activities and capabilities, the BOJ is able to obtain a thorough understanding of each institution's business profile.

Although lacking a formal means of co-operation (for example through the appointment of a 'lead' regulator), in order to avoid the unnecessary duplication of supervisory effort the MOF and the BOJ alternate in conducting biennial on-site inspections/examinations with the aim, in principle, of ensuring that every institution is inspected annually. Moreover, when problems are detected the two authorities will collaborate to enhance the cost-effectiveness of supervision.

On-site examinations by the BOJ   The BOJ's examinations are pre-announced – institutions receive roughly one month's notice – and usually last from two to three weeks. Typically, interviews with senior executives are held on the first day or so of the visit following a preliminary study of the institution prior to the visit; the management and the board of directors attend separately. On the following three or four days the quality of assets (including off-balance-sheet exposures) is assessed, with low-quality assets being classified as 'L' (a likely loss), 'D' (doubtful) or 'S' (slow or substandard), largely on the basis of an estimate of the likelihood of repayment. The ratio of such inferior loans to total loans is also seen as prime indicator of the soundness of the institution.

The appraisal of assets, the longest and perhaps most important part of the examination process, is followed by visits lasting two days or so to the branches of the institution. The subsequent analysis of the information collected attempts to provide an overall assessment of their profitability and risk management systems.

One to two weeks after the examination the BOJ's findings are usually reviewed with the institution, with reports being sent a week or so later to the Director and Deputy Director of the Bank Supervision Department of the BOJ. Banks are classified 'A', 'B', 'C' or 'D' according to a rating system which takes account of asset quality (the main concern), risk management capabilities, management skills more generally and earnings, although the rating given is not disclosed to the institution. In principle, the rating can influence the future form of supervision, including frequency of examination, but in practice a uniform approach has been adopted because of a failure to unearth 'bad' banks (at least this was the position prior to the emergence of the banking scandals in the early 1990s – see note 74).

Inspections by the MOF   Inspections are conducted by the MOF with a view to ensuring the financial soundness of institutions and protecting depositors. Visits are made to the business establishments of financial institutions in order to check how transactions are processed, make an independent assessment of asset quality and examine how loans are screened. Interviews are also used to provide an assessment of management capabilities.

A thorough review of inspection procedures was instituted in the wake of the publication in 1987 of a report by the Financial System Research Council which called for increased cost-effectiveness in banking supervision. This was to be achieved, through: computerization of inspection procedures; the priority allocation of manpower; more efficient data collection, storage and analysis; improved post-inspection follow-up procedures; improved assessment of risk management capabilities; placing greater emphasis on net worth and profitability and the measures being taken to improve both; and paying closer attention to management planning, organizational reform and other policies adopted in the light of an institution's current position and soundness, for example, those adopted in respect of domestic and foreign affiliates. As a result, the MOF concentrated its efforts on understanding banks' risk management systems and providing guidance, when necessary, on how such systems might be improved to help the institution withstand growing risk and prevent excessive risk-taking. Beyond this, the inspection placed greater emphasis on the assessment of profitability and asset quality.

In 1988 a new rating system was also introduced that allowed the MOF to rank institutions on a scale of 1 to 5 on the basis of the following considerations: net worth ratios; asset quality; management control systems; profitability; and liquidity. In principle, the intensity of supervision and frequency of inspection is determined by this ratio, although it remains the MOF's intention to inspect every institution at least once every three years or so.[81]

The use of administrative guidance within the supervisory process Mirroring the BOJ's employment of administrative guidance in the name of monetary policy (in the form of 'window guidance' – see above), the MOF uses such moral suasion extensively in its supervisory capacity. Although its usage is catered for in the provisions of the Banking Law of 1927 (as amended in 1981) it is not legally enforceable; rather, banks are expected to act on it. Moreover, despite the 1981 amendment to the Banking Law, which represented an attempt to shift the emphasis away from the informal approach and towards a more formal regulatory framework depending for its effectiveness upon the use of Cabinet Orders, the MOF retains considerable discretion in the discharging of its supervisory duties.

Administrative guidance comes in a number of guises – 'directives', 'requests', 'warnings', 'suggestions' and 'encouragements' – and is usually transmitted via notifications or official liaison letters. Its advantages lie in the flexibility it provides for the supervisory authorities and the speed with which it can induce remedial action. Against this must be set the potential dangers associated with the authorities' abuse of the system, the imprecision of some of the requirements and the lack of sanctions available to the authorities to enforce the provisions. Moreover, the principle of 'competitive equity' may be breached if some institutions (Japanese rather than foreign?) prove more amenable to persuasion than others.

Licensing provisions   Under Article 4 of the Banking Law of 1981 no firm can engage in banking without first acquiring a licence from the MOF. According to the same article, applicants have to satisfy the following criteria: (i) that they have 'adequate' financial resources (minimum capital of Y1 billion or as specified by Cabinet Order), and that the income and expenses associated with the prospective business operations are 'satisfactory'; (ii) that the personnel to be involved in the banking operation have sufficient knowledge and expertise to enable them to conduct banking business appropriately, fairly and efficiently and to command credibility; (iii) that the proposed banking business can be justified, and not threaten financial instability, in the light of the supply and demand for funds, the business situation of banks and other financial intermediaries, and other economic and financial conditions in the proposed location for the banking business; and (iv) that they satisfy any additional 'public interest' conditions specified by the MOF.

Banking licences may be revoked for violation of any law, articles of incorporation or MOF measures designed to protect the public interest (Article 27), and conditions on a banking licence may be imposed by the MOF as and when it deems necessary in the public interest (Article 4, para. 4).

For firms incorporated outside Japan, additional requirements apply. Banks incorporated overseas can enter Japan as branches, subsidiaries or representative offices. In principle, acquisitions of local banks are also allowed, although the requirements of the Anti-monopoly Law, the Foreign Exchange and Foreign Trade Control Law and Banking Law (Article 9) would all have to be satisfied. To date, no such acquisitions have been made so the MOF's policy on the issue has not yet been tested. For those wishing to operate through branches or agencies (these modes of operation are preferred to the subsidiary route by the MOF, in effect confining operations to the former), a separate licence must be obtained for each branch/agency from the MOF, in accordance with Article 47 of the Banking Law of 1981, although if more than one branch is operated one may be designated to be responsible for the provision of books, documents, reports and other material in a consolidated form as and when required by the MOF, in accordance with Article 48. The criteria applied in the award of such licenses are similar to those employed in respect of locally incorporated institutions: financial strength, size and standing, competence of management and so on, although certain additional requirements apply. These embrace a reciprocity provision, concerned with ensuring that similar rights are available to foreign banks in the country of incorporation in accordance with Article 4, and a provision relating to the length of time the applicant has operated a representative office in Japan. Successful applicants must also undertake to inform the MOF of any substantive changes in the nature of their operations. These include, *inter alia*, changes in capital, the location of the head office and the trading name used, and any plans to merge or cease trading as a bank (in accordance with Article 48).

Prospective operators of a representative office must notify the MOF in advance of the nature of the proposed activities, the proposed location of the office and other matters of concern to the MOF and must also undertake to supply any further information requested by the MOF (in accordance with Article 52).

Finally, for those foreign applicants which are engaged in non-banking business, approval has to be secured from the MOF in accordance with Article 9 of the Banking Law of 1981.

Accounting, auditing and reporting arrangements   Under the Banking Law of 1981 banks are obliged to adopt an annual business term, or basic accounting period, which runs from 1 April to 31 March of the following year. Pursuant to the so-called 'Bank Accounting Standards' developed by the MOF, banks have to account for their business practices in terms of fairness, clarity and continuity. The content of financial statements is governed by the Banking Law of 1981. Article 19 specifies that for each financial year a bank must prepare and submit to the MOF interim and final business reports describing its business activities and financial position; and Article 20 requires each bank to compile a balance sheet and a statement of profits and losses for each business year and make them public within a three month period after the end of each business year. Certified public accountants are appointed by shareholders to validate the accuracy of the published financial statements.

Like other businesses in Japan, banks are also subject to the auditing requirements of the Japanese Commercial Code. A minimum of two auditors and one certified public accountant must be appointed by each bank, the auditors being primarily responsible to the bank's management and the accountant to the bank's shareholders. Auditors are authorized to receive any information that might assist in their determination of the financial position of a bank, and they are legally bound to report any breaches of the law to the Bank's board of directors.

As for reporting requirements, the MOF requires prudential returns covering business activities and financial positions (as noted above) to be submitted twice a year, together with any *ad hoc* reports that it deems desirable, as provided for in Article 24 of the Banking Law of 1981. The latter reports may also be sought from a bank's subsidiary or affiliated company.

Capital adequacy assessment   Apart from satisfying the minimum capital requirement of not less than Y1 billion set by a Cabinet Order, Japanese banks have either to abide by the G10 agreement of July 1988 on the measurement and assessment of capital adequacy for 'internationally-active' banks (guideline proposals were published by the Basle Committee of Supervisors in December 1987 – see BIS, 1987) or otherwise observe a minimum capital ratio of 4 per cent, the ratio being calculated as the sum of capital plus certain reserves as a percentage of the daily average of total assets less some special reserves. Those banks obliged to abide by the former rules comprise those which maintain overseas business establishments. Other banks may also opt to be covered by the G10 rules rather than be subject to the 4 per cent minimum ratio requirement. For all those bound by the G10 agreement, guidance on the implementation of the rules is contained in a circular issued by the MOF in December 1988 (MOF, 1988), full details of which are incorporated in the comparative study in Chapter 8 of this book. In brief, those bound by the rules are committed to observing, on a consolidated basis, a minimum *risk asset ratio* of 8 per cent by the end of March 1993, with *Tier 1* capital amounting to at least 4 per cent of *weighted risk assets* (for a discussion of the risk asset ratio methodology employed, see Hall, 1989).

Despite the continuing efforts of Japanese banks to meet the Basle guidelines (all but one of the major banks reported risk asset ratios in excess of 8 per cent at the close of the 1991–2 financial year having successfully met the interim standard of 7.25 per cent by the end of March 1990 – see Exhibit 6.11) a number of serious problems have recently conspired to hinder them in this task. The problems comprise: a steep fall in local stock prices (by the end of June 1992 the Nikkei index was hovering around the 16,000 level, well below half of the peak recorded in 1990); declining profitability, due largely to a dramatic increase in bad and doubtful debts (especially on property investment and property-related lending), but also to the intensification in competition induced by deregulation and to the decline in loan demand associated with the slowing-down of the real economy; and a secular fall in the value of the yen against the US dollar (although this has been partially reversed since mid-1992).

The decline in the Nikkei index is important for a number of reasons. First, it directly affects banks' capital because 45 per cent of unrealized gains on securities holdings are allowed for inclusion within Tier 2 capital (see IBCA, 1992) and because Japanese accounting rules require the value of individual equity holdings to be written down, leading to valuation losses. Secondly, the potential contribution to profits (which contribute to Tier 1 capital) from those securities that are realised is reduced. And thirdly, the cost and difficulty of raising equity finance is increased for the banks (indeed, an informal ban on equity issues by banks was imposed by the MOF in April 1990).

Exhibit 6.11   Japanese banks' risk asset ratios 1990–2

Type of bank	Bank name	End-March 1990[a]		End-March 1991	End-March 1992
		A	B		
City banks	Bank of Tokyo	8.02	8.02	8.12	8.10
	Dai-Ichi Kangyo	8.28	8.28	8.75	8.24
	Daiwa	10.14	8.41	8.92	8.27
	Fuji	8.24	8.24	9.08	8.04
	Hokkaido Takashoku	8.49	8.33	8.74	8.26
	Kyowa	10.83	8.82	8.97	8.30[c]
	Mitsubishi	8.59	8.46	8.70	8.20
	Saitama	8.26	8.26	8.97	8.30[c]
	Sakura[b]	8.40	7.05	7.35	7.92
	Sanwa	8.45	8.44	8.50	8.10
	Sumitomo	8.44	8.44	8.87	8.43
	Tokai	8.56	7.72	8.05	8.38
Long-term credit-banks	Industrial Bank of Japan	9.56	7.78	8.15	8.33
	Long-Term Credit Bank of Japan	9.94	8.23	8.35	8.27
	Nippon Credit Bank	8.80	7.26	7.66	8.33
Trust banks	Chuo Trust and Banking	10.20	9.20	9.31	8.12
	Mitsubishi Trust and Banking	11.22	11.16	10.36	8.38
	Mitsui Trust and Banking	11.96	10.23	10.53	9.10
	Nippon Trust and Banking	13.88	13.30	12.96	10.37
	Sumitomo Trust and Banking	11.10	11.10	10.34	8.78
	Toyo Trust and Banking	12.48	12.19	10.48	8.55
	Yasuda Trust and Banking	11.79	10.29	10.24	8.42

Notes
[a]   Figures in column A are derived by applying the transitional arrangements provided for in the G10 agreement; the figures in column B (as for end-March 1991 and end-March 1992) are derived by applying the final arrangements applicable to the post-March 1993 period.
[b]   Formed from the merger of Mitsui Bank and the Taiyo Kobe Bank in April 1990.
[c]   The Kyowa and Saitama banks merged to form the Kyowa Saitama Bank in April 1991.

Source: Annual accounts.

Declining profitability also directly impacts on banks' capital positions as it reduces the banks' ability to boost Tier 1 capital from retentions. And finally, a fall in the value of the yen against the US dollar adversely affects the banks' capital ratios because of the high proportion of assets that are denominated in US dollars, while capital is denominated almost exclusively in yen.

The banks have reacted to these adverse conditions in a number of ways. In their search for capital they have increasingly exploited the new opportunities created for them by the MOF. This has involved them in raising additional Tier 2 capital, within the limits provided for in the G10 rules, through the issuance of subordinated bonds and preferred stock (through overseas subsidiaries), through the issuance of convertible bonds, through the issuance of perpetual subordinated bonds, and through the soliciting of subordinated loans from domestic financial institutions (mainly life assurance companies but also the finance subsidiaries of the major manufacturing companies). The last source of capital, however, has to a degree exacerbated the problems associated with raising equity finance because some of the loans have been financed by the lending institutions selling off their holdings of bank stock, thereby further depressing the price of bank shares. Beyond this, they have sought to raise the contribution to capital from retentions by raising lending margins in the face of declining interest rates (and despite the payment of market rates on deposits) and restricting dividend payments (as sought by the MOF in 1988).

On the other side of the coin, they have sought to reduce the total of risk-weighted assets (the denominator of the risk asset ratio) through a combination of: securitization (despite continuing difficulties, which should be eased in the wake of the August 1992 rescue package (see below), some housing and corporate loans, as well as loans to local government, have successfully been securitized); shifting to lower risk-weighted assets, such as housing loans, government bonds and guaranteed loans to small and medium-sized businesses; shifting towards off-balance-sheet fee-based activities such as mergers and acquisitions business; and curtailing asset growth, especially in the fields of overseas and LDC lending and in low-margin/return business, a policy assisted by the MOF through the exercise of administrative guidance over the growth in banks' housing loans (October 1988), loans to local government (July 1989), corporate loans (March 1990) and real-estate lending. The significance of the last course of action was demonstrated in the publication of the banks' balance sheet data for the financial year 1991–2. While the average annual loan growth rate for city banks had fallen to under 3 per cent (in the late 1980s it stood at over 15 per cent plus) the lending of both the Bank of Tokyo and Sukura Bank actually fell in absolute terms.

By these means, as noted earlier, all but one of the major banks recorded risk asset ratios in excess of 8 per cent at the end of March 1992. But after that date the Nikkei index crashed to new lows and most of the banks experienced a deterioration in their bad debt experience. Increasingly, it became clear that if the banks were to remain on track in relation to the G10 agreement – the Japanese authorities had already ruled out a unilateral appeal to the Basle Committee for special dispensation such as an extension in the time allowed before the final standard target risk asset ratio has to be met – and if the local stock market did not pick up substantially before end-March 1993, there was a real danger that a domestic and international credit crunch could result.

While policymakers, especially in the West, have to date taken a fairly relaxed approach to this spectre – weak loan demand associated with sluggish real economic performance has so far staved off localized credit crunches – the warning signs are certainly there. Already, Japanese banks have retreated significantly from overseas markets (including North American), and at a pace probably more rapid than even the more vociferous of the initial supporters of the Basle proposals wanted; and if economic activity picks up in the world economy, as predicted, later in 1993 there can be no certainty that all creditworthy borrowers will be accommodated in the traditional way by the bankers from Japan.

Fortunately for the world economy the Japanese authorities decided to act. The rescue packages put together during August 1992 (see ch. 3, n. 4) should both alleviate some of the capital pressure facing Japanese banks as well as ward off the dangers associated with a local and global credit crunch. Moreover, the resurgence in the local stock market, if sustained, will certainly ease the capital pressures facing many of the banks.

Liquidity adequacy assessment   The assessment of liquidity adequacy features prominently in the MOF's overall assessment of a bank's soundness – it has a direct impact on the rating given (see above) – and to a lesser degree, through its impact on asset quality, in the BOJ's assessment procedures.

Although the MOF has refrained from imposing general liquidity norms it has, nevertheless, encouraged banks to raise the ratio of (average) current assets to total deposits to at least 30 per cent. Special guidelines have also been given in respect of banks' eurocurrency operations because of concerns about the possibility of a credit crisis in the light of the fact that there is no formal lender of last resort to the market. Thus, for example, in February 1983 it was announced that at least 45 per cent of eurocurrency term lending for one year or more had to be funded by (eurocurrency) term deposits or other debt of over one year to maturity, with loans of over three years requiring at least 15 per cent of maturity-matched deposits. These guidelines applied to both Japanese and foreign banks but not to subsidiaries of the former.

More recently, the BOJ has also become concerned with the maturity transformation undertaken by Japanese banks. Accordingly, although setting no formal guidelines, it has encouraged banks to formally use maturity ladders in the assessment of interest rate risk and assesses for itself the risks being run by each bank, giving advice on an *ad hoc* basis. In its analysis, the BOJ breaks down assets and liabilities into five time bands – up to three months, three to six months, six to nine months, nine to twelve months, and over twelve months – focusing heavily on the period of up to one year. Assets are classified into four categories: those with yields which are still regulated; those with yields which are linked to short-term money market rates of interest; those with yields which are linked to the short-term prime rate; and those with yields which are linked to the long-term prime rate. Similarly, deposits are classified according to whether their associated interest payments are regulated (linked to the BOJ's discount rate), linked to short-term money market rates or to the long-term prime rate. The BOJ compares the 'accumulated net mismatched position' (ranging over the whole of the maturity spectrum) with annual earnings, as well as comparing assets and liabilities by maturity.

Measures to limit exchange rate risk   The foreign currency operations of authorized foreign exchange banks are monitored through (pre-announced) on-site examinations by the MOF and banks are required to report their positions, broken down by currency, on a monthly basis. Under Article 11.2 of the Foreign Exchange Law the MOF is authorized to set limits on the foreign exchange positions run by such banks which in practice means the banks have to observe, on a daily basis, limits on the aggregated net dealing positions (on both a spot and spot-plus-forward basis) in all currencies taken together. In principle, the maximum exposure limit set is US $100,000 but, on a case by case basis, this may be varied to take account of various factors such as capital adequacy and daily trading volume. Banks generally keep foreign exchange exposure well below 10 per cent of the capital base.

Measures to limit concentration risk   Measures designed to limit the concentration risks run by banks in Japan comprise the promulgation of loan exposure guidelines, rules relating to loans to directors and the exercise of moral suasion on the extension of property and property-related loans.

Article 13 of the Banking Law of 1981 deals with exposures to single (non-bank) customers or connected groups of borrowers[82] by limiting such credit exposures to a fixed multiple of capital and reserves (unless the MOF approves otherwise for reasons of merger or transfer of operations). The multiple is determined by Cabinet Order and currently stands at $2^1/_2$ (that is, such credit exposures are subject to a maximum of 40 per cent of capital and reserves). Administrative guidance from the Director General of the Banking Bureau of the MOF, however, ensures that the *de facto* limits are stricter than this. The current guidelines mean that ordinary banks are subject to a limit of 30 per cent of capital and reserves for single credit exposures, *sogo* banks and *shinkin* banks to a limit of 20 per cent and long-term credit banks and trust banks to a limit of 38 per cent. Additionally, administrative guidance is used to limit such exposures for *shinkin* banks to Y1.5 billion.

Rules governing the extension of credit to bank directors derive from both banking law and commercial law. Under Article 14 of the Banking Law of 1981, such loans must not prejudice the interests of the bank and have to be approved by a majority vote of the board of at least two-thirds of those present.

Although no attempt is generally made to limit sectoral exposures, banks' property-related lending[83] is the exception. Concern with the rapid escalation in land and property prices first prompted the issuing of administrative guidance in respect of real-estate lending in the mid-1980s but, in March 1990 the MOF went one stage further. Under the so-called 'total amount control', banks were asked to restrict the growth in their lending to real-estate companies to that of total lending for the financial year 1990–1. Although designed as a temporary measure it remained in operation until the end of December 1991, when it was judged that the boom in land prices, at least for the time being, had ended.

Functional separation   Functional separation in Japan – especially the separation of long-term from short-term finance, banking business from securities business and deposit banking from trust banking – is achieved by law and the use of administrative guidance, as noted at the beginning of this chapter. Originally designed to stabilize the financial system, avoid excess concentration and protect consumers in conflict of interest situations, such measures have been considerably relaxed in recent years in the light of changing market needs and a drive for greater efficiency (see pp. 95–8). The result has been a gradual encroachment of intermediaries on each other's territory as a result of the authorities pursuing a policy of balanced deregulation on a *quid pro quo* basis.

Of particular interest is the approach adopted by the authorities to the dismantling of the barriers between banking and securities business. While the issue is covered in depth in Chapter 9, it is worth noting here the policy initiatives that have been taken in recent years. The opening up of securities business to the banks is surveyed in Exhibit 6.12, and this is due to culminate sometime in 1993 in the banks being allowed to engage domestically in the full range of securities operations, except brokerage, through subsidiaries. Similar reciprocal rights will be extended at the same time to the

Exhibit 6.12   The new opportunities created for Japanese banks in the securities business arena

Date of implementation	Reform measure
1979	Banks permitted to issue and deal in CDs
1983	Banks authorized to affiliate with mortgage securities companies
April	Banks started over-the-counter sale of government bonds to the general public
1984	Securities licences granted to subsidiaries/affiliates of some foreign banks with branches in Japan (but equity stakes limited to 50%)
April	Banks began domestic trading in overseas CDs
June	Banks allowed to deal on their own account in public bonds
1985	Foreign banks allowed to enter trust banking Banks authorized to affiliate with securities investment advisory companies
October	Banks began trading in bond futures
1986	City banks authorized to issue L-T mortgage bonds
October	Banks' overseas subsidiaries authorized to underwrite and deal in CP issues abroad
1987	More securities licences granted to foreign bank subsidiaries/affiliates
April	Ordinary banks allowed to issue convertible bonds in Japan (although use of funds raised was limited to investment in their own plant and equipment until January 1990)
May	Banks allowed to deal in foreign financial futures and options markets
June	Banks authorized to engage in private placement of bond issues
November	Banks began activities (both underwriting and trading) in the domestic CP market
1988: October	Banks allowed to securitize home loans
1989: June	Banks begin *broking* government bond futures and foreign securities futures and options
July	Banks allowed to securitize loans to local government
December	Banks begin *broking* foreign government bond futures and domestic securities futures
1990: March	Banks allowed to securitize loans to corporates
April	Banks allowed to enter the pension trust business through their investment advisory companies

subsidiaries of securities companies, thereby enhancing their ability to engage in banking operations which to date have centred on public bond-collateralized loans (first sanctioned in April 1985), the offering of money market funds and the provision of other bank-style products made possible by tie-ups with banks. These activities are, of course, additional to the trading opportunities created by their access to the yen-denominated commercial paper (CP) market, the foreign CP market, the yen-denominated certificate of deposit (CD) market, the foreign CD market and the yen-based bankers' acceptance (BA) market.

As for the separation of short-term from long-term finance, ordinary banks have been allowed to encroach on the traditional terrain of the long-term credit banks by virtue of their acquisition of powers to issue both long-term mortgage bonds and (since 1987) convertible bonds in Japan. Moreover, under the Financial System Reform Bill of 1992 long-term credit banks will be able to engage in ordinary banking activities through separately capitalized subsidiaries.

Finally, the barriers between commercial and trust banking have been gradually eroded through the decisions taken to allow: (i) foreign banks into the trust banking business (the first were admitted in 1985); (ii) ordinary banks into the housing loan mortgage trust business; (iii) ordinary banks into the pension trust business through their investment advisory companies (possible since April 1990); (iv) ordinary banks into the corporate bond trust business (in accordance with the Secured Bond Trust Law); (v) ordinary banks into other trust business, such as land trusts, through tie-ups with trust banks; (vi) ordinary and foreign banks into investment management (in accordance with the Investment Advisory Law of 1987); and (vii) foreign banks into corporate pension fund management. All these developments have served to further blur the distinction between commercial and trust banking in Japan, a situation which will be carried one stage further under the Reform Bill which allows ordinary banks, long-term banks and the Bank of Tokyo, as well as securities firms, to engage in trust banking operations through separately capitalized subsidiaries.

Provisioning guidelines   The MOF first began exercising moral suasion in respect of provisions to be held against loans to financially troubled countries in 1983. While encouraging Japanese banks to establish such loan loss reserves, they were not expected to exceed 5 per cent of a bank's loan portfolio in total. The next move came in January 1984 when the MOF, keen to encourage banks to participate in worldwide moves to boost lending to the developing world, announced that Japanese banks could make tax-deductible provisions against rescheduled and new loans to less-developed countries (LDCs) up to a maximum of 1 per cent of their exposures to the particular countries. The scope for making such tax-deductible provisions remained at this level until 1990 when the MOF, as a means of stimulating the Japanese banks' participation in the Brady Plan for LDC debt reduction,[84] indicated that it would sanction enlarged tax credits. The guideline limit for total provisions against LDC debt was also raised to 25 per cent of loans outstanding (it had previously been raised to 10 per cent in January 1989 and then to 15 per cent in March 1989) before finally being abolished in April 1990.

Today, the MOF categorizes countries which are deemed high-risk,[85] establishing (unpublished) guidelines for the 'appropriate' levels of provisions that should accompany such loans as well as monitoring (on a consolidated basis) the banks' exposures. The tax treatment of such provisions, however, remains a subject of hot debate, demands from the banks for more favourable treatment being stymied by the National Tax Administration.

Deposit insurance   Following the recommendations of the Committee for Financial System Research (CFSR), the Deposit Insurance Law was passed in April 1971. The Deposit Insurance Corporation (DIC) was duly set up in July of that year to protect depositors in the face of an anticipated intensification of competition within the deposit-taking sector. Membership was made compulsory for all private depository institutions except labour credit associations (the scheme was extended to include these in 1986 – see below), and agricultural and fishery co-operatives, which established their own Savings Insurance Corporation for Agricultural and Fishery Co-operatives (for further details, see Suzuki, 1987, p. 60). The DIC was funded by the Japanese Government, the Bank of Japan and the private financial institutions. Its role was to receive the annual premiums paid by the private depository institutions, which were initially set at 0.008 per cent of the level of insured deposits outstanding at the end of the previous year,[86] invest the proceeds in government bonds or other securities or in deposits at financial institutions and meet any valid insurance claims as and when they arose.[87] In the event of any member institution being unable to refund deposits, the DIC undertook to reimburse depositors up to a maximum of Y3 million of (net) principal.

Following further deliberations of the CFSR the Law was amended in May 1986 to reflect the more important role deposit insurance was likely to play in 'maintaining orderly credit conditions'. With effect from 1 July 1986: (i) the DIC was empowered, with MOF approval, to provide financial assistance to facilitate mergers or the acquisition of failed institutions; (ii) insurance coverage was raised from Y3 million to Y10 million per depositor and payments procedures were improved by simplifying the depositor identification process, introducing a suspense payment system (allowing for payments of up to Y200,000 to meet immediate living expenses) and extending by one month the deadline for considering insurance payments; (iii) the foundation of the DIC was strengthened by raising contributions from 0.008 per cent of insured deposits to 0.012 per cent, raising the limit on DIC borrowing from the BOJ from Y50 billion to Y500 billion and by sanctioning DIC borrowing from private financial institutions (to allow for the repayment of BOJ loans); and (iv) labour credit associations were brought into the scheme (DIC, 1986, p. 3).

The first call made on DIC funds occurred in April 1992 when Y8 billion of financial assistance in the form of low-interest loans was provided to Iyo Bank to facilitate the rescue of the Toho Sogo Bank based in West Japan. This was the last of the *sogo* banks to retain that status. More recently, in June 1992 it was announced that Y20 billion of DIC assistance is to be given to Sanwa Bank to facilitate its merger with the Toyo Shinkin Bank.

Finance industry support Both the BOJ and the MOF have in the past intervened directly to support ailing financial institutions with a view to maintaining orderly conditions in financial markets. This systemic interest explains, for example, the BOJ's actions in 1965 to help prevent the collapse of Yamaichi Securities,[88] one of the 'big four' domestic securities firms, and to support Oi Securities, a smaller broking house that had also failed to meet interest payments due.[89] More recently, both the BOJ and the MOF made public announcements in August 1991 to the effect that they stood ready to support the Toyo Shinkin Bank, an Osaka-based credit co-operative hit by fraud (see note 74 to this chapter);[90] and in 1988, the MOF took over the Daiichi Sogo Bank following its loss of confidence in the senior management of the bank (ibid.).

Apart from direct intervention, the authorities are also involved in behind-the-scenes moves to prevent failures by promoting and/or assisting mergers, takeovers or bail-outs of ailing institutions. The rescue package announced in May 1992 for the Taiheiyo Bank is but the latest example of such action,[91] executives from the BOJ and the MOF (as well as from Sakura Bank) being seconded to the bank to assist in its rehabilitation.[92] This followed the DIC-assisted rescue of the Toho Sogo Bank (see above), which involved the BOJ in making a series of concessionary loans for a period after completion of the takeover by the Iyo Bank. Bank takeovers of ailing securities firms might also be allowed, thereby allowing banks direct access to the securities market.[93]

Ownership rules As in most other countries, concerns about concentration of economic power and national interest considerations have caused the Japanese authorities to promulgate laws relating to bank ownership. Domestic commercial entities, for example, have to satisfy Article 11 of the Anti-trust Law while financial institutions' equity stakes in individual banks (like other companies) are limited to 5 per cent of the bank's stock under the Antimonopoly Law of 1947. Securities companies and insurance companies are further circumscribed by the relevant laws governing their operations. Foreign banks in principle receive the same treatment as domestic concerns although they must also satisfy the reciprocity provision contained in Article 4 of the Banking Law of 1981.

Notes

1. Although 'fixed-date' time deposits are permitted, with a maximum term of three years, they are not 'true' time deposits as they can be withdrawn, subject to giving prior notice, once they have been on deposit for one year.
2. The 1950 Law Concerning Bond Issue by Banks, which permitted ordinary banks to issue financial debentures, was repealed in 1952 on enactment of the Long-term Credit Bank Law.
3. This is still true today despite the 1981 revision to the law which repealed the sections relating to the operations of savings bank business and which resulted in the renaming of the law as the Law Concerning Joint Operation of Trust Business by Ordinary Banks.
4. By 1986 Japan had at 50 per cent the highest ratio of all the major economies for long-term government debt as a percentage of GDP.
5. Although this does not generate more cash reserves for the banks as a group, it does alleviate cash reserve pressure as compared with the situation where direct sales to the banks are made.
6. This need was first recognized when a flexible exchange rate regime was introduced in 1973, for it then became clear that a deeper foreign exchange market would be required if the authorities were to be allowed the option of transacting in the foreign exchange markets to moderate exchange rate volatility. The incompatibility of an efficient foreign exchange market and underdeveloped and highly regulated money and capital markets also became apparent at this time.
7. In the late 1980s, Japanese banks' ambitions to become gilt-edged market makers were stalled pending agreement on the number (and timing) of British firms to be admitted to the Tokyo Stock Exchange.
8. The central banks' desire to diversify reserve asset holdings was, however, distinct from this issue although it would ideally require the establishment of a fully fledged Treasury bill market in Japan.
9. As far as the Japanese banks are concerned, their clients' allegiance, partly because of the prevalence of 'main bank' relationships, is legendary as are their funding advantages arising from access to low-cost deposits (because of deposit rate controls) and low-cost capital (because of the relatively high valuation of their shares on the local stock market compared with other countries). Traditionally, low capital requirements, again by international standards, and the passivity of local stockholders are also believed to have contributed to the Japanese banks' success in gaining market share overseas and in retaining it at home.
10. No separate working guidelines were made for the issue of foreign-currency-denominated foreign bonds (*Shogun* bonds) in Japan with the result that from November 1985 the rules applying for yen-denominated foreign bonds were recognized as applicable.
11. That is, those with a good record of issuing yen-denominated foreign bonds.
12. Impact loans of less than one year's maturity were prohibited until June 1979 and Japanese foreign exchange banks were not permitted to make impact loans until March 1980. Euroyen impact loans were not authorized until June 1984.
13. Non-corporate residents were allowed for the first time to hold up to Y3 million with

banks abroad, and residents in general were free to invest abroad in foreign securities and to make foreign loans (subject to prior reporting). Prior to 1986, the purchase of foreign securities by non-bank institutional investors had been severely restricted (see Osugi, 1990, Table 5, p. 19).

14. The Y3 million limit on non-corporate resident holdings of foreign currency deposits with Japanese banks was abolished in December 1980 and the Japanese foreign exchange bank's freedom to accept foreign currency deposits (from residents and non-residents) and make foreign currency loans was enhanced.

15. Non-residents could issue bonds in Japan, subject to prior reporting. They could also purchase and sell Japanese securities without possessing a licence and hold non-resident bank accounts, reducing the 'non-resident free yen accounts' of the Japanese banks.

16. A third, Fitch Investors Service, was added in July 1987.

17. *Unrated* private corporations, however, were still eligible if they satisfied certain size-related criteria relating to minimum capitalisation and other balance sheet ratios (see JCIF, 1988, pp. 58–9).

18. In June 1986 five types of product were available: floating rate notes; zero coupon bonds; deep discount bonds; currency conversion bonds; and dual currency bonds. Prior to this date, only fixed rate products with a minimum term of five years were recognized. And finally, in June 1987, restrictions on the euroyen bond with a four-year maturity were lifted.

19. On condition that the banks exercized self-restraint and refrained from channelling the funds back into the country.

20. That is, domestic sales.

21. With the result that, by the end of the first quarter of 1986, the share of yen-denominated loans in international bank lending rose to nearly 17 per cent. This meant that the yen had become the second most commonly used currency (after the American dollar) in international lending by that date.

22. In line with the recommendations of the Foreign Exchange Council, a consultative body for the MOF, which called for its early establishment in a report issued in 1985. The recommendations of the Council's Special Committee (Foreign Exchange Council, 1985) were duly accepted by the MOF which in July 1986 announced the necessary amendments to the Foreign Exchange and Foreign Trade Control Law and the Special Taxation Measures Law.

23. These related to maximum issue amounts and the eligibility of issuers, the latter subject first arising in July 1972 following the interest stimulated by the Asian Development Bank's foray – the first of any issuer – into the market.

24. The higher one's credit rating, the higher the limit. The term of the issue was also regulated in this way, that is, the higher one's rating, the longer the permitted term. Ceilings on both amounts and maturities were eventually abolished in July 1989 although the restriction on minimum maturities remained.

25. From any one of the following rating agencies: Standard & Poors, Moody's, the Fitch Investors Service, the Nippon Investors Service, the Japan Bond Research Institute and the Japan Credit Rating Agency.

26. Unrated corporations could also qualify by satisfying certain financial ratio requirements (see JCIF, 1988, pp. 49–51, for further details).

27. Sovereign issuers who had previously floated yen bond public offerings in Japan were automatically qualified to make further issues.

28. The ceilings were substantially higher for foreign banks operating in Japan than Japanese banks, so that somewhat ironically the abolition of the ceilings *reduced* the comparative advantage enjoyed by the foreign banks.

29. Resident-owned foreign currency deposits plus a portion of non-resident-owned yen-denominated deposits are not subject to interest rate controls, however. Moreover, the Study Group on Financial Issues delivered a report on the need for deregulation of non-time deposits in the first half of 1991. The future form of the interest rate system under the Temporary Interest Rates Adjustment Law of 1947 is also being considered.

30. With the scrapping in April 1979 of the 'quotation system' on call rates, under which a uniform rate for all transactions is established, and in October 1979 on bill discount rates (see Suzuki, 1987, pp. 155–6).

31. Under this system, the call money market dealers set rates, which applied to all market participants, according to supply and demand considerations and after a consensus between the major borrowers (city banks) and lenders (other financial institutions) had been reached.

32. This was introduced not only because of the demands made by foreign banks active in the markets but also because of the official desire to internationalize Japanese financial markets, which had already resulted in the liberalization of the euroyen and other markets.

33. That is, bills whose maturities cross three month-ends.

34. That is, those that are due on the corresponding day of the month succeeding the month of the transaction or within 15 days of the day after that corresponding day. This means they can mature any time between 30 and 45 days after issue. Two-months bills can mature any time between 45 and 75 days after issue; three-months bills any time between 75 days and 100 days after issue; four-, five- and six-months bills, however, mature on the precise days implied in their titles.

35. From October 1983 to date financial institutions had to hold such bills for at least a month before reselling and, even then, direct sales to other institutions were not permitted – dealers had to purchase them first.

36. Today, there are two basic types of bill which are eligible for discount in the bill market: cover bills (*hyoshi tegata*) and other bills. Cover bills are simply bundles of other bills (e.g. high-grade commercial and industrial bills, trade bills, high-grade promissory notes and yen-denominated fixed-term export and import bills) which are grouped together and used as collateral for bills underwritten by the institutions themselves with money market dealers as payees. Because the underlying securities may not be in perfect order nor in round sums most transactions are in the form of cover bill trades.

37. That is, a circular entitled *Concerning the Dealing of Conditional Transactions in Bonds* issued on 30 March 1976. The guidance covers the following areas: (i) eligibility of participants; (ii) eligibility of securities which can be traded in the market; (iii) price limits for the range of agreed prices; (iv) maximum allowable term of transactions (i.e. under one year); and (v) individual guidance to be given to each company concerning its appropriate trading balance (not to be 'disproportionately large' in relation to its financial position).

38. Eligible securities comprise: national bonds; local bonds; government agency bonds; and corporate bonds (including yen-denominated bonds of foreign countries and companies and, since June 1984, foreign-currency-denominated bonds).

39. All bills of exchange traded in the market must be underwritten by a bank and originate from an exporter's or importer's settling of a trade transaction. In practice, there are five types of bill which may be issued or traded in the yen-BA market: yen-denominated, fixed-term bills of exchange; 'accommodation' bills; *jikihane* bills; refinance bills; and 'cover' bills (for further details, see Suzuki, 1987, p. 124). And to be 'eligible' they must satisfy the following conditions: (i) they must be accepted within 30 days of the loading of the ship (45 days for non-Japanese exporters); (ii) the date of maturity must be within six months of loading (some allowance is also made for mailing); and (iii) a minimum unit issue size of Y100 million must be met.

40. Sales back to the issuers are prohibited.

41. Because the yield offered on other short-term government securities is set below the official discount rate, and hence market rates, almost all the issues are held by the Bank of Japan.

42. One factor retarding its growth is the treatment of withholding tax. As for other discount bonds, tax is withheld at the time of issue but is later deductible from the companies' corporate tax payments. This arrangement complicates matters for overseas purchasers.

43. Claims outstanding at the end of March 1990 totalled Y13.3 trillion.

44. Adherence to the principle of non-deficit financing, laid down in the Finance Act of 1947, had precluded the issue of government bonds as a means of supplementing annual revenue until January 1966.
45. Banks, however, may not act as brokers but only as principals.
46. The most infamous are the bribery and corruption share scandal – the Recruit affair – of 1988, which eventually brought down the then Prime Minister Nakasone the following year; and the revelations of June 1991 that two of Japan's top broking houses, Nomura and Nikko Securities, had compensated favoured corporate clients for stock trading losses, leading to significant tax evasion, and had close business dealings with the criminal fraternity in Japan. Both company presidents subsequently resigned in recognition of the responsibilities they bore, although both remained on the respective boards.
47. Although it has to be said it may take a long time for the damage done by the recent scandals to sentiment within the retail investing community to be exorcized. Thus, the apparently inexorable rise in significance of the institutional investor, at the expense of the personal investor, is unlikely to be halted in the foreseeable future.
48. And even for convertible debentures issues, the overseas market may be preferred because of the more rapid speed of conversion into stocks that overseas issues allow.
49. No collateral, of course, is required in the eurobond market.
50. General industrial bonds are distinct from the bonds issued by the nine electric power corporations, which are all floated through public subscription. They are issued through either public subscription or private placement.
51. For the electric power companies there is no specified collateral, although the investors in the bonds have first claim in respect of the repayment of interest and principal. For the other industrial issuers, the firm's factories, equipment or other assets are usually put up as collateral.
52. Five-year maturities were ruled out of court so as to avoid competition with the debenture issues of the long-term credit banks.
53. Despite their limited room for manoeuvre on interest margins the banks could, however, raise effective loan rates to a degree by increasing the required level of compensating balances asked of borrowing customers.
54. Initially, only ordinary banks (including foreign banks), long-term credit banks and the specialized foreign exchange bank were affected, but since then the range of institutions falling within the remit of the scheme has expanded to include: those *sogo* banks and *shinkin* banks with deposits exceeding a certain level; the *Norinchukin* Bank; and life assurance companies.
55. Liabilities currently subject to reserve requirements comprise: (i) time deposits, CDs, and other yen-denominated deposits (including instalment savings); (ii) all foreign currency liability accounts of non-residents with authorized foreign exchange banks (excluding guaranteed liabilities) and foreign currency deposits from residents (excluding deposits in the name of the Ministry of Finance); (iii) debentures issued by long-term credit banks and the specialized foreign exchange bank; (iv) money trusts with contracts under which deficiencies of principal are recouped (including loan trusts); and (v) the yen deposit liabilities of authorized foreign exchange banks to non-residents.
56. Others subject to such guidance are long-term credit banks, trust banks (in respect of their banking accounts), regional banks, and the larger *sogo* banks, *shinkin* banks and foreign banks.
57. Although a special lending facility has existed since 1981 whereby loans may be taken at rates other than the discount rate (for money market management reasons), in practice the facility has not been used. Typically, the postwar rate charged by the Bank of Japan on its loans has been below the call rate, thereby fuelling the excess demand for central bank credit (Ichinose, 1991).
58. That is, banks of all type, the securities companies, the securities finance companies, the money market dealers, and other financial institutions.
59. These are the so-called 'cost effects' of discount rate operations which may be distinguished from the 'announcement' or psychological effects which may be associated with discount rate changes.

60. If loans (confined to periods of less than two weeks) in excess of the agreed ceiling are (unavoidably) made, a penal rate – discount rate plus 4 percentage points – is charged.

61. Although the yen was not floated until 1973, the Bank of Japan only carried out foreign exchange transactions with the government. It did, however, act as *agent* for the MOF by carrying out foreign exchange transactions with the public using balances held in the Foreign Exchange Fund Special Account. It also engaged in foreign exchange trading on behalf of overseas central banks and international institutions in order to promote international financial co-operation.

62. Eligible collateral comprises government and government-guaranteed bonds, government bills, financial debentures and certain local government bonds and corporate debentures and bills.

63. See Suzuki, 1987, p. 321, for details.

64. Due both to the lack of government debt issues and to the syndicate members' policy of holding such securities to maturity in order to avoid sustaining capital losses, which would have resulted because of the government's policy of holding public bond yields below market rates.

65. Operations in government bills (first started in 1981, with 'Treasury bills' featuring after January 1990), CDs (1986), the bond *gensaki* market (1987) and the CP market (1989) complemented the Bank of Japan's traditional activities in the public bond and interbank markets. Moreover, the Bank of Japan has concentrated its traditional rediscount operations in bills with a maturity of less than one month (as opposed to those with maturities of between one and three months, the previous focus of policy) since November 1988 with a view to allowing the market a greater say in the determination of one to three months' bill yields.

66. Apart from the dearth of paper available, foreign participation was adversely affected by the problems associated with the application of the withholding taxes.

67. Despite the broadening of the interbank market, the establishment of an offshore market and expansion of the yen swap market, all of which aided those foreign organizations without a retail deposit base in Japan.

68. A target for M0 – notes and coin in circulation plus banks' operational deposits held at the central bank plus banks' till money – is still used in the UK today.

69. It should be noted that the effectiveness of monetary policy pre-deposit rate liberalization *relied upon* disintermediation, which largely resulted from the suppression of bank deposit rates relative to open market rates, thereby curtailing the growth in bank credit (see Suzuki, 1987, pp. 332–3).

70. Deposit rate liberalization, along with financial innovation, will also of course complicate interpretation of movements in narrow money such as M1 – notes and coin in circulation plus banks' demand and current deposits. [M2 = M1 plus banks' savings, time and other deposits.]

71. In a fully liberalized financial system this is due to the higher 'own rate' on money which deposit-rate liberalization allows, thereby necessitating a greater absolute change in interest rates in order to achieve the change in interest rate differentials required to secure the desired change in the demand for money. This implies, of course, that (nominal) interest rates are both higher on average and more variable, *ceteris paribus*.

72. Any tax-deductibility of loan charges will, of course, serve to lower this figure.

73. Evidence casts doubt on any monetary authority's ability to identify stable and enduring demand for money functions. Rather, it would appear that apparently stable demand for money functions (such as those identified by Okina, 1985) break down once the aggregate(s) in question is elevated to the status of a target, particularly if direct monetary controls are employed to assist in the attainment of such targets (this is the so-called 'Goodhart's Law'). While the use of 'private' rather than publicly announced targets might improve the situation somewhat, the wider benefits perceived to derive from the public announcement of targets (see Hall, 1982, ch. 7) would of course be lost. Accordingly, few (if any) from amongst the ranks of those advocating the use of monetary targets would advocate the adoption of such a policy.

74. The post-Recruit scandals afflicted much of the securities industry in 1991: 21 broker-

age firms, including the 'Big Four', admitted compensating favoured clients for price falls to the tune of Y173 billion, and some were also accused of stock manipulation, making illegal loans and having close ties with organized crime syndicates. In addition, a number of banks were also implicated in a series of scandals. For example, the Industrial Bank of Japan (IBJ), the largest long-term credit bank, had loans outstanding of Y240 billion at one stage to an Osaka restaurateur and stock speculator Ms Inoue, who was eventually indicted for breach of trust, forgery and fraud in 1991. The small Osaka-based credit co-operative *Toyo Shinkin* Bank was also found to be closely involved in the affair, having issued Ms Inoue with Y342 billion worth of forged CDs, which were then used as collateral for loans from the IBJ and eleven other banks. Other banks subsequently found to have been issuing forged CDs comprised the *Fuji* Bank, the *Tokai* Bank and the *Kyowa Saitama* Bank.

Earlier scandals touched the *Sumitomo* Bank which, in 1990, along with *Mitsui* Trust and Banking, was linked with the notorious Mr Kotani, a stock market speculator indicted on charges of stock manipulation. *Sumitomo* Bank was also involved in the Itoman scandal because of the size of the loan exposure incurred in respect of the trading company. And, finally, the *Daiichi Sogo* Bank was eventually taken over by the MOF in 1988 because of the latter's loss of confidence in the senior management of the bank who had tolerated serious breaches of the Ministry's loan exposure rules relating to loans to single customers.

75. For further details, see pp. 162–3.
76. Provisions also allowed the DIC to borrow from other financial institutions to repay the Bank of Japan.
77. Henceforth, the DIC could provide financial aid to a financial institution that merged with or bought another troubled financial institution, if necessary through the purchase of the bad assets of the failed institution in a situation where *all* the assets and liabilities of the failed institution are being assumed.
78. The previous restriction on the growth of external claims took the form of the imposition of a limit of 14 times capital and reserves (reduced from 15 times in May 1985) on the total amount of claims outstanding on non-residents.
79. That is, those entrusted with the following business: agency business for the parent institution; examination, classification or transportation of cash; management of collateral; development of computer systems and software.
80. A lack of staff in the supervision division (currently 200 or so, of whom some 120 are examiners) precludes more frequent examination.
81. The 'target' inspection cycle for city banks was reduced from three years five months to three years in 1991 in order to allow for more frequent inspection of real-estate exposures. The shorter cycle was to be achieved by reducing the time, staff and resources devoted to the inspection of regional and smaller banks and, in the longer term, by increasing staff numbers at the Bank Inspection Department of the MOF (stuck at under 100 for the last 20 years or so).
82. The law does not apply to national or local government, to credit facilities where the repayment of principal and payment of interest are guaranteed by the government, nor to such similar facilities as designated by a Cabinet Order.
83. The operations of non-banks (many of which are connected with banks) in this area have also come under scrutiny. Traditionally, the monitoring of such activities by the Ministry for International Trade and Industry has been relatively light but, in the light of the surge in activities following the introduction of tough controls on such lending by banks in April 1990, the authorities decided to clamp down. This followed publication of a MOF report in February 1991 which showed that non-banks (i.e. leasing, credit and finance companies) accounted for over 40 per cent of loans outstanding to the property developers and building companies surveyed at the end of September 1990 as compared with the banks' share of 17 per cent. Moreover, the annual growth rate in property loans recorded for non-banks in the year to March 1990 stood at 49 per cent compared with a 29 per cent figure for the banks. As a result, the government announced in May 1991 that non-banks' property-related lending would be regulated to reduce land speculation.

      This involves non-banks with assets of over Y50 billion reporting details on such lending to the government, with the MOF having the authority to monitor such activities.

84. In the event they wrote off nearly 70 per cent of their medium and long-term loans to Mexico.

85. Each Japanese bank, however, is responsible for developing its own country risk evaluation system. Indeed, the Japan Centre for International Finance was set up in 1983 specifically to provide information on country risk to sponsoring banks.

86. To include yen-denominated deposits, instalment savings, mutual instalment savings and money-in-trust where the repayment of principal is guaranteed. Foreign currency deposits, negotiable CDs, deposits from central and local government, public entities, semi-governmental organizations, the BOJ, the DIC and insured financial institutions, deposits made under assumed names and anonymous time deposits are not covered.

87. It may also take possession of the assets of a failed bank in situations where depositors' claims have been met, and retain the liquidation proceeds.

88. The BOJ, in consultation with the MOF, put together a rescue plan which included the provision of BOJ credit on a largely unsecured basis. The decision to intervene was taken mainly because of the banking system's exposure to the securities industry. Yamaichi eventually made a full recovery, repaying the loans over a four-year period.

89. Although the BOJ essentially views its lender-of-last-resort function as extending to liquidity matters only, there is a statutory basis for intervention to deal with a generalized solvency or liquidity crisis. This is contained in Article 25 of the BOJ Law which permits the BOJ to make loans to Japanese banks on special terms if they are deemed 'necessary for the maintenance and bolstering of the credit system'.

90. The Industrial Bank of Japan, Sanwa Bank and the National Federation of Credit Co-operatives were also involved in the support operation.

91. Other recent examples are the MOF-sponsored takeovers of the Heiwa Sogo Bank by Sumitomo Bank and the Toyo Shinkin Bank (*see* note 74) by Sanwa Bank.

92. The Taiheiyo Bank came to grief because of its exposure to the property-speculating company Mogami Kosan which accumulated almost Y100 billion of bad and doubtful debts in the late 1980s. Under the rescue package, Y110 billion of low-interest loans will be made to the bank over the next ten years with Sukura Bank putting up almost 30 per cent and Fuji Bank, Tokai Bank and Sanwa Bank making up the difference.

93. Rescue operations, rather than full-scale takeovers or mergers, were mounted by the Sakura Bank and the Bank of Tokyo to save the broking firms Yamatane Securities and Dainana Securities respectively in the middle of 1992.

References

Argy, V. (1987), *International Financial Liberalisation: The Australian and Japanese Experience Compared* (The Centre for Studies in Money, Banking and Finance, Macquarie University, July).

Bank of Japan (1975), *The Importance of the Money Supply in Japan* (Tokyo: Bank of Japan).

Bank for International Settlements (BIS) (1987), *Proposals for International Convergence of Capital Measurement and Capital Standards*, consultative paper issued by the Committee on Banking Regulations and Supervisory Practices [the Basle Committee] (Basle: BIS).

Deposit Insurance Corporation (DIC) (1986), *Annual Report for 1985* (Tokyo: DIC).

The Economist (1986), *Tokyo 2000: The World's Third International Financial Centre?* (London, Economist Publications).

Federation of Bankers Associations of Japan (FBAJ) (1989), *The Banking System in Japan* (Tokyo: FBAJ).

Federation of Bankers Associations of Japan (FBAJ) (1992), *Japanese Banks '92* (Tokyo: FBAJ).

Financial System Research Council, Financial System Subcommittee (1987), *Report on Specialized Financial Institution System in Japan* (Tokyo: Federation of Bankers Associations of Japan).

Foreign Exchange Council (1985), *The Establishment of the Tokyo Offshore Market*, Report of the Special Committee on the Internationalisation of the Tokyo Markets [Special Committee Report] (Tokyo: Foreign Exchange Council).

Hall, M. J. B. (1982), 'Monetary targets', in G. E. J. Dennis *et al.* (eds), *The Framework of UK Monetary Policy* (London: Heinemann), pp. 213–33.

Hall, M. J. B. (1983), *Monetary Policy Since 1971: Conduct and Performance*, (London: Macmillan).

Hall, M. J. B. (1987), *Financial Deregulation: A Comparative Study of Australia and the United Kingdom* (London: Macmillan).

Hall, M. J. B. (1989), 'The BIS capital adequacy "Rules": a critique', *Banca Nazionale del Lavoro Quarterly Review*, no. 169, June, pp. 207–27.

Hanzawa, M. (1991), 'The Tokyo offshore market', in Foundation for Advanced Information and Research (FAIR), *Japan's Financial Markets* (Tokyo: FAIR).

IBCA (1992), *Japanese Banks and the Stockmarket: The Fall Continues* (London).

Ichinose, A. (1991), 'Why is bank rate below call rates in Japan?', *Okayama Economic Review*, Vols 3/4, February.

Japan Center for International Finance (JCIF) (1988), 'The past and present of the deregulation and internationalisation of the Tokyo money and capital market', JCIF Policy Study Series no. 10 (Tokyo: JCIF).

Kasman, B. and Rodrigues, A. P. (1991), 'Financial liberalization and monetary control in Japan', *Federal Reserve Bank of New York Quarterly Review*, vol. 16, no. 3, pp. 28–46.

Katayama, S. (1985), 'The Japanese economy, the monetary structure, and the monetary policy in Japan after World War II: a comparison between the high economic growth period and the 1970s', *Proceedings of the Seventh International Symposium on Asian Studies* (Hong Kong: Asian Research Service), pp. 201–14.

Ministry of Finance (1988), *Outline of the Official Notification Concerning the Implementation of the Basle Committee's Capital Adequacy Framework* (Tokyo: MOF 22 December).

Nakaishi, A. (1991), 'The foreign exchange market', in Foundation for Advanced Information and Research (FAIR), *Japan's Financial Markets* (Tokyo: FAIR), pp. 245–59.

Nakao, M. and Horii, A. (1991), 'Changes in the monetary control techniques and procedures by the Bank of Japan', *Bank of Japan Research and Statistics Department*, special paper no. 195.

Okina, K. (1985), 'Re-examination of the empirical study using Granger causality: causality between money supply and nominal income', *Bank of Japan Monetary and Economic Studies*, vol. 3, no. 3.

Osugi, K. (1990), 'Japan's experience of financial deregulation since 1984 in an international perspective', *BIS Economic Papers*, no. 26.

Postal Savings Bureau (1987), *Postal Banking in Japan: Fiscal 1986* (Tokyo: Postal Savings Bureau).

Shigehara, K. (1991), 'Financial liberalization and monetary policy', in Foundation for Advanced Information and Research (FAIR), *Japan's Financial Markets* (Tokyo: FAIR).

Suzuki, Y. (1987), *The Japanese Financial System* (Oxford: Clarendon Press).

Suzuki, Y. (1990), 'Monetary policy in Japan' in C. A. E. Goodhart and G. Sutija (eds), *Japanese Financial Growth* (London: Macmillan).

Yoshitomi, M. (1985), 'Japan as capital exporter and the world economy', *Group of Thirty*, Occasional Paper no. 18 (New York: Group of Thirty).

PART III

COMPARISON OF BANKING REGULATION AND SUPERVISION IN THE UK, USA AND JAPAN

7 A comparison of regulatory and supervisory policies

Introduction
In this chapter the major differences and similarities in the regulatory and supervisory frameworks employed for both monetary and prudential purposes in the three countries in question are highlighted. Reference is also made to the courses of action which national authorities might take with a view to enhancing the cost-effectiveness of their policies. Detailed analysis of two of the more important supervisory developments – the implementation of risk-based capital requirements in accordance with the G10 agreement and the lowering of barriers between commercial banking and securities business – is held over to Chapters 8 and 9 respectively.

Regulations employed for monetary policy purposes
As can be seen from Exhibit 7.1, which compares the use of regulations for monetary policy purposes in the three countries, policymakers in the UK may be distinguished from their US and Japanese counterparts by their willingness since 1982 to conduct policy almost without any reliance upon such instruments (see Kasman, 1992, for a comparison of the conduct of monetary policy in the three countries).

Interest rate controls and prescribed[1] reserve requirements are both eschewed[2] – the non-interest-bearing 0.4 per cent of 'eligible liabilities' cash ratio requirement imposed on banks is explicitly designed to fund the run-

Exhibit 7.1 *Monetary controls used in the UK, USA and Japan: a comparison*

Instrument	UK	USA	Japan
Exchange control	No	No	No
Prescribed reserve requirements	No[a]	Yes	Yes
Interest rate controls	No	No	Yes
Administered discount rate	No[b]	Yes	Yes

Notes
[a] The 0.4 per cent of eligible liabilities cash ratio requirement is not a monetary control device.
[b] Exceptionally, a publicly announced rate (minimum lending rate) may be employed.

ning costs of the Bank of England and plays no part in monetary policy, although on occasions (such as when a very public announcement of a change in policy stance is thought desirable)[3] officials have lapsed back into using an *administered* discount rate.[4]

In contrast, the Japanese authorities, despite the liberalization of interest rates and the movement towards open market operations as the main basis for the conduct of monetary policy (see Chapter 6), still employ interest rate controls to support policy alongside an administered discount rate and pre-scribed reserve requirements.[5] The US authorities, in turn, occupy the middle ground, eschewing interest rate controls but relying upon an administered discount rate and prescribed reserve ratios although in recent times the latter have become non-binding.[6]

Despite the differences which exist today, however, further convergence is already in the pipeline. This reflects a general recognition that the use of direct monetary controls is likely to breed inefficiency, distort the meaning of financial indicators and the competitive balance existing in the market place between different types of financial intermediary, and achieve at best a cosmetic change in monetary aggregates (see Hall, 1991, sections 5.4 and 5.5). Differing announcement effects,[7] however, may explain the retention of an administered discount rate; and the stabilizing effects of prescribed reserve requirements may enhance the monetary authorities' ability to control and stabilize interest rates (Kasman, 1992).[8] It is also possible that the employment of different instruments may be associated with different interest rate responses although, in the absence of segmentation of financial markets or under-developed markets, it is not intuitively obvious why open market operations alone should not suffice. Whatever the strength of the case for retaining the use of regulations within the monetary authorities' armour, however, policymakers remain wary of dispensing with them totally.

Prudential regulation and supervision
The major differences in the policies adopted towards the prudential regula-tion and supervision of banks in the three countries are highlighted in Ex-hibit 7.2. The first point to make is that the supervisory system administered in the UK is distinct from those operated in the other two countries by virtue of the significance attached to the management interviews (see Chapter 4). The US and Japanese systems, in contrast, are still largely inspection-based, relying heavily for their effectiveness upon formal on-site bank examina-tions. While it is true that this difference in approach is being narrowed somewhat, as a result of the increasing use of on-site inspections in the UK and of the growing significance attached to the assessment of managerial skill, competence and integrity in the US and Japan, the contrast is still stark; and, arguably, it is for the Bank of England to change tack if a further

Exhibit 7.2   *The prudential framework operating in respect of banks*
incorporated in the UK, USA and Japan

Element of policy	UK	USA	Japan
Bank examination	Possibly[a]	Yes	Yes
Management interviews	Yes	Yes	Yes
Licensing requirements			
Minimum capital requirement?	Yes[b]	Yes	Yes
'fit and proper' test?	Yes	Yes	Yes
'convenience and needs of community' test?	No	Yes	Yes
Capital adequacy assessment			
risk-based approach?	Yes	Yes	Yes[c]
gearing approach?	No	Yes	Yes[d]
Liquidity adequacy assessment			
formal measure(s) employed?	Yes[e]	No	No
Exposure Limits			
re. single borrowers or connected parties?	No[f]	Yes	Yes
re. loans to directors?	No	Yes	No[h]
re. property-related lending?	No[g]	No	Possibly[i]
re. sectoral exposure?	No	No	No
re. exchange rate risk?	No[j]	No	Yes
re. country risk?	No	No	No
Provisioning guidelines for LDC debt exposure	Yes	Yes	Yes
Deposit protection schemes			
risk-related premia?	No	Yes[k]	No
co-insurance principle applied?	Yes	No	No
Ownership rules			
statutory provisions?	Yes	Yes	Yes
'fit and proper' test?	Yes	Yes	Yes
'reciprocity' provisions?	Yes	No[l]	Yes
'moral suasion'?	Yes	No	Yes

Element of policy	UK	USA	Japan
Separation of banking from commerce			
statutory provisions?	No	Yes	No[m]
moral suasion?	Yes	No	Yes
Separation of banking from securities business	No	Yes	Yes[n]
Separation of banking from insurance business	No[o]	Yes	Yes[p]
Finance industry support facilities			
extending to securities firms?	No	Yes	Yes
Branching restrictions	No	Yes	Yes
Merger restrictions	Yes	Yes	Yes
Consumer protection legislation	Yes	Yes	Yes

Notes

[a] Either as part of a routine inspection (by either Bank of England staff or a team of auditors) or as part of a more specific inquiry (which may be conducted by a team of reporting accountants).

[b] Only needs to be satisfied on the date of authorization.

[c] Applies to all Japanese banks which either maintain overseas business establishments or which otherwise *voluntarily* choose to abide by the G10 agreement on capital adequacy assessment.

[d] For those banks not observing the G10 agreement.

[e] That is, the 'accumulated net mismatched position'.

[f] Formal statutory limits apply from 1 January 1993 under EC law. Before that there were only reporting requirements.

[g] Moral suasion may, however, conceivably be exercised.

[h] No statutory limits apply, but the terms of such loans are governed by statute.

[i] Currently in abeyance but used throughout the 1986–91 period.

[j] No statutory limits apply, only agreed guidelines (for dealing positions).

[k] A crude system is currently in operation but a more sophisticated system is supposed to be operational by mid-1994.

[l] These may, however, evolve depending on the progress of the Fair Trade in Financial Services Bill through Congress and its ultimate form should it be enacted.

[m] Although there is no outright prohibition on commercial entities taking equity stakes in commercial banks they are subject to the provisions of the Antimonopoly Law and Anti-trust Law.

[n] This is being eroded under the Financial System Reform Bill which was passed by the Diet in June 1992 and will take effect some time in 1993. Henceforth, interpenetration of banking and securities business by securities companies and commercial banks respectively will take place via separately capitalized subsidiaries.

[o] Moral suasion, however, might be used.

[p] Again, this demarcation is likely to break down once insurance business is accommodated within the structure of the Financial System Reform Bill.

narrowing is to be achieved. Inevitably this change in supervisory style would involve, however, a further downgrading of the role to be played by moral suasion in the supervisory mix, a trend already firmly established as a result of the UK's enforced adoption of various EC Directives (see Chapter 4) yet lamented by the Bank of England (Quinn, 1991). Adoption of Lord Justice Bingham's recommendations in the wake of the BCCI fiasco will further accelerate this process (see Chapter 4).

Moving away from considerations of style and on to the nitty gritty of prudential regulation and supervision, it can be seen that when it comes to *licensing* banks much the same approach is adopted whatever the bank's country of incorporation. Accordingly, both a 'fit and proper' test and minimum capital requirements are employed in all three countries although it is instructive to note that, in respect of the latter, the Bank of England's requirement is deliberately set at a very low level (so as to minimize its impact as a barrier to entry) and need only be satisfied at the time of authorization. More significantly, no 'needs test' is applied in the UK at the licensing stage, in stark contrast with the situation obtaining in Japan and, more especially, the US.

In the *assessment of capital adequacy*, the Bank of England is unique in not employing any gearing measures although, to be fair to the Japanese, they are only applied there to those banks which are not required to observe the G10 agreement on risk-based assessment (see Chapter 8) or which otherwise are allowed to opt out of risk-based assessment. The superiority of the risk-based approach is, accordingly, recognized in all three countries, although the US authorities see merit, at least for the time being while the risk-based approach is still being refined, in complementing this with a gearing ratio requirement. (For a full discussion of the individual approaches adopted towards implementation of the G10 agreement, see Chapter 8.)

Other factors which set the UK and US approaches apart from the Japanese are the eagerness of the authorities in the former countries to take the management factor and *all* risk exposures into account in the assessment process and their willingness to set requirements on an individual basis.

In respect of *liquidity adequacy assessment*, the Bank of England's approach is distinctive in that it alone employs formal measures (that is, the 'accumulated net mismatched position') within its assessment process. This does not mean that maturity transformation is not considered in the other two countries; far from it. Rather, it is a reflection of the Bank of England's determination to include some formal quantitative element of assessment[9], within its overall subjective evaluation of liquidity adequacy which, as in the other countries, will also focus on, *inter alia*, management capabilities, the liquidity mix and internal controls.

The approaches adopted towards the setting of *exposure limits* differ markedly between the three countries. The Bank of England alone eschews all such limits, preferring on principle to maximize the flexibility of supervision by allowing itself maximum discretion in this area of policy. Accordingly, although dealing position guidelines are agreed on an individual basis with UK banks, no formal limits to exchange rate risk apply.[10] Similarly, and despite the fact that the major part of Johnson Matthey Bankers' problems derived from over-exposure to just two borrowing parties (Hall, 1987c), no statutory limits on single loan exposures currently apply in the UK, only reporting requirements.[11] Other than this, moral suasion *may* be exercised, for example to retard the growth in size of property and property-related exposures.

The Japanese authorities, in contrast, employ formal limits to restrict exchange rate risk and exposures to single borrowers (or connected parties), and moral suasion may be used to limit other kinds of exposure.

In between come the US authorities, which apply statutory limits to loans to directors and single borrowers (or connected parties) but which otherwise forgo the application of exposure limits.

With regard to the policies adopted in respect of *provisions to be held against LDC debt*, a common line is taken. Formal guidelines are employed in each of the three countries to establish appropriate floors to the levels of provisions held.

On the subject of *deposit protection*, it is clear that, although schemes exist in all three countries, there is room for improvement in each.[12] The first reform which needs to be considered is the introduction of risk-related premia as a means of reducing the moral hazard created for banks' management by the application of flat rate premia and of the costs and competitive distortions that are associated with such a premium structure. While the US authorities have already taken a step in this direction and are expected to be operating a more sophisticated system by the middle of 1994, neither the UK nor the Japanese authorities have signalled any intention to follow in their path. This is regrettable given the potential contribution that options pricing theory can make to the design of risk-related premia.[13]

Secondly, in order to reduce the moral hazard facing the depositor, the US and Japanese authorities should give serious thought to introducing the principle of 'co-insurance' whereby the depositor is asked to shoulder some of the risk within the scope of *de jure* coverage. Systemic considerations, however, require that the degree of co-insurance be kept low – perhaps in the 5 to 10 per cent range – suggesting that the 25 per cent figure imposed on UK depositors is undesirably high.

Finally, in the US at least, there is a strong case for reducing the extent of *de jure* protection (the level of *de facto* protection currently enjoyed by US depositors is already under attack – see Chapter 5), if only to reduce taxpayer exposure. This could be done, for example, by applying the current level of coverage ($100,000) on a customer-only basis. By comparison, the *de jure* protection enjoyed by UK depositors is decidedly niggardly and should perhaps be raised nearer the US and Japanese levels, with the levels then being indexed in all three countries to allow them to rise in line with inflation. In this way, 'reasonable' levels of protection would be assured for all time and the potential dangers of destabilization associated with the adoption of markedly different levels of protection in different countries avoided.[14]

In the end, however, the systems that evolve at the national level will reflect local judgment on what constitutes the optimal balance between meeting the requirements of investor protection and a stable financial system on the one hand, and satisfying the desire to instil sufficient market discipline to eradicate the moral hazards facing both the investor and bank manager/director on the other. What is clear is that none of the systems currently obtaining in the three countries can by any stretch of the imagination be called 'optimal', leaving plenty of room for raising the cost-effectiveness of such regulatory requirements.[15]

When it comes to determining who or which institutions are allowed to *own* commercial banks, a similar range of considerations apply in each country. Statutory provisions, incorporating a 'fit and proper' test, are common to each country. The use of moral suasion, however, does not feature in the US approach, unlike in the UK and Japan. As for the treatment of foreign stakebuilding in the local commercial banking sectors, all three countries adopt a broadly similar approach: it is allowed in law and prospective stakebuilders are generally subject to the same range of prudential safeguards as are domestic entities (the principle of 'national treatment'), although the US is the only country in which reciprocity provisions do not currently feature.[16] Finally, in respect of stakebuilding by non-financial concerns, legal hurdles, designed to separate banking from commerce in the US, have to be overcome in both the US and Japan, with moral suasion alone being exercised in the UK.

Functional separation is also common to all three countries although less prevalent in the UK. As just noted, moral suasion is used to deter non-financial companies from taking controlling stakes in domestic banks in the UK, a practice repeated in respect of banks' links with the insurance industry. In contrast, statutory provisions are used extensively in Japan and the US to separate banking from insurance and securities business and, in the US, to separate banking from commerce. Additionally, as noted in Chapter 6, the Japanese authorities use both the rule of law and moral suasion (that is, administrative guidance) to effect the separation of long-term from short-term finance and commercial from trust banking.

The UK authorities, unlike those in the US and Japan (see Chapter 9), do not seek to deny opportunities in the *securities* arena to locally-incorporated banks; the UK banking sector conforms more closely to the universal banking model prevalent in Germany and Switzerland. But this does not mean that they overlook the potential 'dangers' associated with the joint offering of such services (the dangers are discussed at length in Chapter 9). Rather, they seek to maximize the potential economies of scope that commercial banks can enjoy by allowing such joint operations and restricting 'firewall' requirements to those deemed essential as prudential safeguards. Accordingly, unlike in the US and Japan, local banks operating in the UK are generally allowed to engage freely[17] in securities (and other financial and many non-financial) activities provided that: (i) they agree to observe any capital requirements specified by the Bank of England and/or other relevant supervisory authorities (self-regulatory organizations (SROs), such as the Securities and Futures Authority, in respect of securities activities – *see* Hall, 1990a);[18] (ii) they abide by any other rules or requirements which may be specified by the Bank of England and/or other relevant supervisory authorities.[19] Additionally, assurances may be sought from large shareholders that they accept ultimate responsibility for the liabilities of their securities subsidiaries; and restrictions may be placed on the scope of activities of a securities subsidiary and on the nature of transactions which can take place between the subsidiary and related entities.[20]

While the UK approach to the separation of banking from securities business undoubtedly provides banks with significant opportunities to reap the benefits of the alleged synergies, it is not clear that the prudential safeguards are adequate. As noted in Hall (1987a), for example, the use of dedicated capital as a device for limiting the spread of contagion is seriously flawed, calling into question the adequacy of the authorities' policies for handling systemic risk. Similarly, it can be argued that too sanguine a view is taken towards the ability of Chinese Walls and industry rulebooks to protect investors adequately from potential conflict of interest abuse. This suggests that, as in the US and Japan (see Chapter 9), there is a case for reassessing the balance struck between maximizing efficiency gains and optimizing prudential policy, although competitive pressures, as the US and Japanese authorities have found, render standing out against the worldwide drift towards universal banking[21] a costly option. Without further convergence in supervisory practice, however, serious competitive distortions will remain.

The nature of the *finance industry support facilities* available in the three countries also merit close scrutiny. Although the traditional 'lender-of-last-resort' liquidity facility is available to the commercial banking fraternity in each country, the merits of extending this to the securities industry have not yet been officially acknowledged in the UK, despite the Bank of England's willingness to tolerate potentially greater systemic risk by virtue of the approach it adopts towards the separation of banking from securities business. It is not clear that such ostrich-like behaviour serves any useful purpose in the light of the uncertainty generated and the certainty that the markets will call the Bank of England's bluff in the event of a major financial collapse.

As for solvency support (assuming one can differentiate it in practice from liquidity support), although the mechanism for providing it may differ between countries – assisted mergers are favoured in the Japan, 'purchase and assumptions' under FDIC management in the US and 'lifeboats' in the UK – the end results are much the same. In particular, potentially serious moral hazards are created[22] if central banks give the impression that banks of a certain size or standing will never be allowed to fail. While the US authorities (who, to be fair, have most cause to be concerned) are grappling with their so-called 'too-big-to-fail' doctrine, it is not evident that either the UK authorities nor, more significantly, their Japanese counterparts are earnestly seeking solutions to the dilemmas posed by ailing banks. Yet few would claim that the authorities in any of the three countries have struck an appropriate balance between ensuring systemic stability on the one hand and limiting moral hazard and efficiency losses on the other.

Finally, it should be noted that although *merger restrictions* and *consumer protection legislation* apply in all three countries – the former are more stringent in the US and Japan than in the UK, while the latter are most irksome in the US (see Chapter 5) – no branching restrictions are imposed in the UK, unlike the situation obtaining in Japan and the US. The fight for abolition of the legislative hurdles to inter- and intra-state branch banking in the US, however, is likely to continue with undiminished fervour despite the setback received in 1991 when Congress rejected the Treasury's proposals for reform.

Concluding observations

Despite common objectives and the pressures created for convergence in regulatory and supervisory practice, the regulatory and supervisory regimes currently in place in the UK, USA and Japan are likely to retain a significant degree of distinctiveness for a considerable time to come. Accordingly, it is instructive to note the differences in approach adopted in these countries in respect of banking regulation and supervision with a view to understanding the sources of competitive distortion faced by international banks and the reasons for the continued fragility of the international banking system.

Whatever the outcome of international agreements – multilateral or bilateral – and irrespective of differences in legal and fiscal systems, institutional structure or accounting conventions, national differences in approach will always exert a powerful influence on the fortunes of internationally active banks and the stability of the international banking system because of the degree of discretion which will always reside with national governments and regulatory authorities. While acknowledging this fact of life, it is nevertheless incumbent upon academics and others to indicate the desired course for regulatory and supervisory reform if global welfare is to be maximized. In the process it is to be hoped that, from a public policy perspective, national arrangements may also be improved. The distinctive features of the regulatory and supervisory regimes applying in the US, UK and Japan have accordingly been highlighted in this chapter, together with the scope remaining for improvements at the national level. The case for reform of the international arrangements governing the regulation and supervision of banks is not developed here but may be assessed by referring to Hall (1992 and forthcoming).

Notes

1. In the UK the fulcrum for official money market operations is provided by the clearing balances *voluntarily* held by the clearing banks at the Bank of England, the banks being obliged to assist the latter in its daily forecasting of the cash reserve position of the banking system by indicating their target levels for such balances.
2. As is exchange control. All three countries adopt a similar line on this together with a (managed or free) float of their currencies. (Sterling left the exchange rate mechanism of the European Monetary System in September 1992.)
3. The old concept of minimum lending rate (see Hall, 1991) is occasionally reactivated, usually as a means of defending sterling on the foreign exchange markets.
4. The official discount rate is otherwise market-determined.
5. Moral suasion, concerning both the growth and direction of lending, remains in the authorities' armoury although it is currently in abeyance. Similarly, moral suasion, at least in respect of the direction of commercial bank lending (e.g., to the property sector), cannot be ruled out in either a US or UK context.
6. In this respect, the US conduct of policy is edging towards that of the UK (see Kasman, 1992). For a discussion of the conduct of US monetary policy under non-binding reserve requirements, see Sternlight (1992).
7. 'Seignorage' considerations may, in practice, also play a part.
8. Although their absence in the UK has not caused any apparent difficulties in the conduct of policy.
9. Its proposal to introduce a 'high quality stock requirement' was withdrawn following opposition from the banking (primarily the overseas segment) industry (see Hall, 1989, ch. 14).
10. Exchange rate risk, along with sectoral exposure, is, however, considered at the capital adequacy assessment stage.
11. This, however, will change once the EC's Directive on Large Exposures becomes effective.
12. The need for such schemes is not challenged here. As noted in Hall (1991, p. 171), however, there are some who argue that the drawbacks associated with the schemes outweigh the potential benefits accruing to both depositors and the wider community. Such critics point to the following:

(i)   that dangerous moral hazards may be created as the schemes, according to their design, may discourage the investing public from undertaking adequate appraisal of prospective risk-adjusted rates of return and/or encourage bank management to take on higher risk business for a given pattern of expected rates of return;

(ii) that, because imperfect pricing of premiums is unavoidable, deposit insurance creates a need for increased regulation of banks to deal with the resultant moral hazards;

(iii) that the inequities created (between large and small banks, domestic and foreign, and between banks and non-bank financial intermediaries) and costs incurred, both direct and indirect, might outweigh the benefits – principally systemic stability, but also avoidance of disruption to the payments system and to bank–customer relationships, which can damage the real economy (see Diamond and Dybvig, 1983). The benefits, however, might be achieved by alternative means; for example, systemic stability might be achieved through judicious use of the lender of last resort facility and/or official open market operations;

(iv) that its existence might impair the provision of an adequate risk-return spectrum of investment opportunities; and

(v)   that, according to its design, it might result in an unacceptable level of exposure for taxpayers.

13.   It was Merton (1977) who first noted such a role for options pricing theory. In his words: 'deposit insurance is isomorphic to a put option with the bank's asset portfolio being the underlying security and the value of the insured deposits corresponding to the exercise price' (Merton and Brodie, 1992). Since then the idea has been subject to intense analysis (see, for example, Ronn and Verma, 1986; Crouhy and Galai, 1991; Pennacchi, 1987; and Marcus and Shaked, 1984), with some still doubting its feasibility because of: (i) the opaqueness of parts of the commercial banks' balance sheets; (ii) the possibility that asset variability might be 'unbounded' and/or subject to significant unilateral change by the insured after the premium has been set (Merton and Bodie, 1992); and (iii) the fact that individual bank failures cannot always be treated as independent random events.

14.   The European Commission's proposals for a Directive on Deposit Guarantee Schemes (EC, 1992) would, if implemented, serve this aim – at least within the EC arena – as they would involve Member States in providing at least a common minimum level of protection for local depositors. More contentiously, however, they would also involve the arrangements being applied on a home country basis (rather than on the present host country basis) which, although serving to further stem the drift towards competition in supervisory laxity, does raise a number of thorny issues which cannot be ignored (see Key and Scott, 1991; and Schoenmaker, 1992).

15.   For a discussion of the range of options open to the US authorities for reforming federal deposit insurance arrangements, see Hall (1990b); and for suggestions as to how the UK's Deposit Protection Scheme ought to be reformed, see Hall (1987b).

16.   This, however, is likely to change if a Fair Trade in Financial Services Bill is enacted.

17.   It is important to note that although *direct* bank provision of securities services is not prohibited, unlike in the US and Japan, the Bank of England may insist that certain operations (such as stock exchange money-broking, gilt-edged inter-dealer broking or gilt-edged market-making – see Hall, 1989, Appendices 2 and 3) are conducted through separately capitalized subsidiaries with their own dedicated capital which cannot be readily withdrawn by the parent.

18.   A *lead regulation* principle is employed to ensure supervisory overlap or underlap does not occur where more than one supervisory authority is involved.

19.   For example, the rules set out in SRO conduct of business rulebooks which cover, *inter alia*, such issues as the handling of conflicts of interest, information disclosure, advertising, the keeping of records and accounts, the protection of clients' money, the protection of investors against unsolicited calls, compliance and enforcement procedures and reporting requirements.

20.   Both types of restriction, for example, apply to the operation of Gilt-Edged Market

Makers (see Hall, 1989, Appendix 2). Typically, however, these 'firewall' requirements are less onerous than those applied in the US and Japan (see Chapter 9).
21. Accelerated by the EC's decision to adopt a universal banking approach under its Second Banking Co-ordination Directive (EC, 1989), which took effect on 1 January 1993.
22. See Hall (1987c) for a discussion of the ramifications of the Bank of England-sponsored rescue of Johnson Matthey Bankers in 1984.

References

Crouhy, M. and Galai, D. (1991), 'A contingent claim analysis of a regulated depository institution', *Journal of Banking and Finance*, vol. 15, February, pp. 73–90.

Diamond, D. W. and Dybvig, P. H. (1983), 'Bank runs, deposit insurance, and liquidity', *Journal of Political Economy*, vol. 91, no. 3, pp. 401–19.

European Community (EC) (1989), The Second Banking Co-ordination Directive, 89/646/ EEC.

European Community (EC) (1992), *Proposal for a Council Directive on Deposit Guarantee Schemes*, COM (92).

Hall, M. J. B. (1987a), 'Reform of the London Stock Exchange: the prudential issues', *Banca Nazionale Del Lavoro Quarterly Review*, no. 161, pp. 167–81.

Hall, M. J. B. (1987b), 'The deposit protection scheme: the case for reform', *National Westminster Bank Quarterly Review*, August, pp. 45–54.

Hall, M. J. B. (1987c), 'The JMB affair: have the lessons been learnt?' *Journal of International Securities Markets*, vol. 1, Autumn, pp. 59–71.

Hall, M. J. B., *Handbook of Banking Regulation and Supervision*, (London: Woodhead-Faulkner).

Hall, M. J. B. (1990a), 'The Financial Services Act and its consequences for Europe', *Wirtschaft und Recht*, special edition on 'Capital market law and its reform', vol. 42, December, pp. 211–36.

Hall, M. J. B. (1990b), 'The reform of federal deposit insurance: the options', *Banca Nazionale Del Lavoro Quarterly Review*, no. 175, pp. 441–58.

Hall, M. J. B. (1991), 'Financial regulation in the UK: deregulation or reregulation?', *Surveys in Monetary Economics*, vol. 2 (Oxford: Basil Blackwell), pp. 166–209.

Hall, M. J. B. (1992), *Towards Better Banking Regulation and Supervision*, consultancy report (Geneva: International Federation of Commercial, Clerical, Professional and Technical Employees (FIET).

Hall, M. J. B. (forthcoming), 'The G10 agreement on capital adequacy assessment: a critique, in C. A. Stone and A. Zissu (eds), *Risk-based Capital Regulation: Asset Management and Funding Strategies*, (Philadelphia: Business One Irwin).

Kasman, B. (1992), 'A comparison of monetary policy operating procedures in six industrial countries', *Federal Reserve Bank of New York Quarterly Review*, vol. 17, no. 2, pp. 6–24.

Key, S. J. and Scott, H. S. (1991), 'International trade in banking services: a conceptual framework', Group of Thirty, Occasional Paper no. 35 (Washington, D.C.: Group of Thirty).

Marcus, A. and Shaked, I. (1984), 'The valuation of FDIC deposit insurance using option pricing estimates', *Journal of Money, Credit and Banking*, vol. 16, November, pp. 446–60.

Merton, R. C. (1977), 'An analytic derivation of the cost of deposit insurance and loan guarantees: an application of modern option pricing theory', *Journal of Banking and Finance*, June, pp. 3–11.

Merton, R. C. and Brodie, Z. (1992), 'Deposit insurance reform: a functional approach', paper presented at the *Carnegie–Rochester Public Policy Conference*, Rochester, New York, April.

Pennacchi, G. G. (1987), 'A re-examination of the over- (or under-) pricing of deposit insurance', *Journal of Money, Credit and Banking*, vol. 19, no. 3, pp. 340–60.

Quinn, B. (1991), 'The influence of the Banking Acts (1979 and 1987) on the Bank of England's traditional style of banking supervision', in J. J. Norton (ed.), *Bank Regulation and Supervision in the 1990s*, (London: Lloyd's of London Press).

Ronn, E. I. and Verma, A. K. (1986), 'Pricing risk-adjusted deposit insurance: an option-based model', *Journal of Finance*, vol. 41, no. 4, pp. 871–95.

Schoenmaker, D. (1992), 'Home country deposit insurance, LSE Financial Markets Group Special Paper no. 43 (London: London School of Economics).

Sternlight, P. D. (1992), 'Report submitted to the Federal Open Market Committee', adapted and reprinted as 'Monetary policy and open market operations during 1991', *Federal Reserve Bank of New York Quarterly Review*, vol. 17, no. 1, pp. 72–95.

8 Implementation of the BIS rules on capital adequacy assessment: a comparative study of the approaches adopted in the UK, the USA and Japan

Background

In December 1987 the Basle Committee of Supervisors, operating under the auspices of the Bank for International Settlements, published guideline proposals for the measurement and assessment of the capital adequacy of internationally active banks (see Hall, 1989 and forthcoming, for a critique). With minor amendments, these proposals were formally accepted by the bank supervisors of the Group of Ten (G10)[1] countries plus Luxembourg in July 1988. Inevitably, in order to secure the widest possible degree of political acceptance – most of the financially developed world now abides by the spirit if not the letter of the agreed rules – compromises on principles were required, and a substantial degree of discretion, in respect of both the interpretation and implementation of the rules, was left with the national supervisory authorities, particularly in the run-up to the deadline for full implementation of the agreed package on 31 December 1992.

The major aims of the Basle Committee in promulgating the proposals were 'to achieve convergence in supervisory regulation and standards of capital adequacy' (BIS, 1987, para. 8). These aims, in turn, were to be achieved through the establishment of a 'common framework of capital adequacy measurement' and a 'common minimum target capital standard' for internationally-active banks (ibid., para. 1).

The agreed rules

Under the agreement of July 1988, the supervisors of the G10 nations are obliged to impose a *minimum risk asset ratio* of 8 per cent on all internationally active banks falling within their jurisdiction by the end of 1992 at the latest (transitional arrangements – see below – allowed for the phasing-in of this requirement). This ratio is derived by expressing the adjusted capital base as a percentage of the total of weighted risk assets. The numerator is calculated by summing allowable components of Tier 1 and Tier 2 capital, subject to prescribed limits, and then deducting certain items. The denominator, in turn, is derived by summing the products of the nominal balance sheet amounts of each asset and their corresponding risk weights (designed,

Exhibit 8.1   Derivation of the risk assets ratio

In mathematical terms:

$$RAR(\%) = \frac{ACB}{TOWRA}$$

where *ACB* is the adjusted capital base, and

$$TOWRA = \sum_{i=1}^{s} \sum_{j=1}^{t} (A_{ij}W_j)$$

$$+ \sum_{i=1}^{u} \sum_{j=1}^{v} \sum_{k=1}^{w} (B_{ijk}X_kW_j)$$

$$+ \sum_{i=1}^{x} \sum_{j=1}^{y} \sum_{k=1}^{z} [(C_{ijk}X_k + M)W_j)]^*$$

A_{ij} being the value of the ith asset with risk weight, W_j;

B_{ijk} being the notional principal amount of off-balance-sheet activity i with risk weight W_j and conversion factor X_k; and

C_{ijk} being the notional principal amount of the interest or exchange rate related activity i with risk weight W_j and conversion factor X_k;

s the number of distinct asset components;

u the number of distinct off-balance-sheet activities (excluding interest rate and exchange rate related activities);

x the number of distinct interest and exchange rate related off-balance sheet instruments;

M the 'mark-to-market' value of the underlying contract,

where $x < u < s$; $v \leq t = 5$; $y \leq t = 5$; $w = 4$; and $z = 4$.

---

* 'Current exposure' assessment method employed.

---

primarily, to reflect credit risk), and adding this figure to the sum of the weighted loan equivalents arising from off-balance-sheet activities (see Hall, 1990b, and Exhibit 8.1). Apart from permitting a phasing-in of the minimum ratio requirement, the transitional arrangements also allow for temporary inclusion of Tier 2 elements of capital within Tier 1, the gradual introduction of limits (expressed as a percentage of weighted-risk assets) on the inclusion of general provisions within Tier 2 capital, and delay (until the end of 1992) in deducting goodwill from Tier 1 capital and limiting the proportion of term subordinated debt that may rank as Tier 2 capital (see Table 8.8).

Modifications resulting from the European Community's Own Funds and Solvency Ratio Directives

All Member States of the European Community (EC) which, of course, includes the UK, were obliged to implement in full the provisions of the Own Funds Directive (89/299/EEC of 17 April 1989) and the Solvency Ratio Directive (89/647/EEC of 18 December 1989) by 1 January 1993 at the latest. Although these Directives were deliberately drafted in such a way as to minimize the differences with the earlier Basle agreement, certain mainly minor disparities still emerged (for full details, see Price Waterhouse, 1991, Annex 5, pp. 124–30).

In respect of the definition of capital, the Own Funds Directive does not refer to 'Tier 1' and 'Tier 2' capital, the terms used by the Basle Committee, but rather to 'original' and 'additional' capital. However, the limits introduced under Article 6 on the inclusion of certain items within total capital effectively create a tiering of capital very close to that used by the Basle Committee, thereby facilitating discussion of the Directive's contents using the terminology which evolved in Basle.

Adopting this approach, one can assess the impact of the Directive on the definitions of Tier 1 and Tier 2 capital and hence on the capital base (that is, total capital). Starting with Tier 1 capital, the major items of note relate to the Directive's treatment of *interim profits* and *revaluation reserves*. According to Article 2(1)(2), interim profits may only be included if they have been: (i) verified by external auditors; (ii) evaluated in accordance with the Bank Accounts Directive (86/635/EEC of 8 December 1986); and (iii) calculated net of any foreseeable charge or dividend. And the Directive requires that all revaluation reserves be confined to Tier 2.

The Bank of England's response to the new legally binding requirements, as set out in its Notice of December 1990 (see Bank of England, 1990(a)) did not involve any immediate changes of policy (see Bank of England, 1988). Accordingly, the Bank of England determined to continue with its current policy of allowing the inclusion in Tier 1 capital of the current year's retained earnings (net of foreseeable charges and distributions) where they have been published in the form of an interim statement, including retained earnings of authorized subsidiaries within banking groups which publish interims even if not separately disclosed, but to require verification by external auditors from 1 January 1993. As for its treatment of revaluation reserves, the Bank of England determined to continue with its present policy of including revaluation reserves relating to tangible fixed assets within Tier 2 capital and other revaluation reserves, including those relating to fixed asset investments, within Tier 1 capital until the end of 1992. From 1 January 1993, however, the latter would only be eligible for inclusion in Tier 2 capital.

In respect of the definition of Tier 2 capital, the only Article of significance is that dealing with *unpublished profits*. Article 3(1)(c) states that they will only be eligible for inclusion if they have been verified by internal audit (eventually, external audit may be required). Again, the Bank of England's response was to continue with prevailing policy, which places unpublished current year profits in Tier 2 capital but, from 1 January 1993, to make eligibility for inclusion dependent on verification by internal audit.

The final item of note on the definition of capital front, at least from a UK perspective (other elements of capital set out in Article 2(1), covering such items as funds for general banking risks and permitted value adjustments, are not relevant in the UK), concerns the deductions to be made from total capital. For, under Articles 2(12) and 2(13), full deduction of the following is required: (i) holdings of another credit or financial institution's capital instruments which constitute more than 10 per cent of the equity of the institution in which the investment is made; and (ii) such holdings which constitute less than 10 per cent of the equity of the institution in which the investment is made but which, in aggregate, exceed 10 per cent of the own funds of the reporting institution (the excess amount must be deducted).

The Bank of England's response was, once again, to continue with existing policy, which entails full deduction (in line with Article 2(12); however, this may be waived if such holdings are temporary, resulting from a financial rescue of an institution) from total capital of all holdings of another credit institution's capital, subject to the market-making concessions granted (as set out in Bank of England, 1986), but to agree to limit such concessions from 1 January 1993 in line with the requirements of Articles 2(12) and 2(13).

Switching discussion towards the Solvency Ratio Directive, the significant discrepancies with the Basle agreement occur in the assignation of risk weights to balance sheet items. (Article 10(1) prescribes an 8 per cent minimum standard, identical to that agreed on in Basle, to be determined in similar methodological fashion to that prescribed by the Basle Committee.) The approach adopted within the Directive is to lay down the *minimum* risk weightings (Article 6) which should be applied by the 'competent authorities' of the Member States, the latter retaining the discretion to apply higher weightings if they deem fit. Again, this is similar to the approach adopted by the Basle Committee.

As far as the Bank of England was concerned, the changes necessitated by the adoption of the Solvency Ratio Directive (all measures except implementation of the minimum capital standard requirement had to be put into effect by 1 January 1991) related to its treatment of the following items: (i) on-balance-sheet claims in gold and silver bullion on the non-bank market-making members of the London Bullion Market Association; (ii) mortgage-

Table 8.1   Allowable components of Tier 1 (i.e., 'core') capital

UK approach	Japanese approach	US approach[e]
1. *Permanent shareholders' equity* (i) Allotted, called up and fully paid share capital/ common stock (net of any own shares held at book value) (ii) Perpetual, non-cumulative preferred shares, including such shares redeemable at the option of the issuer and with the Bank's prior consent; and such shares convertible into ordinary shares	*Permanent stock-holders' equity* (i) Common stock (ii) Non-cumulative, perpetual preferred stock[c]	*Common stockholders' equity*[f]
2. *Disclosed reserves* in the form of general and other reserves created or increased by appropriations of retained earnings, share premiums and other surplus[a]	*Disclosed reserves*	*Qualifying non-cumulative perpetual preferred stock*[g]
3. *Published interim retained profits*[b]	*Published retained earnings*[d]	*Minority interest in equity accounts of consolidated subsidiaries*
4. *Minority interests* arising on consolidation from interests in permanent shareholders' equity	*Consolidated subsidiaries' minority interests*	

Notes
[a]   Including capital gifts and capital redemption reserves.
[b]   That is, net of anticipated dividends and any other appropriations. These must be verified by external auditors with effect from 1 January 1993.
[c]   They are allowed, in principle, although Japanese company law precludes preference share issues in Japan. It does not preclude, however, foreign issues by overseas subsidiaries.
[d]   That is, net of anticipated tax and value of outflow (dividend and executive directors' bonus payments).

backed securities; (iii) claims on regional governments and local authorities of another Member State; (iv) claims secured by cash deposited with and held by an agent bank acting for a syndicate of which the reporting institution is a member; (v) Multilateral Development Banks; (vi) loans secured on residential property; (vii) deferred tax assets; (viii) guarantees received from a banking subsidiary; (ix) commodity-related transactions and equity options.

The policy changes were set out in full in the Bank of England's Notice of December 1990 (see Table 8.4; and Bank of England, 1990b) and took effect on 1 January 1990. While the Bank of England contends that none of the policy changes were substantive, the new policy adopted in respect of the treatment of mortgage-backed securities (MBS) is worthy of a second mention. This is because the Directive, by not specifically covering MBS, has forced the Bank of England to ascribe a 100 per cent risk weighting to them (albeit only from 1 January 1993), which is double the weighting currently used. Unless the Directive is amended by the Comitology procedure, such action might retard the growth of the market in such instruments in the UK (and, indeed, in the EC), a development likely to be viewed in an unfavourable light by the UK authorities.

Comparison of the UK, the US[2] and Japanese approaches adopted towards the implementation of the agreed rules

The definition of capital

Tier 1 capital As can be seen from Table 8.1, there is little difference in the approaches adopted towards the classification of capital components eligible for inclusion in Tier 1 capital by the three countries. Unlike in the UK and

---

e   For state member banks. The main difference in treatment *vis-à-vis* that of bank holding companies is that the latter may include cumulative as well as non-cumulative perpetual preferred stock in Tier 1 capital, subject to a limit of 25% of Tier 1 capital. The limit on *non-cumulative* perpetual preferred stock was lifted in January 1992 as part of a package, which included lenient valuation of property loans by regulators and, somewhat later (April 1992), a cut in reserve requirements, designed to increase banks' capacity to lend and hence avoid a credit crunch.

f   Includes: common stock; related *surplus*; and *retained earnings*, including *capital reserves* and adjustments for the cumulative effect of foreign currency translation, net of any treasury stock.

g   Adjustable-rate non-cumulative perpetual preferred stock may be included but *not* auction rate perpetual preferred stock (although this may be included in Tier 2 capital). Banks are also asked to avoid placing undue reliance on such preferred stock as a source of Tier 1 capital.

Sources: Bank of England, 1990(a), p. 4; Japanese Ministry of Finance, 1988; Board of Governors of the Federal Reserve System, 1989, Attachment II, p. 21.

Table 8.2   Allowable components of Tier 2 (i.e., 'supplementary') capital

UK approach	Japanese approach	US approach[l]
1. *Undisclosed reserves* and *unpublished* current year's *retained profits*[a]		
2. *Reserves* arising from the *revaluation* of tangible fixed assets[b] and, from 1 January 1993, of fixed asset investments (previously included in Tier 1 capital)	1. 45% of *latent revaluation reserves* related to securities holdings	
3. *General provisions* (i.e., those held against possible or latent loss but where these losses have not as yet been identified), subject to a limit[c,d]	2. *General loan loss reserves*, subject to a limit[g]	1. *Allowance for loan and lease losses,*[m] subject to a limit[n]
4. *Hybrid capital* instruments: (i) perpetual, cum- ulative preferred shares, including such shares redeem- able at the option of the issuer and with the prior consent of the Bank, and such shares convertible into ordinary shares (ii) perpetual sub- ordinated debt which meets the conditions for 'primary' perpetual subordinated debt (see Bank of England, 1986), including such debt which is convertible into equity	3. 'Allowable'[h] *hybrid capital* instruments (i) convertible subordinated bonds; (ii) perpetual, cumulative preferred stock and limited life redeemable preferred stock; (iii) perpetual subordinated bonds (e.g., FRNS) and loans	2. *Hybrid capital* instruments and qualifying[o] mandatory convertible debt securities in the form of equity-contract notes 3. Perpetual preferred stock[p]
5. *Subordinated term debt*, subject to a limit;[e] (i) dated preferred shares (irrespective of original maturity); (ii) convertible sub- ordinated bonds not included in 4(ii) above;	4. 'Allowable'[i] *sub- ordinated term debt*, subject to a limit[j] (i) subordinated loans;[k] (ii) subordinated bonds	4. *Subordinated debt* and *intermediate-term pre- ferred stock* (with an original weighted average maturity of 5 years or more),[q] subject to a limit[r]

(iii)   'allowable'[f] sub-
         ordinated term loan
         capital

6. *Minority interests*
arising on consolidation
from interests in Tier 2
capital items

Notes

[a]   Undisclosed reserves will only be allowed until the end of 1992, in accordance with the EC's Bank Accounts Directive (EC, 1986) (Funds for 'general banking risks' are not relevant in the UK.) Unpublished current year's retained profits must be verified by internal audit from 1 January 1993.

[b]   Capitalized property revaluation reserves could, however, be counted as Tier 1 capital until the end of 1992.

[c]   At the moment, the limit is 1.25% of weighted risk assets. Provisions earmarked or held specifically against lower valuations of particular claims or classes of claims are *not* included in capital.

[d]   This policy remains in force pending further agreement in Basle on a more precise definition of unencumbered provisions. (For the latest Basle Committee proposals, see BIS, 1991.)

[e]   That is, up to 50% of Tier 1 capital.

[f]   That is, it has an original term to maturity of over five years and otherwise meets the conditions set out in Bank of England, 1986 (e.g., it is subject to a straight line amortization in the last five years, leaving no more than 20% of the original amount outstanding in the final year before redemption).

[g]   That is, up to 1.5 percentage points of weighted risk assets for the period running from the end of fiscal 1990 to prior to the end of fiscal 1992 (i.e., 31 March 1993) and 1.25 percentage points of weighted risk assets thereafter.

[h]   That is, they must be unsecured, subordinated, fully paid-up, available to participate in losses and redeemable only at the initiative of the issuer.

[i]   That is, it must have an original term to maturity of over five years and be subject to straight line amortization in the last five years.

[j]   This limit, which comes into force only at the end of fiscal 1992, is a maximum of 50% of Tier 1 capital.

[k]   The recipients are confined to banks which abide by the BIS capital adequacy rules and the lenders must be financial institutions whose business is lending money.

[l]   For state member banks (although basically the same approach is adopted with respect to bank holding companies).

[m]   Excluding allocated transfer risk reserves and reserves created against identified losses.

[n]   That is, up to 1.25 percentage points of weighted risk assets from the end of 1992 (for transitional arrangements, see Table 8.8). Amounts in excess of limitations are permitted but do not qualify as capital.

[o]   That is, those that meet the criteria set out in Regulation Y (12 CFR 225), Appendix B.

[p]   Including related surplus and long-term preferred stock with an original maturity of 20 years or more (with maturity being defined as the earliest date at which the holder can put the instrument back to the issuing bank).

[q]   Such instruments must be amortized for capital purposes as they approach maturity, and those with a remaining maturity of less than one year are excluded from Tier 2 capital. Prior approval from the Federal Reserve must also be received if banks wish to redeem subordinated debt before the stated maturity.

[r]   That is, a combined maximum of 50% of Tier 1 capital.

Sources: Bank of England, 1990(a), pp. 4–5; Japanese Ministry of Finance, 1988; Federal Reserve System, 1989, Attachment II, p. 21.

the US, however, Japanese banks have not to date been able to make any issues of non-cumulative, perpetual preferred stock because under Japanese company law preference shares cannot be issued in Japan. The competitive position of Japanese banks has improved, though, since the Basle Committee of Supervisors gave its permission for such stock issues where made by the banks' *overseas vehicle subsidiaries* to rank as Tier 1 capital, although the Director General of the Banking Bureau at the Ministry of Finance still has to sanction such overseas issues (as was, presumably, the case with the Mitsui Taiyo Kobe Bank's Y100 billion euromarket offering of yen-denominated convertible preferred stock in March 1992).[3]

Tier 2 capital Close inspection of the elements of capital included within Tier 2 capital within the three countries indicates that it is here that the fundamental differences in approach to the definition of capital reside. As is evident from Table 8.2, UK-incorporated banks have by far the most scope for raising Tier 2 capital. This is due partly to differences in accounting conventions (which, for example, preclude the inclusion of *any* revaluation reserves by US banks and the inclusion of undisclosed reserves and unpublished retained profits by either US or Japanese banks), to differences in company law (which, for example, prohibit preference share issues in Japan) but also to differences in the *discretionary* policies adopted by the supervisory authorities.

This last point can be illustrated by contrasting the UK and Japanese approaches to the treatment of *revaluation reserves*. In Japan, the authorities take full advantage of the concession granted under the BIS rules enabling banks to count up to 45 per cent of their latent gains on securities holdings as Tier 2 capital but choose to disallow property and fixed asset revaluation reserves;[4] in stark contrast, the Bank of England chooses (it is now also obliged under the EC's Own Funds Directive) to disallow undisclosed latent gains on securities holdings (which are insignificant for most UK banks anyway) while allowing property revaluation reserves, a portion of which indeed could be counted (but only until the end of 1992) as Tier 1 capital on capitalization.[5]

Further disparities arising from differences in the discretionary policies adopted by the supervisory authorities are evident in the treatment of *general provisions/loan loss reserves*. As annotated in Table 8.2, the Bank of England excludes from Tier 2 all provisions which reflect lower valuations of particular assets, notably against less-developed country (LDC) debt; the remaining, unearmarked provisions are eligible for inclusion up to an agreed limit. No such exclusion of sovereign debt provisions is insisted upon in either the US or Japan although the latest Basle Committee proposals (BIS, 1991), if adopted, would ensure their exclusion in the two countries by the end of 1993 at the latest. The Japanese authorities have indicated, however, that if and when this situation arises, they will allow their banks to deduct provisions made against third world debt from their totals of weighted risk assets in the calculation of their risk asset ratios. This decision has been taken with a view to encouraging Japanese banks to make such provisions.

Turning to the treatment of *hybrid capital* instruments, it is clear that Japanese banks are at a comparative disadvantage by virtue of their limited availability in Japan. Although convertible subordinated bond issues have been sanctioned since 1987, with associated restrictions being removed in January 1990,[6] no perpetual debt issues have been forthcoming in Japan.

Finally, in comparing the treatment of *subordinated term debt* instruments, it is clear that once again the Japanese banks are at a competitive disadvantage, despite their ability (since June 1990) to issue subordinated bonds and take subordinated loans (perpetual issues in overseas markets were also sanctioned in the Autumn of 1992). This is because of the restrictions placed on the latter – the lenders must be financial institutions – and the complications created for the former issues by the legal separation of long-term credit and commercial banking in Japan, which confines debenture issues to the long term credit banks.[7] With respect to the differences in the UK and US approaches, it should be noted that those instruments qualifying as Tier 2 in the US are excluded once they fall under the one-year-to-maturity threshold whereas in the UK and Japan 20 per cent of the amounts outstanding would still be eligible for inclusion.

Deductions from capital   Although *goodwill* must be deducted from Tier 1 capital by the banks incorporated in each of the three countries,[8,9] potentially serious disparities arise from the treatment of items to be deducted from total capital (see Table 8.3). The main point at issue here is the treatment of holdings of the capital instruments of other depository institutions. The Bank of England once again adopts the toughest stance, insisting upon full deduction of all holdings of other banks' and building societies' capital instruments for all UK-authorized institutions other than those which qualify for concessions as primary or secondary market makers in such instruments (see Bank of England, 1986). The concessions granted, however, are subject to certain limits from 1 January 1993 in line with Articles 2(12) and 2(13) of the EC's Directive on Own Funds (89/299/EEC April 1989). By way of contrast, banks incorporated in the US and Japan need only deduct intentional reciprocal holdings of banking organizations' capital instruments, creating doubts about the extent of *de facto* deduction in those countries. While on the face of it, this would appear to put UK-incorporated banks at something of a competitive disadvantage, close monitoring of the policies adopted by commercial banks in the US and Japan by their respective super-

Table 8.3   Deductions to be made from capital

Type of deduction	UK approach	Japanese approach	US approach[d]
Deductions from Tier 1	(i) Goodwill and other intangible assets[a] (ii) Current year's unpublished losses	(i) Goodwill	(i) Goodwill[e]
Deductions from total capital (i.e., Tier 1 + Tier 2 capital)	(i) Investments in unconsolidated subsidiaries and associates (ii) Connected lending of a capital nature (iii) All holdings of other banks' and building societies' capital instruments[b]	(i) 'Intentional'[c] reciprocal holdings of capital instruments of banks aimed at raising capital ratios	(i) 'Intentional' reciprocal holdings of banking organizations[f] capital securities (ii) Investments[g] in unconsolidated subsidiaries (iii) Other deductions (such as other subsidiaries or joint ventures) as determined by supervisory authority

Notes
[a] This includes mortgage servicing rights unless it can be demonstrated that there is an active and liquid market in which they can be reliably traded (as in the US).
[b] Existing concessions (as set out in Bank of England, 1986), which apply to primary and secondary market makers in such instruments, will remain in place after 1992 but will be subject to amendment to accommodate Articles 2(12) and 2(13) of the EC's Own Funds Directive of April 1989.
[c] All such holdings are, in principle, to be deducted although individual banks are given the opportunity to explain to the authorities why this should not occur.
[d] For state member banks. The treatment of bank holding companies differs to the extent that, until the end of 1992, bank holding companies could count goodwill acquired before 12 March 1988 as Tier 1 capital.
[e] Except previously grandfathered goodwill approved in supervisory mergers.
[f] This may be done on a case-by-case basis or as a matter of policy after formal rulemaking.
[g] Generally, investments for this purpose are defined as equity and debt capital investments and any other instruments that are deemed to be capital in the particular subsidiary. 'Advances', even if deemed not to be capital, may however also be deducted, at the discretion of the Federal Reserve.

Sources: Bank of England, 1990(a), pp. 4–5; Japanese Ministry of Finance, 1988; Federal Reserve System, 1989, Attachment II, p. 21.

visory authorities and the allocation of a 100 per cent risk weight to such investments not so deducted (see below) is likely to mitigate the competitive distortions in practice.

Finally, with respect to investments in unconsolidated subsidiaries and associates, competitive equality is more or less assured by virtue of the fact that, although not formally obliged to deduct such items from total capital (as are UK and US-incorporated banking organizations), all banking and financial subsidiaries and associated companies have to be consolidated for accounting purposes in Japan, regardless of the 'significant impact rule'.[10]

The risk weight framework
Table 8.4 provides a comparison of the three sets of risk weights applied in the three countries to banks' balance sheet items. The differences arise, of course, in those instances where the Basle Committee determined to allow for national discretion. In virtually all such cases,[11] the Japanese authorities have seen fit to adopt the lowest weights permissible under the BIS agreement. In the process, no attempt is made in Japan to capture either interest rate risk or foreign exchange rate risk within the risk weight framework, in stark contrast to the situation obtaining in the UK and, for some items,[12] in the US. The cumulative effect of this policy is to lighten the regulatory burden imposed on Japanese banks as compared with the positions faced by banks incorporated in the US and more especially in the UK, *ceteris paribus*.

In contrasting the policies adopted within the UK and the US, it is clear that, overall, UK-incorporated banks face the stricter regime although, on certain items, such as items (4), (9) and (16), they are treated more favourably than their US counterparts. The implications of this disparity in treatment are less clear, however, when it comes to the setting of trigger or target risk asset ratios (see Hall, 1990b), as a whole host of factors, such as interest rate risk, liquidity risk, funding risk, market risk, asset quality, managerial competence and skill, the quality and level of earnings, investment and loan portfolio concentrations, and loan and investment policies,[13] are taken into account in determining a final assessment of an organization's capital adequacy.

The treatment of off-balance-sheet (OBS) items
The conversion factors applied to the OBS activities of banks incorporated in the UK, the US and Japan in the conversion of OBS risks to balance sheet credit risk equivalent amounts are identical and presented in Tables 8.5 and 8.6. The main[14] competitive distortion introduced thus relates not to the conversion factor framework adopted but rather to the range of institutions forced to adopt the current exposure method (see Hall, 1990b) in their assessment of the credit risks associated with interest-rate-related and ex-

Table 8.4 Risk weights to be applied to asset items

Asset item	BIS-recommended risk weight (%)	Risk weight applied in the UK (%)	Risk weight applied in Japan (%)	Risk weight applied in the US (%)
1. Cash[a]	0	0	0	0
2. Gold	0	0	0	0
3. Loans to OECD[b] central governments and central banks including claims on the European Communities	0[c]	0	0	0[x]
4. Claims fully collateralized by cash	0	0	0	20
5. Claims fully guaranteed by OECD central governments and central banks	0[d]	0	0	0[y,z]
6. Loans to non-OECD central governments and central banks denominated in local currency and funded in that currency	0[e]	0	0	0
7. Loans guaranteed by non-OECD central governments or central banks, where denominated and funded in local currency	0[f]	0	Not available	0[z]
8. Holdings of fixed interest securities issued (or guaranteed) by OECD central governments with a residual maturity of up to 1 year, and floating rate and index-linked OECD central government securities of any maturity	Zero or a 'low' weight (e.g., up to 20%) if an interest rate risk proxy is applied[g]	10	0	0
9. Claims fully collateralized by OECD central government fixed interest securities of up to 1 year, and similar floating rate securities of any maturity	Zero or a 'low' weight[h]	10	0	20[aa]
10. Holdings of non-OECD central government securities with a residual maturity of up to 1 year denominated in local currency and funded by liabilities in the same currency	Zero or a 'low' weight[i]	10	0	0

11.	Holdings of OECD central government (guaranteed) fixed securities of a residual maturity of over 1 year or claims collateralized by such securities	Zero or a 'low' weight[j]	20	0	0 and 20 respectively
12.	Holdings of non-OECD central government securities of a maturity of over 1 year denominated in local currency and funded by liabilities in the same currency	Zero or a 'low' weight[i]	20	0	0
13.	Claims on multilateral development banks[k] and claims fully guaranteed by or fully collateralized by the securities issued by these institutions	0 or 20	20	20	20
14.	Claims on credit institutions incorporated in the OECD and claims guaranteed (or accepted or endorsed) by OECD-incorporated credit institutions[l]	20[m]	20	20	20[bb]
15.	Claims on credit institutions incorporated outside the OECD with a residual maturity of up to 1 year and claims of the same maturity guaranteed by non-OECD credit institutions	20[p]	20	20	20
16.	Claims on OECD public-sector entities (excluding central government) and claims guaranteed by such entities[o]	0, 20 or 50	20[p]	10 or 20[q]	20, 50 or 100[cc]
17.	Cash items in the process of collection	20	20	20	20
18.	Loans fully secured by mortgage on residential property owned or rented out by the borrower	50	50[r]	50[s]	50[dd]
19.	Claims on the non-bank private sector	100	100	100	100
20.	Claims on credit institutions incorporated outside the OECD with a residual maturity of over 1 year	100	100	100	100

Asset item	BIS-recommended risk weight (%)	Risk weight applied in the UK (%)	Risk weight applied in Japan (%)	Risk weight applied in the US (%)
21. Claims on central governments and central banks outside the OECD (unless denominated in the national currency and funded in that currency)	100	100	100	100
22. Claims guaranteed by non-OECD central governments or central banks which are not denominated in local currency and funded locally	100	100	100	100
23. Claims on commercial companies owned by the public sector	100	100	100	100
24. Claims on PSEs outside the OECD	100	100	100	100
25. Premises, plant and other fixed assets	100	100	100	100
26. Capital instruments issued by other banks (unless deducted from capital)	100	Not applicable[t]	100	100
27. Real estate, trade investments[u] and other assets not otherwise specified[v]	100	100	100	100[e,ff]
28. Aggregate net-short open foreign exchange position	Not specified	100[w]	Not applicable	Not applicable

Notes

[a] Denominated in local and foreign currency.

[b] Comprises countries which are full members of the OECD or which have concluded special lending arrangements with the IMF under the Fund's General Agreements to Borrow (see Annex 1 for the full list). In Bank of England 1990(b) these countries are classified as 'Zone A' countries.

[c] The original BIS-recommended risk weight was 100% unless the claim was on a domestic central bank or domestic central government.

[d] The original BIS-recommended risk weight was 100% unless the claims were fully-guaranteed by domestic central governments.

[e] The original BIS-recommended risk weight was 20% and this applied to such loans given to any foreign central government.

[f] The original BIS-recommended risk weight was 100% as this item was not identified and hence fell within the category of all other assets.

[g] The initial BIS view was that such claims on foreign central governments (unless in local currency financed by local currency liabilities, in which case the recommended risk weight was 20%) should attract a risk weight of 100%. Holdings of domestic central government securities, however, were to have been subject to either a zero or 'low' risk weight, according to whether or not attempts were being made to take account of investment risk by incorporating an interest rate risk proxy.

h   Under its initial proposals, these weights would only have been applied to such claims fully collateralized by domestic central government securities; a risk weight of 100% would have applied in all other cases.

i   The initial BIS-recommended risk weight was 20% and this would have been applied to all such claims on foreign central governments.

j   See notes g and h for the initial stance adopted by the BIS.

k   As far as the Bank of England is concerned, the list comprises the IBRD (including the IFC), the IADB, the AsDB, the AfDB, the EIB, the EBRD, the CDB and the NIB. (For explanation of abbreviations, see Bank of England, 1990b, Annex 6, p. 15.)

l   The Bank of England includes building societies within this context.

m   Initially, the BIS took the view that this weight should only apply to claims on domestic and foreign banks with an original maturity of under 1 year and to claims on domestic banks with an original maturity of 1 year and over and to loans guaranteed by domestic banks. All other claims and banks would have attracted a risk weight of 100%.

n   Loans with a residual maturity of 1 year guaranteed by non-OECD banks were not separately distinguished in the original BIS paper and so, presumably, would have attracted a risk weight of 100%.

o   In the UK such entities (PSEs) are defined as regional governments, local authorities and 'other PSEs', as identified in Bank of England (1990b, Annex 5 – see Annex II below).

p   In line with Article 7(2) of the EC's Solvency Ratio Directive, the Bank will consider applying a zero weighting on a case-by-case basis.

q   The 10% weight applies to claims on Japanese local governments (as defined in the Local Autonomy Law) and Japanese government agencies (comprising those corporate bodies established by specific laws – but excluding corporations established according to commercial company legislations and agencies which conduct commercial business – and in which (i) the government is a majority shareholder or (ii) the government is a shareholder and whose budgets and settlements of account are subject to the approval of the Diet or of the Minister in charge). [Local government securities which are serviced only from the revenue obtained from a specific undertaking are excluded.] It also applies to claims guaranteed by non-domestic PSEs. Japanese local governments and Japanese government agencies. The 20% weight applies to claims on and loans guaranteed by non-domestic PSEs.

r   In the UK, this weight only applies to such loans (either to individuals or to housing associations registered with the Housing Corporation, Scottish Homes and Tai Cymru) where they are for the sole purpose of residential occupation and which are fully secured by a first equitable or legal charge. The 50% weight is also applied to:

(i)   holdings of securities issued by special purpose mortgage finance vehicles where the risk to the security holders is fully and specifically secured against residential mortgage loans which would themselves qualify for the 50% weight or by assets which qualify for a weight of less than 50% (since 1 January 1993 such claims have been weighted at 100%), as long as the mortgage loans are fully performing on origination of the vehicle;

(ii)   mortgage sub-participations, where the risk to the sub-participating bank is fully and specifically secured against residential mortgage loans which would themselves qualify for the 50% weight.

s   In principle, the concessionary weight is restricted to the first mortgage; and loans to a body engaged in speculative residential construction or property development are given a risk weight of 100%, regardless of circumstances.

t   Because all such holdings are fully deducted from total capital (see Table 8.3).

u   In the UK, this excludes holdings of capital instruments issued by credit institutions which are deducted from total capital, and holdings of capital instruments of other financial institutions which must be deducted according to Articles 2(12) and 2(13) of the EC's Own Funds Directive.

In the UK, this excludes items in suspense, except items arising from transactions which can be identified with counterparties which attract a weight of less than 100% – these items will be treated in line with other claims on those counterparties. It also excludes the following items (in a UK context):

(i)   certificates of tax deposit (these attract a 0% risk weight);
(ii) loans to discount houses, gilt edged market makers, institutions with a money-market dealing relationship with the Bank of England and those Stock Exchange money brokers which operate in the gilt-edged market, where the loans are secured on gilts, UK Treasury bills, eligible local authority and eligible bank bills, or London CDs (these attract a 10% risk weight);
(iii) on balance sheet claims in gold and other bullion on the non-bank market making members of the London Bullion Market Association (these currently attract a 20% risk weight but, from 1 January 1993 such claims will be weighted at 100% unless they are unconditionally, explicitly and irrevocably guaranteed by an OECD bank);
(iv) claims on and guaranteed (or accepted) by discount houses which are unsecured or secured on assets other than gilts, UK Treasury bills, eligible local authority and eligible bank bills, or London CDs (these also attract a risk weight of 20%); and
(v)   claims secured by cash deposited with and held by an agent bank acting for a syndicate of which the reporting institution is a member (they also receive a 20% weighting).

w This is a proxy weight for a bank's foreign exchange risk, and will remain in effect until an international framework for capturing foreign exchange risk is agreed. Net short open positions in gold, silver, platinum and palladium are included here pending further discussion with the banking community.

x Including loans to the US Treasury and US government 'agencies' (defined as 'instrumentalities of the US government whose obligations are fully and explicitly guaranteed as to the timely payment of principal and interest by the full faith and credit of the US government'). The list of government agencies includes: the Government National Mortgage Association; the Veterans Administration; the Federal Housing Association; the Commodity Credit Corporation; and the Small Business Administration.

y Including claims fully guaranteed by the US Treasury and US government agencies (see note'). Claims on, and the portions of claims that are guaranteed by, US government-sponsored agencies (defined as agencies originally established or chartered to serve public purposes specified by the US Congress but whose obligations are not explicitly guaranteed by the full faith and credit of the US government) attract a risk weight of 20%.

z Claims conditionally guaranteed attract a risk weight of 20%.

aa This includes claims fully collateralized by any securities issued or guaranteed by the US Treasury, the central governments of other OECD countries, US government-sponsored agencies or US government agencies.

bb This includes claims on, and the portions of claims that are guaranteed by, US depository institutions (defined to include branches, foreign and domestic, of federally insured banks and depository institutions chartered and headquartered in the 50 states of the US, the District of Columbia, Puerto Rico, the US territories and possessions).

cc General obligation claims on and the portions of claims that are guaranteed by the full faith and credit of local governments and political subdivisions of the US and other OECD local governments attract a 20% risk weight. Revenue bonds or similar claims that are obligations of US state or local governments, or other OECD local governments, but for which the government entity is committed to repay the debt only out of revenues from the facilities financed attract a risk weight of 50%. Obligations issued by US state or local governments, or other OECD local governments (including industrial-development authorities and similar entities), repayable solely by a private party or enterprise attract a risk weight of 100%.

dd To attract this risk weight the loans must be fully secured by first liens on one- to four-family residential properties and have been made in accordance with prudent underwriting standards (including a conservative loan-to-value ratio), are performing in accordance with their original terms, and are not past due or in nonaccrual status. The 50% weight also applies to certain privately issued mortgage-backed securities representing indirect ownership of such loans.

ee The trade investments relate to those investments in any unconsolidated subsidiaries, joint ventures or associated companies, if they are not deducted from capital.

ff The 100% risk weight does *not* apply to:
  (i)   certain privately issued securities representing indirect ownership of mortgage-backed US government agency or US government-sponsored agency securities (these attract a risk weight of 20%);
  (ii) investments in shares of a fund whose portfolio is permitted to hold only securities that would qualify for the zero or 20% risk categories (these also attract a risk weight of 20%).

Sources: Bank of England, 1990b, Annex 1, pp. 7–9; BIS, 1987; Hall, 1990b; Japanese Ministry of Finance, 1988; Federal Reserve System, 1989, Attachment III, pp. 22–3.

Table 8.5   Credit conversion factors to be applied to banks' off-balance-sheet transactions to determine the corresponding 'deemed credit risk equivalents'

Instruments	Credit conversion factor applied in the UK, US and Japan (%)
1. Direct credit substitutes, including general guarantees of indebtedness, standby letters of credit serving as financial guarantees, acceptances and endorsements (including *per aval* endorsements)	100
2. Sale and repurchase agreements and asset sales with recourse, where the credit risk remains with the bank	100
3. Forward asset purchases, forward forward deposits placed and the unpaid part of partly-paid shares and securities, and any other commitments with a certain drawdown	100
4. Certain transaction-related contingent items not having the character of direct credit substitutes (e.g., performance bonds, bid bonds, warranties and standby letters of credit related to particular transactions)	50
5. Short-term, self-liquidating, trade-related contingent items (e.g., documentary credits collateralized by the underlying shipments)	20
6. Note issuance facilities and revolving underwriting facilities	50
7. Other commitments (e.g., formal standby facilities and credit lines) with an original maturity of over 1 year	50
8. Similar commitments with an original maturity of up to 1 year, or which can be unconditionally cancelled at any time	0
9. Endorsements of bills (including *per aval* endorsements) which have previously been accepted by a bank	0

Sources: Bank of England, 1990b, Annex 2, p. 10; Japanese Ministry of Finance, 1988; Federal Reserve System, 1989, Attachment IV, p. 24.

Table 8.6   *Conversion factors to be used to determine the 'deemed credit risk equivalents' associated with interest-rate-related and exchange-rate-related off-balance-sheet activities (according to the current exposure method)[a] by UK-incorporated, Japanese and US state member banks and bank holding companies[b]*

Residual maturity	Interest rate contracts (%)	Exchange rate contracts (%)
One year or less	0	1.0
Over one year	0.5	5.0

Notes
[a]   This method has to be adopted by *all* US state member banks and bank holding companies. In Japan and the UK, however, the *original exposure method* may instead be adopted by some banking organizations. (For details of the conversion factors to be used by these banks see Table 8.7.)
[b]   In the US, exchange rate contracts with an original maturity of 14 days or less and instruments traded on exchanges that require daily payment of variation margin are excluded from the risk-based ratio calculation.

Sources: Bank of England, 1990b, Annex 3, p. 11; Japanese Ministry of Finance, 1988; Federal Reserve System, 1989, attachment IV, p. 24.

Table 8.7   *Conversion factors to be used by those Japanese and UK banks allowed to adopt the original exposure method for determining the 'deemed credit risk equivalents' associated with interest-rate-related and exchange-rate-related off-balance-sheet activities*

Original maturity	Foreign-exchange-related transactions	Interest-rate-related transactions
One year or less	2.0%	0.5%
Over one year	[a]	[b]

Notes
[a]   3.0% times years of original maturity minus 1.0%
[b]   1.0% times years of original maturity minus 1.0% (fractions of years count as one whole year).

Source: Bank of England, 1990b, Annex 3, p. 12; Japanese Ministry of Finance, 1988.

change-rate-related activities. As noted in Table 8.6, *all* banking organizations in the US have to adopt this approach whereas in Japan and the UK the original exposure method may instead be adopted by some (see Table 8.7). In Japan, this concession applies to those banking organizations which do not conduct a 'significant' volume of business in such transactions or, as an interim measure, to those which do not have the proper office facilities or procedures for adopting the current exposure method. And in the UK it applies mainly to those banks which do not actively trade in such instruments or for whom such instruments form an insignificant part of their treasury operations.[15]

The exercise of discretion in other areas
As noted by Dale (1990), the actual impact of the BIS agreement on the world's internationally active banks will depend in large degree on the manner in which national supervisory authorities exercise the discretion available to them under the agreement. The areas in which such discretion resides encompass the following (Hall, 1990a):

(i)   in the specification of risk weights and conversion factors;
(ii)   in the determination of which, and to what degree, items are included in supplementary capital, subject to the limits and restrictions laid down by the Basle Committee;
(iii) in the approach adopted towards the deduction, from total capital, of banks' holdings of capital issued by other banks or deposit-taking institutions;[16]
(iv)   in the general approach adopted during the transitional period (that is, until end-1992, according to the BIS document, although the Japanese authorities have interpreted this to mean the end of fiscal 1992 namely, the 31 March 1993); and
(v)   in the specification of the target standard ratios for individual banks, subject to the minimum ratio prescribed by the Basle Committee.[17]

The exercise of discretion in areas (i)–(iii) listed above has already been covered, leaving items (iv) and (v) for further comment.

The transitional period   The discretion exercised within permissible bounds during this period by the UK, the US and Japanese supervisory authorities is contrasted in Table 8.8. It is clear that the Japanese authorities have availed themselves of most of the opportunities[18,19] for delaying implementation of the 'final' BIS requirements, in stark contrast to the approach taken by the Bank of England. Accordingly, the interim and final standard target ratios will be adopted at the latest possible moments in Japan, whereas the final standard has served as a floor to the individually agreed, trigger RARs in the UK since the end of June 1989. (All the major UK-incorporated banks had risk asset ratios in excess of the 8 per cent minimum standard by this date.) In a similar vein, the maximum advantage is taken in Japan of the transitional arrangements allowing the inclusion of supplementary elements of capital within core capital and limiting the inclusion of term subordinated debt within supplementary capital. In the UK the 'final' arrangements (that is, those agreed for the post-1992 period) have applied since the new capital adequacy assessment regime was first implemented at the end of June 1989.[20] While this disparity in approach no doubt reflects market realities – compared with their UK-incorporated counterparts, Japanese banks have traditionally operated with lower levels of capital – it does serve as a reminder of the competitive inequalities that internationally active banks (and, indeed, other credit institutions)[21] face, at least until the end of March 1993, as a result of the differential application of capital requirements, a situation that will be worsened by the Japanese treatment of the agreed minimum standard target ratios as *de facto* maxima requirements.

As for the US approach to the transitional period, the Federal Reserve, like its Japanese counterpart, has seen fit to avail itself of some of the discretionary provisions which allow for a temporary shielding of its charges from the full rigours of the agreed final proposals. (Calls from a number of US banks, mirroring the demands of some of their Japanese counterparts, for a go-slow on the implementation of the 1988 agreement have, to date at least, been resisted by the Basle Committee.) Thus, for example: full advantage was taken of the provisions allowing for the inclusion of general loan loss reserves within Tier 2 capital; full advantage was taken of the provisions allowing for the temporary inclusion of supplementary elements of capital within core capital; and the agreed minimum target standard risk asset ratio was phased in (no standard was specified for the period before the end of 1990). Contrariwise, state member banks were required to deduct goodwill from Tier 1 capital throughout the period, in spite of the available concession to delay implementation of this policy until end-1992, although this reflected internal accounting conventions rather than a conscious policy choice on the part of the Federal Reserve.

The specification of target standard ratios The final but overwhelmingly important factor which impinges upon the competitiveness of internationally active banks is the choice of trigger risk asset ratios which the banks are actually asked to observe. Whilst we know that these will be set, for all banks subject to the BIS rules in Japan,[22] at the agreed minimum of 8 per cent from the end of March 1993, the bulk of their UK and US competitors will be subjected to much higher requirements, according to their individual

Table 8.8   The discretion exercised during the transitional period: a contrast of the approaches adopted in the UK, US and Japan

The bounds of discretion[a]	The UK approach	The Japanese approach	The US approach[p]
1. Minimum standard for the risk asset ratio (RAR)			
(a) initial position: the level prevailing at end-1987	The level prevailing at end-1987[b]	The level prevailing at end-1987[c]	None
(b) end-1990 position: 7.25%	8%[d]	7.25%	7.25%[c]
(c) end-1992 position: 8.0%	8%[e]	8%[f]	8%[q]
2. Measurement formula for the RAR			
(a) initial position: core elements[g] plus 100%	Core elements plus 100%[h]	Core elements[j] plus 100%	Core elements[j] plus 100%
(b) end-1990 position: core elements[g] plus 100% (3.625% plus 3.625%)	4% + 4%	3.625%[k] + 3.625%	3.625%[k] & 3.625%
(c) end-1992 position: core elements plus 100% (4% plus 4%)	4% + 4%	4% + 4%	4% + 4%
3. Supplementary elements of capital allowed to be included in core			
(a) initial position: maximum 25% of total core	None[l]	Maximum 25% of total core (incl. supplementary elements)	Maximum 25% of total core (incl. goodwill
(b) end-1990 position: maximum 10% of total core (i.e. 0.3625%)	None	Maximum 10% of total core (incl. supplementary elements)	Maximum 10% of total core (incl. goodwill
(c) end-1992 position: none	None	None	None
4. Limit for inclusion within supplementary capital on general loan loss reserves/general provisions which reflect lower valuations of assets or latent but unidentified losses present in the balance sheet[m]			
(a) initial position: no limit	Up to 1.5% of risk weighted assets[n]	No limit	No limit[t]
(b) end-1990 position: up to 1.5 percentage points of risk-weighted assets or, exceptionally, up to 2.0 percentage points of risk-weighted assets	Up to 1.5% of risk-weighted assets[n]	Up to 1.5% of risk-weighted assets	Up to 1.5% of risk-weighted assets
(c) end-1992 position: up to 1.25 percentage points of risk-weighted assets or, exceptionally and temporarily, up to 2.0 percentage points	Up to 1.25% of risk-weighted assets[n]	Up to 1.25% of risk-weighted assets	Up to 1.25% of risk-weighted assets

5. Limit on term subordinated debt in supplementary elements

(a) initial position: no limit	Maximum of 50% of Tier 1[o]	No limit	Combined maximum of 50% of Tier 1[u]
(b) end-1990 position: no limit	Maximum of 50% of Tier 1	No limit	Combined maximum of 50% of Tier 1
(c) end-1992 position: maximum of 50% of Tier 1	Maximum of 50% of Tier 1	Maximum of 50% of Tier 1	Combined maximum of 50% of Tier 1

6. Deduction for goodwill from core capital

(a) initial position: discretionary	Deducted	Deducted	Deducted
(b) end-1990 position: discretionary	Deducted	To be deducted	Deducted
(c) end-1992 position: compulsory	To be deducted	To be deducted	To be deducted

Notes

a As set out in the BIS document of December 1987 (Annex 4). It is important to note, however, that the Japanese authorities have interpreted the calendar years as fiscal years, thereby allowing themselves an extra three months period of grace in each case.

b In practice, the agreed minimum trigger (Hall, 1990b) RARs are likely to have been substantially in excess of this level.

c For those institutions which needed to improve capital levels to attain the interim and final standards (not even temporary diminutions in capital levels were allowed).

d The minimum ratio of 8% became effective at the end of June 1989. Henceforth, all trigger RARs had to be in excess of this level, with each bank agreeing on an individual basis with the Bank of England what its actual trigger RAR should be for the ensuing period.

e Again, in practice, the individually agreed minimum trigger RARs are likely to be substantially in excess of 8.0% for most, if not all, banks.

f This minimum is also likely to be a *de facto* maximum requirement for most, if not all, institutions and no attempt will be made to differentiate between banks so as to tailor requirements to their particular circumstances.

g Including supplementary elements up to a maximum of 25% of core capital.

h From the date of application of the new RAR methodology (i.e., end-June 1989), the minimum trigger RARs became subject to a floor of 8%, with a minimum of half of this (i.e., 4 percentage points) to be represented by core capital. Prior to this date, trigger RARs were calculated using the methodology set out in Hall (1990b).

i Including supplementary elements up to a maximum of 25% of core capital (including supplementary elements).

j Including supplementary elements up to a maximum of 10% of core capital.

k This contribution from core elements includes supplementary elements up to a maximum of 10% of core capital (including supplementary elements).

l Once the new regime took effect at the end of June 1989.

m The limits apply until agreement is reached on a consistent basis for including unencumbered provisions or reserves in capital. (For the latest proposals which push back the end-1992 requirement until the end of 1993 but narrow the limit to a strict 1.25% of weighted risk assets, see BIS, 1991.)

n This limit only applies to general provisions which are held against possible or latent loss but where these losses have not as yet been identified. All provisions held against value-impaired assets, including provisions against problem country debt, are excluded from capital.

o This limit (equivalent to a limit of 25% of the capital base) was introduced at the end of June 1989 and contrasts with the previous limit applied of 33⅓% of the capital base (Hall, 1990b).

p For state member banks. The main difference in their treatment *vis-à-vis* that of bank holding companies is that the latter, until the end of 1992, could count goodwill acquired before 12 March 1988 as Tier 1 capital (i.e., no deduction was required).

q This is very much a minimum. In general, banking organizations will be expected to operate well above this level particularly if they are contemplating significant expansion or have high or inordinate levels of risk.

r Including supplementary elements up to a maximum of 25% of the sum of Tier 1 capital plus goodwill.

s Including supplementary elements up to a maximum of 10% of the sum of Tier 1 capital plus goodwill.

t In the US, the limits relate to allowances for loan and lease losses.

u In the US, this limit relates to subordinated debt and intermediate-term preferred stock.

Sources: Bank of England, 1990a and 1990b; BIS, 1987; Hall, 1990b; Japanese Ministry of Finance, 1988; Federal Reserve System, 1989, Attachment VI, p. 26.

circumstances.[23] This, more than anything else, indicates how dependent internationally active banks are on the discretionary policies adopted by their supervisors within the field of capital adequacy assessment.

Conclusions

Mainly because of the process of political compromise that was deemed necessary to ensure widespread acceptance of its guideline proposals, the Basle Committee allowed national supervisory authorities a substantial degree of discretion in the interpretation and implementation of the agreed proposals on capital adequacy assessment, most especially in the run-up to the end of 1992. Such action, although no doubt increasing the number of countries willing to abide by the spirit if not the letter of the agreement, is likely to have involved a sacrifice of some net competitive equity gains. The sacrificial burden is, of course, borne by the international banks themselves, as they are only too well aware.[24] Examples of the resulting competitive inequalities (as well as those resulting from other factors), as faced by banks incorporated in the UK, the US and Japan, are clearly identified within the text.

Notes

1. Belgium, Canada, France, Germany, Italy, Japan, The Netherlands, Switzerland, the UK, the USA and Sweden.
2. The analysis of US policy is focused mainly on the approach adopted towards state member (i.e., of the Federal Reserve System) banks (which is the same as the approach adopted by the OCC in respect of national banks and by the FDC in respect of FDIC-insured state non-member banks), although the main differences in their treatment *vis-à-vis* bank holding companies are noted in the text. The risk-based measure is applied on a consolidated basis to all state member banks and bank holding companies with consolidated assets of $150 million or more. For other bank holding companies it is applied on a bank-only basis.
3. It should be noted that preference share issues made by overseas *banking* subsidiaries, as opposed to special-purpose offshore subsidiaries, would rank as Tier 1 capital at the consolidated level.
4. The prevailing tax situation (in respect of capital gains tax) also deters banks from revaluing property.
5. This was agreed by the Basle Committee in 1990. The Bank of England, on a bank-by-bank basis, agrees what proportion of such revaluation reserves should be capitalized, which to date has taken place through scrip issues. The Bank of England's view is that a 'reasonable' proportion of the reserve should remain uncapitalized in order to absorb future declines in property values before the current year's profit and loss account is affected.
6. Prior to this date, the money so raised had to be restricted to 'investment (i.e., physical) facilities' and not used as a general fund for lending.
7. The Sumitomo Bank was the first bank to circumvent the rules by using a Caribbean-based subsidiary to make subordinated bond issues in the US and Europe in June 1990, the proceeds being on-lent by the subsidiary on a subordinated basis to the parent bank. Later issues involved the parents being distanced even further as the proceeds were used to repay loans made by foreign banks to the Japanese banks' overseas affiliates.

8. In the US, bank holding companies could postpone deduction of goodwill acquired before 12 March 1988 until the end of 1992.
9. In the US, previously grandfathered goodwill approved in supervisory mergers is exempt from deduction.
10. Under this Securities and Exchange Law rule, a parent company need not consolidate any of its subsidiaries the assets, the sales and the profits of which are all below 10 per cent of those of the combined total for the parent company and its consolidated subsidiaries.
11. The exceptions to the rule are: (i) claims on multilateral development banks and claims fully guaranteed by or fully collateralized by the securities issued by these institutions (a risk weight of 20 per cent is adopted, despite the availability of an option to impose a zero risk weight); and (ii) claims on OECD public-sector entities (excluding central government) and loans guaranteed by such entities (risk weights of either 10 or 20 per cent are adopted in the light of options which would allow for the adoption of zero, 20 or 50 per cent risk weights).
12. Interest rate risk proxies are applied to items (9) and (11). Separate studies are still being conducted on market risk, exchange rate risk, interest rate risk and liquidity risk, the outcome of which is likely to be further modification of the risk weight framework. A draft proposal on a methodology for incorporating interest rate risk within risk-based capital adequacy assessment procedures used within the thrift industry was released for comment by the Office of Thrift Supervision in July 1990 (see Office of Thrift Supervision, 1990). Implementation of this proposal, however, has been deferred. Notwithstanding this, all federal banking agencies have been mandated under the Federal Deposit Insurance Corporation Improvement Act of 1991 to take account of interest rate risk (as well as concentration of credit risk, the risks of non-traditional activities, and loss experience associated with multi-family mortgages) in their risk-based measures by June 1993 at the latest.
13. These are the factors addressed in the US. For a contrast with the approach taken by the Bank of England, see Hall, 1990b.
14. The UK and US authorities, however, exercised the discretion granted in the Basle Committee's proposals to allow their banks the option of measuring *commitments* on a residual maturity basis until the end of 1992 rather than on an original maturity basis. The decision was taken with a view to facilitating data collection in the two countries and to minimizing the reporting costs incurred by banks.
15. Those which are actively engaged in trading such instruments may, exceptionally, also be allowed to adopt this approach, subject to agreement with the Bank of England.
16. Although the Basle Committee fully recognized the potential systemic dangers of such 'double gearing' it baulked at demanding full deduction of all holdings of other banks' capital on the grounds that 'to do so could impede certain significant and desirable changes taking place in the structure of domestic banking systems' (BIS, 1987, p. 9). Notwithstanding this, the Committee determined to closely monitor the situation and did not rule out the possibility of introducing constraints at a later date.
17. In December 1987 the Committee had not endorsed any particular minimum figure for this standard but it was agreed during 1988 that the minimum ratio should be set at the 8 per cent level.
18. Though not all! The discretion to wait until the end of 1992 before deducting goodwill from Tier 1 capital was not exercised (although, presumably, this was ruled out by local standard accounting practices); nor has any attempt been made to seek 'exceptional' status for general loan loss reserves.
19. It might also be argued that the Japanese interpretation of the end of calendar year requirements as end of *fiscal* year requirements has allowed them to extend the periods of grace beyond those provisionally agreed. Moreover, their interpretation of the amounts of supplementary capital allowed to be included in core capital during the transitional period – they assess it as a maximum percentage of total core, *including* supplementary elements (see item 3 in Table 8.8) – further indicates their determination to stretch the rules to the limit.

20. Apart from the Bank of England's decision, noted earlier, to exercise the discretion granted in the Basle Committee's proposals to allow UK-authorized banks the option of measuring commitments on a *residual* maturity basis until the end of 1992 rather than on an original maturity basis.

21. It should be noted that the EC's Solvency Ratio Directive applies to *all* credit institutions operating within the EC.

22. That is, those Japanese banks which either maintain overseas business establishments or which otherwise *voluntarily* choose to adopt the BIS rules.

23. In the US, for example, banks contemplating significant expansion or which are exposed to high or inordinate levels of risk will be asked to observe ratios significantly above the minimum allowed, a policy reflected in the UK where even the clearing banks run risk asset ratios typically in the 9–10 per cent range. It is also likely that UK and US banks will eventually be asked to observe the requirements on a (moving?) average daily basis rather than just on reporting dates, so that less window-dressing than in Japan is likely to be tolerated.

24. The concern most frequently expressed by the banks whose views on the impact of the Basle agreement were recently canvassed by Price Waterhouse was over 'the inter-country differences emerging in the areas of national discretion, particularly with regard to the elements of Tier 2 capital and the setting of individual target ratios above the 8 per cent minimum' (Price Waterhouse, July 1991, p. 8). Those banks which feel most strongly about being disadvantaged *vis-à-vis* banks in other countries are located in the UK, Germany, Norway, Canada, Belgium, France and Spain, according to this study. Of the UK respondents, almost two thirds cited the setting of minimum target ratios substantially in excess of the agreed 8 per cent minimum as a cause for dissatisfaction.

References

Bank for International Settlements (BIS) (1987), *Proposals for International Convergence of Capital Measurement and Capital Standards*, consultative paper issued by the Committee on Banking Regulations and Supervisory Practices [the Basle Committee] (Basle: BIS).

Bank for International Settlements (BIS) (1991), *Proposals for the Inclusion of General Provisions/General Loan Loss Reserves in Capital*, Consultative paper issued by the Basle Committee (Basle: BIS).

Bank of England (1986), *Subordinated Loan Capital Issued by Recognised Banks and Licensed Deposit-takers*, BSD/1986/2 (London: Bank of England).

Bank of England (1988), *Implementation of the Basle Convergence Agreement in the United Kingdom*, BSD/1988/3 (London: Bank of England).

Bank of England (1990a), *Implementation in the United Kingdom of the Directive on Own Funds of Credit Institutions*, BSD/1990/2 (London: Bank of England).

Bank of England (1990b), *Implementation in the United Kingdom of the Solvency Ratio Directive*, BSD/1990/3 (London: Bank of England).

Dale, R. (1990), 'Japan's banking regulation: current policy issues' in C. A. E. Goodhart and G. Sutija (eds), *Japanese Financial Growth* (London: Macmillan), pp. 33–45.

European Community (EC) (1986), *Directive on the Annual Accounts and Consolidated Accounts of Banks and Other Financial Institutions* [Bank Accounts Directive] (86/635/EEC).

European Community (EC) (1989a), *Directive on the Own Funds of Credit Institutions* [Own Funds Directive] (89/299/EEC).

European Community (EC) (1989b), *Directive on the Solvency Ratio for Credit Institutions* [Solvency Ratio Directive] (89/647/EEC).

Federal Reserve System (1989), *Capital Adequacy Guidelines*, (Washington, D.C.: FRS Board of Governors).

Hall, M. J. B. (1989), 'The BIS capital adequacy "rules": a critique', *Banca Nazionale del Lavoro Quarterly Review*, no. 169, pp. 207–27.

Hall, M. J. B. (1990a), 'Comment' on Dale's paper, in C.A.E. Goodhart and G. Sutija (eds), *Japanese Financial Growth* (London: Macmillan), pp. 46–51.

Hall, M. J. B. (1990b), 'The Bank for International Settlements' capital adequacy "Rules": implications for banks operating in the UK', *Service Industries Journal*, vol. 10, no. 1, pp. 147–71.

Hall, M. J. B. (forthcoming), 'The G10 agreement on capital adequacy assessment: a critique', in C.A. Stone and A. Zissu (eds), *Risk-based Capital Regulations: Asset Management and Funding Strategies* (Philadelphia: Business One Irwin).

Ministry of Finance (Japan) (1988), *Outline of the Official Notification Concerning the Implementation of the Basle Committee's Capital Adequacy Framework* (Tokyo: Ministry of Finance).

Office of Thrift Supervision (1990), *Regulatory Capital: Interest Rate Risk Component*.

Price Waterhouse (1991), *Bank Capital Adequacy and Capital Convergence* (London: Price Waterhouse).

Annex I: Members of the OECD and those countries which have concluded special lending arrangements with the IMF associated with the Fund's general arrangements to borrow

Australia	Finland	Ireland	New Zealand	Sweden
Austria	France	Italy	Norway	Switzerland
Belgium	Germany	Japan	Portugal	Turkey
Canada	Greece	Luxembourg	Saudi Arabia	United Kingdom
Denmark	Iceland	Netherlands	Spain	United States

Source: Bank of England, 1990b, Annex 4, p. 13.

Annex II: UK public bodies classified as public sector entities

Local authorities and regional governments
London borough councils, county and district councils in England, Northern Ireland and Wales, and district and regional councils in Scotland together with their departments (for example, gas departments and water service departments but not transport departments); those bodies formed on 1 April 1986 to take over the assets and functions of the former metropolitan councils and the GLC; and the state governments in the Channel Islands and the Isle of Man government.

Other public sector entities
Those UK non-commercial bodies deemed eligible to receive the same capital treatment as local authorities and regional governments are identified on a Bank of England list which is updated from time to time. As of July 1989, the list comprised the following:

(a) Local bodies

Central Scotland Water
  Development Board
Fire services
Fire service colleges
Forth Road Bridge Joint Board
Humber Bridge Board
Inner London Education Authority
Magistrates' Court

Police colleges
Police forces (including
  Metropolitan Police)
Probation Service in England and
  Wales
Scottish colleges of education
Scottish River Purification Boards
Teacher-training colleges

(b) Non-commercial public corporations

Audit Commission
Black Country Development
  Corporation
Bristol Development Corporation
Cardiff Bay Development
  Corporation
Central Manchester Development
  Corporation
Covent Garden Market Authority
Development Board for Rural
  Wales
Don Valley Development
  Corporation
English Industrial Estates
  Corporation
Her Majesty's Stationery Office
Highlands and Islands Development
  Board
Independent Broadcasting Authority
Leeds Development Corporation
Letchworth Garden City

London Docklands Development
  Corporation
National Dock Labour Board
New Town Commission (and new
  town development corporations
Northern Ireland Housing Executive
Oil and Pipeline Agency
The Pilotage Commission
Royal Mint
Scottish Development Agency
Scottish Homes
Sheffield Development Corporation
Trafford Park Development
  Corporation
Tyne & Wear Development
  Corporation
United Kingdom Atomic Energy
  Authority
Urban Development Corporations
Welsh Development Agency
Welsh Fourth Channel Authority

Source: Bank of England, 1990b, Annex 5, p. 14.

9 The separation of banking and securities business: a comparative study of the approaches adopted in the US and Japan

Background
Given that much of the legislation separating banking and securities business in Japan was introduced by General Headquarters of the Supreme Commander Allied Powers (SCAP) in the aftermath of the Second World War and was modelled on the then existing US legislation, it is unsurprising that the regulatory regimes employed in the two countries exhibit a number of similarities. Notwithstanding this, however, important differences remain, both in legislative frameworks and *de facto* administrative interpretation and implementation. These differences reflect, in part, the differing rationales for the implementation of the legislative provisions and the contrasting institutional features of the two countries' financial systems. Whatever the differences, however, common forces have been at work creating pressure for reform, if not repeal, of the offending legislation. The background to this reform debate and its likely outcome in the two countries in question, together with the other issues touched upon above, are examined in detail below.

THE US APPROACH TO THE SEPARATION OF BANKING AND SECURITIES BUSINESS

The regulation of US banking organizations' domestic securities activities

The legal framework
The primary legislative provisions governing US banks' domestic securities activities arise from the following: the National Bank Act of 1864; the Federal Reserve Act of 1913; the McFadden Act of 1927; the Glass–Steagall Act of 1933; the Bank Holding Company Act of 1956; and state laws (US General Accounting Office, 1990, Appendix VI).

The National Bank Act of 1864 This Act precludes national banks[1] (that is chartered by the Office of the Comptroller of the Currency (OCC)) from underwriting corporate securities directly but does not prohibit them from engaging in such (or other) securities activities through affiliated organizations, such as state-chartered securities affiliates.

Under regulatory guidance from the OCC, national banks are allowed to engage in the following securities-related activities: the full range of government securities activities; private placement of corporate securities; the purchase and sale of all types of securities (including mutual fund shares) on an agency basis for customers; the purchase and sale, for their own account, of a limited amount[2] of corporate bonds, provided they are marketable and of investment quality; the sale of mortgage pass-through certificates representing interests in mortgage loans originated by the bank; the sale of units in unit investment trusts; the offering of brokerage services and investment advice.

The Federal Reserve Act of 1913   Sections 23A and 23B of this Act, which governs the activities of all national banks and state-chartered member banks, impinge upon the securities activities of these banks. Under section 23A, a member bank is prohibited from extending credit to, or purchasing assets from, an affiliate in excess of 10 per cent of the bank's capital; and a limit of 20 per cent of capital is applied to the aggregate of such transactions. Additionally, the provisions require that, as a minimum, any bank loans to an affiliate be fully collateralized, with up to 130 per cent of the loan amount being required depending on the composition of the loan collateral. Section 23B, in contrast, deals with covered transactions between banks and their affiliates (for example, the sale of assets or services purchased under contract) and requires that such transactions be undertaken on substantially the same terms as those prevailing at the time for comparable transactions involving non-affiliates.[3]

The McFadden Act of 1927   Under this law, the authority of national banks to buy and sell investment securities was reaffirmed.

The Glass–Steagall Act of 1933   The Glass–Steagall Act is the present day label applied to four sections of the US Banking Act of 1933 namely, sections 16, 20, 21 and 32. The legislation was enacted to enforce, at least partially, physical separation of investment and commercial banking activities, in the light of the publicity given to excesses in both the stock market and commercial banking industries at that time and widespread assertions that commercial banks' securities operations contributed significantly to the banking collapse of the Great Depression (for a refutation of this belief, see Benston, 1990). The legislation was founded on the implicit assumption that separation is necessary both to reduce risk for the bank intermediaries and to protect consumers from the abuse of conflict of interest situations.[4]

Section 21 is the broadest in scope, prohibiting individuals and organizations in the investment banking business from engaging in deposit banking at the same time. The other three sections apply only to member banks of the Federal Reserve System. Section 16 relegates member banks'[5,6] securities activities, in the main, to a pure agency brokerage role, prohibiting the underwriting of securities and stock and dealing in securities (other than those investments sanctioned by the Comptroller of the Currency) for their own account. The caveat introduced concerning allowable investment activity means, however, that member banks are *not* prohibited from dealing in and underwriting obligations of the United States government or general obligations of the States and their political subdivisions and, when permitted by law, a member bank may purchase corporate stocks for its own account in a few situations.

The other two sections essentially support section 16. Section 20, for example, prohibits member banks from using securities affiliates to achieve what was denied to the banks themselves. Similarly, section 32, which deals with personnel affiliations with securities firms, reinforces section 20 by covering those cases in which affiliation would not amount to a control situation.

In spite of the extensive scope of the legislation, a number of significant exceptions to the general prohibitions exist. First, section 21, although prohibiting securities firms from accepting deposits directly, does not preclude a securities firm from having a subsidiary or an affiliate that accepts deposits.[7] Secondly, as noted earlier, sections 16, 20 and 32 relate only to member banks.[8] Thirdly, securities brokerage (for either individual or institutional clients) is not prohibited for member banks under section 16.[9] And fourthly, section 16 prohibitions do not extend to dealing in for one's own account or underwriting US government, state and municipal general obligation securities (the so-called 'bank eligible' securities operations).[10]

Finally, it should be noted that although there is no explicit reference to bank holding companies in the Glass–Steagall Act, in 1966 Congress clarified the statute to bring holding companies, as one form of affiliation, within the reach of section 20. Moreover, the Federal Reserve Board has made clear that it applies Glass–Steagall policy to bank holding companies. The Glass–Steagall Act, however, does *not* extend to US institutions' overseas activities (see below) nor to foreign banks, which are not considered banks under the definition contained in either the National Banking Act or the Bank Holding Company Act (for the regulation of their financial activities in the US, see below).[11]

The Bank Holding Company Act of 1956 (BHCA)   The BHCA is implemented by the Federal Reserve Board and governs the operations of bank holding companies and their non-bank subsidiaries but not the direct activities of the banks themselves. The scope of activities in which bank holding companies (and their subsidiaries) can engage is determined according to section 4(c)(8) of the Act. These activities must be deemed to be 'closely related to and a proper incident to banking' and for new approvals the Board

Table 9.1   Activities closely related to banking and approved for bank holding companies under Regulation Y

Activities	Securities-related
Making and servicing loans	No
Industrial banking	No
Trust company functions	Yes
Investment or financial advice	Yes
Leasing personal or real property	No
Community development	No
Data processing	No
Insurance agency and brokerage in connection with credit extensions	No
Underwriting insurance related to an extension of credit	No
Providing courier services	No
Management consulting to non-affiliated bank and non-bank deposit institutions	No
Issuing and selling money orders, savings bonds and travellers' cheques	No
Real estate and personal property appraising	No
Arranging commercial real estate equity financing	No
Securities brokerage	Yes
Underwriting and dealing in government obligations and money market instruments	Yes
Foreign exchange advisory and transactional services	No
Future commission merchant	Yes
Investment advice on financial futures and options on futures	Yes
Consumer financial counselling	No
Tax planning and preparation	No
Cheque-guarantee	No
Operating a collection agency	No
Operating a credit bureau	No

Source: US General Accounting Office, 1990, Table VI.1, p. 91.

is required to determine that activities may reasonably be expected to produce net public benefits. As can be seen from Table 9.1, six securities-related activities had been approved by the Board as of October 1989 under this section of the Act – Regulation Y – and, in addition to the 24 activities listed in the table, a further 25 activities had been approved following the direct submission of applications by individual bank holding companies. Authorization of 'section 20' companies, with expanded securities powers (see below), proceeded through the latter route – that is, the approval of individual applications rather than the amendment of Regulation Y – and the Board used its authority under the Act to impose requirements regarding revenue limitations, capitalization and firewalls.

Finally, under the Act bank holding companies are required to comply with the provisions of the Glass–Steagall Act.

State laws   State-chartered banks' operations are governed by both federal and state law. Accordingly, some are permitted to engage in some securities activities that are denied national banks.

The interpretation and implementation of the legal provisions
As has already become clear, the specific powers available to a US bank depend on: (i) the identity of its chartering authority (states or the OCC); (ii) the provisions of federal statutes (such as the Glass–Steagall Act, as amended and interpreted by the OCC, the Federal Reserve Board and the courts); and (iii) the rules established by its primary federal regulator (the OCC for national banks,[12] the FDIC for state-chartered non-member banks, and the Federal Reserve for state-chartered member banks). The permissible activities for US banks' affiliated companies are, in turn, established by the Glass–Steagall Act and the BHCA, as amended and interpreted by the Federal Reserve Board and the courts.

Given their reluctance or inability to amend statutes, policymakers have therefore been forced down the road of seeking judicial support of regulatory reinterpretation to accommodate demands for reform. Firmly in the vanguard of such action, the Federal Reserve Board has since the mid-1980s actively sought to expand the scope of permissible securities activities for member banks. Relatively recent Supreme Court rulings have established that bank affiliates can provide discount brokerage services (1984) and/or investment advice (1988)[13] without contravening section 20 of the Glass–Steagall Act. Further, since March 1988,[14] US commercial banks have been allowed, through wholly owned non-bank 'section 20' subsidiaries, to trade and underwrite commercial paper, mortgage-related[15] and asset-backed securities, consumer-receivable-related securities and municipal revenue bonds, subject to certain revenue limitations and other requirements.[16] These deci-

Table 9.2 Securities activities of US commercial banks[a] (April 1990)

Permissible	Year started[b]
Underwriting, distributing, and dealing	Always
US Treasury securities	Always
US federal agency securities	Various years
Commercial paper	1987
Mortgage and other asset-backed securities	
Collateral originated by other banks	1987
Collateral originated by issuing bank	1989
Municipal securities	
General obligation	Nearly always
Some revenue bonds	1968
All revenue bonds	1987
Corporate bonds	1989
Corporate equity	1990
Financial and precious metal futures brokerage and dealing	1983[c]
Private placement (agency capacity)	Always
Sponsor closed-end funds	1974
Underwrite deposits with returns tied partially	
to stock market performance	1987
Offshore dealing in eurodollar securities	Always
Mergers and acquisitions	Always
Trust investments	
Individual accounts	Nearly always
IRA commingled accounts	1982
Automatic investment service	1974
Dividend investment service	Always
Financial advising and managing	
Closed-end funds	1974
Mutual funds	1974
Restricted	Always
Brokerage	
Limited customer	Always
Public retail (discount)	1982
Securities swapping	Always
Research advice to investors	
Separate from brokerage	1983
Combined with brokerage	
Institutional	1986
Retail	1987

Non-permissible
Mutual funds underwriting and distributing

Notes
[a] Federal Reserve member banks or non-bank affiliates of bank holding companies.
[b] After the Civil War. Different dates may apply to national and state banks. With some exceptions the earliest date is shown. Regulatory rulings frequently concluded that a specific activity was permissible before the date of ruling. If the activity was halted by enactment of the Glass–Steagall Act, the date of renewed activity is given.
[c] Restricted to futures contracts for which banks may hold the underlying security or that are settled only in cash.

Source: Kaufman and Mote, 1990, p. 419 (amended).

sions meant that, as of March 1988, the main areas of continuing prohibition related to the underwriting and trading of equities through subsidiaries and, of course, to the offering of a wide range of securities activities direct by commercial banks.

Further erosion of the investment/commercial banking barriers occurred in September 1990 when the Federal Reserve made a far-reaching decision to allow J. P. Morgan, the New York commercial bank, to underwrite corporate equities through a subsidiary, a situation presaged by the Fed when it approved commercial bank applications to underwrite any corporate debt in January 1989.[17] As in its earlier decision, however, extensive firewalls would have to be applied (see US General Accounting Office, 1990, pp. 99–106)[18] to limit potential abuse and conflicts of interest and to insulate insured bank affiliates from the risks associated with the section 20 subsidiaries' activities, capital adequacy requirements would have to be met and no more than 10 per cent of gross revenues could be earned by the subsidiary from the underwriting of corporate debt, equities and related securities.

The decision meant that as at September 1990[19] over 20 commercial banks were operating section 20 subsidiaries, the majority of which were engaged in underwriting commercial paper (the major activity), municipal revenue bonds, mortgage-backed securities and consumer-receivables-backed securities. Two of them were engaged in underwriting corporate bonds and one was also about to engage in underwriting corporate equities. In most cases, these activities were additional to those securities operations, such as the underwriting and trading of government bonds, not prohibited by Glass–Steagall, that is, the 'bank-eligible' securities operations (see Table 9.2 for a comprehensive list).

In summary, despite the legislative impediments, regulatory interpretation of the law and judicial rulings have allowed US commercial banks, directly or through section 20 affiliates, to engage (albeit often subject still to restrictions and limitations) in virtually every conceivable form of securities activity except the underwriting and trading of mutual fund shares.

The regulation of US banking organizations' overseas securities operations

As noted earlier, the provisions of the Glass–Steagall Act do not apply to US banks' foreign activities. This factor and other aspects of the federal regulatory structure (see below) ensure that domestic commercial banks and bank holding companies are able to compete in international markets by allowing them to engage in a broader range of securities activities overseas than is permitted domestically.

As far as organizational structure is concerned, the international securities business may be conducted in foreign branches or in foreign bank and non-bank subsidiaries, Edge Act corporation subsidiaries[20] or joint venture companies, where non-controlling interests in foreign banks and financial companies are held. Whatever the structure adopted, however, compliance with relevant US law (regarding powers, capitalization and transactions within the holding company, for example) and the banking laws and regulations of the host country is mandatory.

The legal framework

The Federal Reserve Act of 1913   Section 25 of this Act allows national banks[21] to set up foreign branches, take stakes in foreign banks and engage in other activities, including securities activities to a limited degree, that are 'usual' in connection with the conduct of banking in the overseas markets where the foreign branches transact business. The branches' underwriting and distribution activities are confined, however, to the government securities of the country of location.

As noted earlier, section 25(a) also authorizes national banks to set up Edge Act corporations which are allowed to engage in a broad range of investment activities abroad. And finally, sections 23A and 23B place restrictions on transactions between the domestic bank and the bank holding company parent or its affiliates.

The Bank Holding Company Act (BHCA) of 1956   Under section 4(c)(13) of the BHCA, bank holding companies are allowed to make direct foreign investments.

Implementation

Regulation K of the Federal Reserve Board implements key sections of the above two federal laws by describing the activities that banks and bank holding companies may engage in abroad and specifying the rules and limitations under which such activities can be conducted.

As far as the permitted activities are concerned, generally the list will encompass all domestic banking powers plus, in the case of branches, some additional banking powers, such as issuing guarantees, and, in the case of subsidiaries, some additional investment banking powers, for example, underwriting and dealing in equity securities. US banking organizations may generally engage in such activities to the extent permitted by host country regulators and, subject to prior Board approval, they may also engage in activities that are not prescribed in Regulation K but which nevertheless are permitted in the host country.

As for restrictions and limitations, the Board does *not* impose on the foreign operations of US banking organizations all the firewall provisions that apply to non-traditional domestic activities (for example, there are no restrictions on interlocking boards of directors or joint marketing activities between a bank and a non-bank affiliate), although it does require that all such overseas operations be conducted in accordance with high standards of banking and financial prudence. Additionally, however, specific limitations are imposed on some of the permitted activities. For example, the aggregate commitment of a banking organization and its subsidiaries to the underwriting of the shares of an issue is not allowed to exceed $15 million; and the total loans and extensions of credit, including underwriting commitments, to any one person by an Edge Corporation or foreign bank subsidiary of a member bank, when aggregated with loans and extensions of credit by the member bank to that person, cannot exceed the member bank's limitations on loans and extensions of credit to any one person.[22]

Finally, it should be noted that the international activities of US banking organizations are subject to supervisory examinations and inspections by the Federal Reserve, the OCC and the FDIC.[23] They are also subject to the BIS rules on capital adequacy assessment (Hall, 1989) and to broad supervisory guidelines agreed by the Basle Committee of Supervisors.

The regulation of foreign banks' securities activities in the US

The legal framework
Under the International Banking Act of 1978 (IBA), a policy of 'national treatment' (Key, 1990) is adopted towards the US operations of foreign banks.[24,25] The provisions of the Act resulted in the then existing non-banking activities of foreign banks being grandfathered, with *future* non-banking activities, whether offered direct or indirect (through a US subsidiary of a foreign affiliate of the foreign bank, for example), becoming subject to section 4 of the BHCA (which specifies permissible business activities for US bank holding companies) for those foreign banks with US agencies and branches.[26] This substantially improved the competitive position of US banks *vis-à-vis* foreign banks as far as their ability to engage in securities operations was concerned.[27]

Implementation
Under US law, foreign banks' subsidiaries are treated as bank holding companies by the Federal Reserve Board. This means that, unlike their US commercial bank counterparts, they *can* fund their US section 20 subsidiaries, which engage in bank-ineligible securities transactions. With only minor modifications, however, the other firewalls applicable to US banks' section 20 operations are applied, although not on the non-US operations of the foreign bank.

As for foreign banks' US agencies and branches, they are treated by the Board as banking affiliates, and hence subject to the relevant firewalls, and not as part of the foreign bank in its capacity as a bank holding company.

Summary
Although substantive federal legislation, most notably the Glass–Steagall Act, is devoted to achieving the separation of banking and securities business in the US, the large number of exceptions and exemptions from the legal provisions render this objective incomplete. Moreover, the determination of bank regulators (especially the Federal Reserve Board), backed by court rulings, to extract the maximum possible flexibility from existing statutes has resulted in significant erosion of the barriers in recent years. This is not to argue, however, that legislative reform is unnecessary; rather, as is demonstrated later, it suggests the need for a thorough reappraisal of the rationale for separation, with the most cost-effective reform measures being implemented to secure the identified policy objectives.

THE SEPARATION OF BANKING AND SECURITIES BUSINESS IN JAPAN

The regulation of Japanese commercial banks' domestic securities operations

The legal framework
The major components of the statutory framework governing the domestic operations of Japanese commercial banks are the Banking Law of 1981, Article 65 of the Securities and Exchange Law of 1948 and the Antimonopoly Law of 1947.

The Banking Law of 1981　Under Article 2 (clause 2), banking business for an ordinary bank is defined as 'the taking of deposits or instalment savings, along with the lending of funds or the discounting of bills, and/or the handling of funds transfer'. Article 3 goes on to establish that the taking of deposits or instalment savings is the exclusive prerogative of banks, thereby denying securities companies access to the deposit-taking business.

Permissible (that is, ancillary or securities) non-banking business activities for ordinary banks are set out in Articles 10 (ancillary) and 11 (securities), and Article 12 prohibits engagement in any other lines of non-banking business. However, this does not preclude other forms of non-banking business – the so-called 'peripheral' business activities – being offered through domestic affiliates although, should this option be chosen, the banks become

Table 9.3   Classification of Japanese banks' associated companies

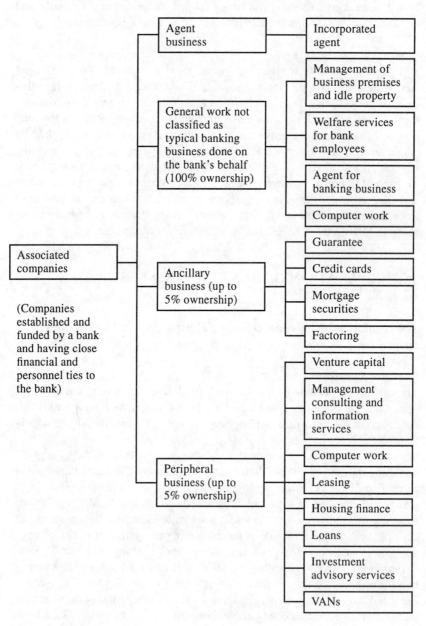

Source: FBAJ, 1989, Fig. 3.6, p. 73.

subject to strict rules concerning the capital subscription rate: 100 per cent in cases where the affiliate acts as the institution's agent or engages in 'non-essential' segments of the institution's business, and no more than 5 per cent in cases where the affiliate engages in business corresponding to ancillary or peripheral business. Moreover, the types of business permitted to affiliates with close staffing or funding ties with the institution are limited to those specified by notification of the Director General of the Banking Bureau at the Ministry of Finance (MOF) (see Table 9.3).

The ancillary business permitted under Article 10 (clause 2) comprises the following: the guarantee of liabilities and acceptance of bills; the purchase and sale of securities; dealing in major index securities futures, in securities options, and in foreign securities futures (but only for investment purposes or on receipt of a written request for a customer); the lending of securities; the underwriting of government bonds, local government bonds, and government-guaranteed bonds (but not for subsequent sale) and placement of bonds underwritten; the acquisition and ceding of monetary claims, as designated by ordinance of the MOF; the provision of subscription agency services for local government bonds, corporate bonds and other securities; the provision of agency services for banks and other entities engaged in financial business; the handling of money transactions on behalf of national and local government bodies and corporations; the safekeeping of securities, precious metals and other items; the changing of money; and dealing in financial futures on a custodial basis (FBAJ, 1989, pp. 43–4). Additionally, ancillary business is supposed to be of a similar nature to bank business, should not exceed bank business in volume terms and should be conducted on proper business lines, that is, it should generate income.

Permissible securities activities listed in Article 11 comprise various operations in connection with government and other bonds, including underwriting and offering for subscription and sale. Notwithstanding this, banks must still obtain permission from the MOF to engage in such securities activities, in accordance with Article 65 of the Securities and Exchange Law. Further securities activities are sanctioned as ancillary business under Article 10 of the 1981 Banking Law, as has just been noted.

Trust business is permitted under the Concurrent Trust Business Law of 1981 and may also be conducted through affiliates.

The Securities and Exchange Law of 1948   Under Article 65 banks (and trust companies and certain other forms of financial institutions, such as insurance companies) are prohibited from engaging in any form of securities business[28] except in cases where: (i) a bank purchases or sells securities on the written order and for the account of its customers; or (ii) a bank purchases and sells securities for its own investment purposes in accordance with the provisions of other laws or for the account of a trust or pursuant to a trust agreement; or (iii) a bank engages in securities transactions with respect to national government bonds, local government bonds or government-guaranteed bonds. (Special approval has to be obtained from the MOF to engage in these activities, however.)

The separation of securities and banking business effected by Article 65 applies not only to the banking and securities companies themselves but also to their Japanese subsidiaries. The law does not apply to Japanese companies' overseas operations, however.

The Antimonopoly Law of 1947 (as amended in 1977)   In spite of the provisions of the Banking Law and the Securities and Exchange Law, Japanese ordinary banks can, of course, diversify into securities business indirectly through their own and their subsidiaries' and affiliates' investments in Japanese securities companies. While Article 11 of the Antimonopoly Law limits such equity stakes to 5 per cent, multiple holdings within a banking group would allow for much larger exposure to be built up if not effective control to be secured. In recognition of this danger, somewhat belatedly some might argue, the MOF moved in May 1988 to limit the extent of such ties by instructing banks to limit *group* holdings of securities houses' equity to less than 50 per cent of the total outstanding.

Implementation and interpretation of the legal provisions
As is evident from Table 9.3, securities business does not feature among the lines of business which ordinary banks are allowed to offer through affiliates with close staffing or funding ties. This means that, *de facto*, banks' securities opportunities arise in the main from the exclusions to the general prohibition incorporated in Article 65 of the Securities and Exchange Law. Thus, ordinary banks *can* in law: buy and sell securities domestically on the written order and for the account of their customers; buy and sell securities domestically for the account of a trust or pursuant to a trust agreement; buy and sell securities domestically for their own investment purposes and, with MOF approval, engage in a wider range of securities activities abroad (see below); and, again with MOF approval, engage domestically in securities operations with respect to public bonds.

The last two categories are significant as they indicate the extent to which banks are dependent upon the whims of the MOF in respect of their securities operations. Moreover, extensive MOF administrative guidance has also to be adhered to. As far as *domestic* securities operations are concerned, ordinary banks were prohibited until 1983 from engaging in *any* securities activities other than the underwriting of public bonds – all banks belonged to the government bond underwriting syndicate – and the buying and selling of securities for investment purposes, despite the additional concessions available under Article 65. Since then, however, the MOF has taken a more liberal line and gradually relaxed the constraints imposed on banks' domestic securities activities. For example, in April 1983 banks were permitted to sell long-term public bonds[29] which they had underwritten to the general public[30,31] and, in June 1984, general dealing in public bonds was permitted.[32] These two moves necessitated amendments to the Banking and Securities and Exchange Laws but, in line with Article 65 of the latter, prior authorization was still required from the MOF.

More recently, opportunities have arisen for the banks in the commercial paper[33] and government bond options and futures markets.[34] They are also permitted to engage in housing-loan mortgage trust activities (that is, operations in mortgage-backed securities)[35] and, subject to obtaining a discretionary fund management licence, in the management of new money destined for certain kinds of pension funds. Finally, apart from their trust business activities, they also engage in investment advisory activities according to the Investment Advisory Law of 1986 and can act as intermediaries for the private placement of public or private bonds. The advisory services, however, are usually provided through affiliations with securities investment advisory companies.

The regulation of Japanese commercial banks' securities operations overseas
As noted earlier, Article 65 of the Securities and Exchange Law does not apply to Japanese banks' overseas operations. Nevertheless, such overseas activities are constrained not only by virtue of the application of foreign laws but also by MOF administrative guidance. Accordingly, since the early 1970s, Japanese banks have only been allowed to engage in such activities through merchant bank subsidiaries incorporated overseas. Moreover, the precise type and nature of the permissible activities have been strictly defined.

In the early days, the merchant bank subsidiaries engaged primarily in euromarket activities, such as underwriting corporate and sovereign bonds, but even here the so-called 'Three Bureau' guidance precluded them from lead managing issues for Japanese companies.[36] They were allowed, however, to lead manage euroyen issues for non-Japanese borrowers and also for Japanese corporate subsidiaries located overseas provided that the issue was made on the strength of the subsidiary's name and did not involve the issue of a parental guarantee. Restrictions also prevented them from selling euroyen bonds directly into Japan within 90 days of the issue date.

The traffic was not all one way, however. For example, in October 1986 the MOF gave permission for the banks' overseas securities subsidiaries to deal in commercial paper issued overseas – this is denied to the Japanese banks' overseas branches – and in January 1989 the Industrial Bank of Japan, with the agreement of the MOF, became the first Japanese bank to engage in equity market-making overseas (hitherto it had confined its overseas activities to debt and equity warrant activities but the new plans involved making markets in ten leading Japanese stocks), although it was prohibited from dealing with Japanese clients from its London operation.

Apart from London, merchant bank activities also proved popular in Switzerland, West Germany (both 'universal banking' centres) and the US, with the last-mentioned also proving a popular site for the establishment of mergers and acquisitions boutiques.[37] These US activities followed on from the acquisition of primary dealerships[38] and the setting up of trust companies, brokerage subsidiaries[39] and leasing operations[40] in the late 1980s.

In the UK, while the underwriting of new eurobond issues and the selling and trading of eurobonds remain their core business, some of the longer-established firms offer a fuller range of services, including investment management, loan syndication, market-making (for example, in equity warrants, Japanese equities, Ecu Treasury bills[41]), swaps and mergers and acquisitions business. And, aided by the MOF's easing of the restrictions on Japanese corporations issuing euroyen commercial paper in the mid-1980s, many of the subsidiaries are now also active in these markets in addition to dealing in the sterling commercial paper market.[42] Finally, it is worth noting that a Japanese regional bank, the Bank of Yokohama, secured entry into the UK merchant banking industry through a successful bid for Guinness Mahon in 1989.

The regulation of overseas financial companies' operations in Japan

Overseas banks' securities operations in Japan
The establishment of foreign-owned securities companies in Japan is governed by two securities laws: the Law on Foreign Securities Firms of 1971 and the Securities and Exchange Law. The former law was designed to administer the entry and regulation of foreign securities firms although it relates primarily to the establishment of a *branch*, which requires a MOF licence. The establishment of a *representative office*, which is not allowed to conduct business, requires prior notification being given to the MOF; while a firm contemplating the setting up of a *subsidiary* has to comply with the provisions of the Securities and Exchange Law.[43]

The acquisition or takeover of a Japanese securities firm is regulated by Japanese antimonopoly law, and approval from the Japan Fair Trade Commission has to be secured for all holdings in excess of 5 per cent of the outstanding equity.

Table 9.4   *Foreign securities companies' operations in Japan at 31 December 1988*

Date of branch opening	Company	Membership of TSE
July 1972	Merrill Lynch	•
December 1978	Merrill Lynch – Osaka	
November 1985	Merrill Lynch – Nagoya	
March 1988	Merrill Lynch – Yokohama	•
October 1978	Citicorp Vickers	•
January 1980	Prudential Bache	•
June 1980	Smith Barney	
May 1981	Jardine Fleming	•
September 1982	Salomon Brothers	•
June 1983	Kidder Peabody	•
September 1987	Kidder Peabody – Osaka	•
November 1983	Goldman Sachs	•
June 1984	Morgan Stanley	•
January 1985	S.G. Warburg	•
March 1985	W.I. Carr	•
July 1985	First Boston	
December 1985	Drexel Burnham	
December 1985	Kleinwort Benson	•
March 1986	Schroder	•
April 1986	Hoare Govett	•
April 1986	Pain Webber	•
May 1986	DB Capital Markets (Deutsche Bank)	•
May 1986	Shearson Lehman	•
June 1986	Cazenove	•
September 1986	Baring	•
October 1986	Dresdner ABD Securities (Dresdner Bank)	
October 1986	SBCI (Swiss Bank Corporation)	
October 1986	County Natwest	
December 1986	DG Securities (DG Bank)	
February 1987	SoGen Securities (Société Générale)	
February 1987	UBS Phillips and Drew	
April 1987	Morgan Grenfell	
June 1987	James Capel	
June 1987	Commerz Securities (Commerzbank)	
June 1987	Amro (Amsterdam–Rotterdam Bank)	
June 1987	WESTLB Securities (Westdeutsche Landesbank)	
June 1987	Paribas Capital Markets (Banque Paribas)	
June 1987	Chase Manhattan Securities	
June 1987	Midland Montagu	
September 1987	Barclays de Zoete Wedd	
October 1987	BT Asia (Bankers Trust)	
October 1987	BV Capital Markets (Bayerische Vereinsbank)	
November 1987	JP Morgan (Morgan Guaranty Trust)	
December 1987	Credit Lyonnais Finanz	
December 1987	Manufacturers Hanover Asia	
February 1988	BHF Securities (Berliner Handels und Frankfurter Bank)	
February 1988	Chemical Securities (Chemical Bank)	
April 1988	Smith New Court	
June 1988	BNP Securities (Banque Nationale de Paris)	

Note: All branches are established in Tokyo unless otherwise indicated. Each firm is listed in order of its first branch opening in Japan, thereafter each branch of a given firm is listed in date order.

Source: Trenchard, 1990, p. 119.

As for supervision, the companies fall within the purview of the securities bureau of the MOF and most hold all four securities business licences: the licence to underwrite security issues; the licence to distribute securities; the licence to deal in securities as a principal; and the licence to deal in securities as an agent.

The first foreign banks to be allowed to establish securities subsidiaries in Japan were Deutsche Bank and Security Pacific National Bank. They both received the green light in December 1985. Prior to this date, foreign banks' securities affiliates had been refused permission by the MOF to establish offices or branches in Japan on the grounds that banking and securities business was legally separated in Japan. Following pressure from those countries entertaining Japanese banks engaged in securities activities, notably West Germany, the MOF eventually relented and decided that bank affiliates in which the parent bank holding did not exceed 50 per cent could conduct securities business in Japan. The reasoning behind this approach was that a legally independent entity could not be held to be in breach of Article 65 of the Securities and Exchange Law. Other foreign banks soon followed in the footsteps of the Deutsche Bank and the Security Pacific National Bank (see Table 9.4) and one was even allowed to enter in its own name and not through the restricted equity holding route. By the end of 1986, twelve US investment banks had licences to operate securities branches in Japan together with a number of British and European commercial banks.

Another source of contention for overseas firms and governments was access to the Tokyo Stock Exchange. Although numerous securities broking licences had been awarded to foreign-owned companies prior to 1986, this involved the overseas companies in the payment of 27 per cent of the commission received on the buying and selling of shares to member Japanese securities companies. Not unnaturally, and especially in the light of the asymmetry in the national treatment of foreign securities companies, foreign companies, often backed by their governments,[44] campaigned vociferously for easier access to the Tokyo Stock Exchange. The Japanese authorities eventually relented and in 1986 foreign firms were admitted for the first time.[45] Foreign membership has been expanded at periodic intervals since then, with further admissions occurring in 1988 and 1990.[46]

In addition to securities broking and dealing,[47] foreign firms (including banks) have successfully entered the following markets in Japan: trust banking (since 1985);[48] government bond auctions;[49] funds management;[50] and investment advisory services.

Overseas securities firms' banking operations in Japan
Apart from engaging in much the same range of securities operations in Japan as do the overseas banks (for example, securities underwriting, trading

and broking, investment management and advisory services), foreign securities firms may also engage in banking operations. The precedent was created in January 1991 when the MOF granted the European-based banking subsidiaries of three US-based securities houses – Morgan Stanley, Salomon Brothers and Goldman Sachs – preliminary licences to open branches in Japan to offer banking services. The foreign securities houses, however, are limited to a 50 per cent stake in their banking units. The banking services planned comprise mainly foreign exchange dealing and currency and interest rate swaps.

Summary
Despite a fairly extensive legislative framework, the separation of banking and securities business in Japan is far from complete. This is due partly to the exemptions and exclusions from the legal prohibitions on the joint offering of banking and securities services, partly to the administrative decisions made by the MOF[51] and partly to the natural evolution of the financial market place, which has witnessed a general fusion of banking and securities business, as in many parts of the globe. Like their US counterparts, the Japanese authorities tolerate, while not actively encouraging, their securities firms[52] and commercial banks to diversify into a wide range of banking and securities activities respectively overseas. Their treatment of foreign companies – be they banks or securities firms – in Japan diminishes the case for continued strict separation of banking and securities business for domestic concerns in Japan.[53]

As in the US, commercial banks can and do actively participate in many securities activities[54] but, as is demonstrated below, much the same range of pressures that have arisen in the US are relevant to the reform debate in Japan. The quest is on for the optimal (that is, most cost-effective) reform package.

THE US AND JAPANESE APPROACHES COMPARED

Given the American influence in the drafting of much of the legislation that separates banking and securities business in Japan after the Second World War[55] (that is the Securities and Exchange Law) one would expect to find a high degree of similarity in the legislative frameworks applying in the two countries. This appears in the common prohibitions on securities firms engaging in deposit-taking, effected through section 21 of the Glass–Steagall Act in the US[56] and Article 3 of the 1981 Banking Law in Japan, and on banks' *direct* involvement in many kinds of non-public bond business, such as the underwriting of corporate bonds and equities. Apart from this, however, the differences are more marked than the similarities. For example, although in both countries commercial banks are allowed to deal in and underwrite a variety of forms of public bond,[57] the buying and selling of other types of security for their own account is prohibited for US commercial banks but not for their Japanese counterparts. On the other hand, while US commercial banks are not prohibited from engaging in securities brokerage their Japanese counterparts are.[58] As for their *indirect* involvement in securities activities, the range of permissible activities and the terms and conditions on which they can be undertaken differ quite markedly in the two countries.

As far as the commercial banks' *overseas* operations are concerned, neither countries' banks are subject to the general prohibitions on the joint offering of banking and securities services, although the exact nature and regulation of securities activities undertaken abroad once again differ for the two sets of banks. Similarly, different regulatory approaches, although subject to the same external pressures arising from demands for reciprocity and a rapid globalization and integration of banking and capital markets, ensure that differing degrees of separation of banking from securities business are effected in respect of the activities of foreign financial companies in Japan and the US. While competitive and other external pressures will serve to narrow these differences, it is far from clear that even far-reaching reform (see below) in both countries will secure total convergence. In part, this reflects the different philosophical approaches adopted towards such regulatory matters. The Japanese, for example, are as much concerned with the strengthening of their capital market and support of their securities companies as with the prevention of conflicts of interest, the achievement of competitive equity and the stabilization of the banking system (FBAJ, 1989, p. 16; Suzuki, 1986, p. 40; Fundamental Research Committee of the Securities and Exchange Council, 1990, p. 33), involving differences in the allocation of priorities to regulatory objectives.[59]

In summary, the conclusion is that marked differences exist today in Japan and the US in the extent to which banking and securities business is separated, *de jure* and *de facto*. It only remains now to see how this position might be changed in the future.

FUTURE REFORM

The case for reform

In attempting to establish a case for reform of the legislative framework surrounding commercial banks' involvement in securities business, a convenient starting point is a reassessment of the original rationale for the establishment of the relevant primary legislation in the two countries. Of particular interest, given America's influence in the drafting of both sets of legislative provisions, is the Glass–Steagall Act and Article 65 of the Securities and Exchange Law of the US and Japan respectively.

In respect of the Glass–Steagall Act, a thorough review has already been conducted by Benston (1990). He identifies seven[60] reasons which have been or might possibly be advanced for continuing with the separation of commercial and investment banking effected under the Glass–Steagall Act of 1933:

(i)   to help protect customers from conflict of interest abuse (for example, from receiving biased investment advice);

(ii)   to reduce individual bank risk;

(iii)   to remove the temptation for banks to make loans to support the price of securities held (or underwritten) directly or by affiliates;

(iv)   to help stabilize the banking system (that is, to reduce systemic risk through routes (ii) and (iii));

(v)   to reduce taxpayer exposure and to prevent the misallocation of resources which intervention might entail (a requirement to limit banks' engagement in riskier activities is deemed necessary because of their access to the so-called federal safety net through discount window borrowing and deposit insurance arrangements, implicit guarantees and so on);

(vi)   to ensure that competitive equity prevails between the banks on the one hand and securities brokers and underwriters on the other (again, this is held to warrant the limiting of banks to traditional commercial banking operations because of their privileged access to the federal safety act which, it is alleged, provides access to cheap deposits which can be used for cross-subsidization); and

(vii)   to avoid an excessive concentration of power and reduction in competition which abolition of the existing restrictions might eventually lead to.

Each of these arguments, however, can be challenged.

(i)   On the issue of the need to shield consumers from conflict of interest abuse, it should be noted that there may be alternative and more cost-effective means available than the option of outright prohibition on the undertaking of certain activities (Hall, 1987), assuming of course that the maintenance of a good reputation is an insufficient incentive for the institutions to refrain from taking advantage of their customers.

(ii)   On the subject of risk, it is not intuitively obvious that securities activities are inherently more risky than traditional, or even more modern, commercial banking activities (for example, operations in the swaps, options and futures markets). Even if they were shown to be so, their returns might still justify investment in them.[61] Secondly, whatever the riskiness of individual activities, it should be remembered that, in principle, diversification into such areas may offer the prospect of a reduction of overall portfolio risk, where this is measured as the variability in portfolio returns (Jensen, 1972).[62]

(iii)   The problem of banks being tempted to support security prices can be dealt with adequately in differing ways. For example, the appropriate use of firewalls (such as the Federal Reserve Board's rules 23A and 23B),[63] codes of conduct, monitoring and sanctions for breaches of the rules and regulations should reduce the temptation and the associated potential risks for both the banks and the wider system.

(iv)   With regard to preserving the stability of the banking system, it can be argued that stability is best promoted by allowing commercial banks the widest possible freedoms in the longer term, subject to necessary checks and safeguards to protect consumers from possible conflict of interest and other abuse, to ensure the prudent operation of the business,[64] and to prevent abuse arising from excessive concentration of economic and political power (see below).

(v)   In respect of the need to contain taxpayer exposure and reduce the chances of resources being misallocated through official intervention, there is no *a priori* reason why allowing banks to engage in a wider range of securities activities should lead to adverse results on either front.[65] This is because such diversification need neither result in an increase in risk nor in an institution's propensity to take risk. Indeed, if diversification did lead to a reduction in risk, the impact in the two areas of concern would actually be positive. Moreover, the regulatory authorities could always take restraining measures (such as through manipulation of the risk-based solvency requirements – see Hall, 1989) should they wish to deter certain kinds of activity.

(vi)   On the thorny subject of competitive equity, it is not clear that provision of a federal safety net confers a competitive advantage on commercial banks. For example, costs, both explicit and implicit, are borne by those covered by the safety net in the form of: insurance premiums (albeit mispriced);[66] examinations; supervision; regulations; reporting requirements; fees; interest-free loans (that is, required reserves) to the Federal Reserve; and the lodging of security against discount window lending. It should also be appreciated that there probably already exists (implicitly if not explicitly: actions taken in the wake of the stock market crash of October 1987 point to the latter) a federal safety net for securities firms, which is almost certainly underpriced, to the benefit of such firms.

(vii)   Finally, on the subjects of concentration and competition, the existing concentration in the securities underwriting industry might lead one to support reduction of the barriers to entry imposed on commercial banks. But even if the worst fears of the anti-reform lobby are realized and, perhaps because of their competitive advantages (federally-derived or otherwise) and the existence of potentially large and unexploited economies of scale and scope, 'universal banks' come to dominate the financial arena, remedies remain for dealing with any undesirable consequences. For example, the risk of failure could be reduced through expeditious use of risk-based capital requirements and other supervisory techniques, and 'appropriate' resolution policies;[67] antitrust laws can be used to deal with the problems arising from the concentration of power; and the existing array of legal and market remedies, such as Chinese Walls,[68] for handling conflicts of interest, backed up if necessary by more intensive monitoring and stiffer penalties for abuse, can be employed to deal with the likely increase in conflict of interest situations that banks would face.

In short, little of the original rationale for enforcing the separation of commercial and investment banking stands up to scrutiny, and any legitimate fears that remain can be adequately dealt with through alternative and more cost-effective means. Bearing this in mind, the growing clamour for change, arising from considerations of efficiency and the domestic and international competitiveness, soundness and stability of US commercial banks, amongst others (see below),[69] is likely to prove irresistible. But what form should the reform take and what is the likely outcome of present deliberations on the subject? These issues will be addressed in the next section.

Turning to the reform debate in Japan, the defenders of the status quo stress their concerns about the proliferation of conflicts of interest that reform would induce, the imbalances in competitive conditions[70] that might favour banks with expanded powers, with concomitant implications for concentration and competitiveness in the financial sector, and the possible damage that reform might do to the stability of the banking sector.

As we have just seen, these concerns feature also in the US debating arena, and each can be allayed in the manner described above. This is not to be dismissive of deeply felt fears, but rather to point out the superiority of alternative approaches, which would continue to embrace both market and legal deterrents to fraud and malpractice, so necessary to instilling public confidence in the integrity of the capital market, but dispense with the outright prohibition on the undertaking of certain business activities.

Apart from the weakness of the traditional case for continuing with the enforced separation of securities and banking business, yet further pressures for reform have emerged in both countries. These embrace, *inter alia*: the banks' desire to meet changing client requirements as the distinction between banking and securities business becomes increasingly blurred and technological advances in communications and computing systems dramatically increase the range of possible business options; the desire of banks (and regulators, for stability reasons) to be given access to new sources of revenue because of the impact of competition, deregulation and securitization on their traditional lending margins;[71] the authorities' wish[72] to deal with the competitive and regulatory anomalies which have emerged because of the differential treatment of foreign and domestic financial institutions' activities in the home market and of domestic institutions' home and overseas activities;[73] and the regulators' need to respond to underlying structural changes in their domestic markets as a result of structural changes in their economies. Above all, governments are keen to improve the efficient functioning of financial institutions and markets,[74] the former being aided by allowing institutions to reap economies of scope and by enhancing their risk-management capacity (for example, by allowing for further diversification and access to additional hedging mediums), and the latter benefiting from promotion of competition and financial innovation.

In the light of this apparently overwhelming case for reform it only remains to determine the optimal course of action in each country.

The options for reform in the US[75]

Continuing piecemeal reform within the confines of the Glass–Steagall Act

The role of the Federal Reserve Board   Although the Federal Reserve Board has certainly been the main driving force behind the gradual fusion of investment and commercial banking in recent years, it is somewhat harsh to characterize its actions as usurping the legislative role of Congress, as the Securities Industry Association (SIA) has done. This is because of the relatively tough line taken on the erection of firewalls,[76] in spite of the Chairman's concern that unnecessarily rigid arrangements may prevent the desired economic benefits from materializing, and the Board's stated opposition to piecemeal reform which is viewed as artificially distorting capital markets. Moreover, the Board has sponsored the organizational (holding company) structure recommended for adoption under the Financial Modernization Bill of 1987 which, unfortunately, failed to be enacted owing to opposition in the House of Representatives.

This Bill was introduced by Senators Proxmire and Garn in November 1987 in an attempt to reduce the high level of concentration of economic power in the underwriting industry and abolish the loopholes and exceptions contained in the securities law. The Bill sought the repeal of the key sections (20 and 32) of the Glass–Steagall Act which restricted affiliations between banks and securities firms, while retaining the prohibition on the joint operation of a deposit-taking business and an investment banking business (section 21). Accordingly, banks and securities firms would have been allowed to be affiliated through the common ownership of a bank holding company, though banks would not have been allowed to engage directly in securities activities nor would securities firms have been allowed to engage directly in banking activities. The securities affiliates of the banks would have had to have been separately capitalized.

In order to ensure the stability of the overall system, a number of safeguards were suggested to limit the potential for the securities affiliate to infect its sister bank and to remove the necessity for the safety net to be extended beyond the deposit-taking sector. Yet further safeguards, or firewalls, were suggested to limit the potential for abuse arising from the conflicts of interest created and to ensure competitive equity *vis-à-vis* non-bank-affiliated securities firms. The firewalls proposed meant that: loans to or on behalf of a bank's securities affiliate would have been prohibited; a bank would not have been able to make a loan to finance the purchase of securities underwritten by its affiliate; securities affiliates that manage underwriting syndicates would have been prohibited from selling securities to their affiliated banks during the underwriting period and for 30 days thereafter; loans to companies for the purpose of paying the principal or interest on securities underwritten by securities affiliates would have been prohibited; staff interlocks between the bank and its securities affiliates would have been prohibited; the exchange of confidential information between the bank and its securities affiliate would have been prohibited unless the customer's consent had been given; and securities affiliates would have been obliged to disclose to their customers that their obligations were in no way backed by their affiliate banks nor insured by the federal government.

It was also recommended that the securities affiliates be regulated by the SEC and that their assets and liabilities should *not* be consolidated with their bank holding companies for the purpose of Federal Reserve Board regulation.

The Bill was redrafted in March 1988 to give the banks the power to underwrite any type of security, except corporate equities, within six months of enactment, with Congress being mandated to decide by 1 April 1991 whether the underwriting of equities should also be allowed. And to prevent the formation of oligopolies, the previously recommended prohibition on affiliations between major banks and securities houses (that is, those with assets of more than $30 billion and $15 billion respectively) was retained. In the event, however, despite gaining the support of the Senate Banking Committee, the Bill failed to gain House of Representatives backing.

Views on the extension of bank powers through section 20 affiliates   The likelihood of reform continuing through this route will depend, *inter alia*, upon how well the system is perceived to be operating. For this reason, a review of the regulators' and banking and securities industries' views on the subject is in order.

(a)   *Views of the General Accounting Office (GAO)*   The most extensive review of the subject was conducted by the General Accounting Office of Congress, which published a report in March 1990 (US General Accounting Office, 1990). This document incorporates not only the GAO's own views but also those of the regulators and officials from the industries affected, and so provides a convenient starting point.

Given the short period of time in which section 20 affiliates had been operating prior to the GAO's investigation, their main conclusion is hardly surprising, namely, that it is 'too early to draw conclusions about Section 20 firms' impact on the market, their profitability, their riskiness or the adequacy of the regulatory system within which they operate'. Nevertheless, their rigorous analysis of these issues does provide pointers to the likely future evolution of the regulatory structure surrounding the joint offering of banking and securities-related services.

As to the appropriateness of the section 20 reform route as the means of expanding bank powers, the GAO derives comfort from the fact that the controls enforced, such as separate corporate identity and regulation by the SEC,[77] and the phased nature of expansion are all consistent with its earlier published views (US General Accounting Office, 1988) on the long-term solution to the linkage of banking and securities activities. Some of the finer details of the arrangements, however, were subjected to closer scrutiny.

On the subject of risk, the GAO noted that 'regulatory officials have found no evidence that any section 20 firm has damaged the financial condition of a bank or bank holding company'. Nevertheless, the GAO argues, it is too early to provide a definitive answer as to whether or not risk has actually been increased as a result of the activities of section 20 subsidiaries.

In principle, of course, the sanctioning of new securities activities for banks provides them with the means to further diversify away risk. Moreover, the risks of cross contamination are reduced by the Federal Reserve

Board's restrictions/limitations on the scope and pace of development for the new activities and on ties between section 20 firms and their affiliates. Capital requirements, the assessment of management capabilities and systems, and monitoring all serve to further reduce risks. Nevertheless, as the GAO points out, some of the arrangements may serve to actually increase rather than reduce risk. For example, some bank holding companies argued that the regulatory structure hampered their ability to manage their overall exposure to a single customer or market segment and thus the risks associated with such exposures. Moreover, some of the individual firewalls may serve to increase risk. An example of this is the absolute prohibition on a bank making loans to its section 20 affiliate if the affiliate is authorized to deal in corporate debt and equity, a requirement which could weaken the overall structure of a banking organization during a liquidity crisis. The GAO acknowledges this risk and accordingly would prefer to see banks allowed to lend to their securities affiliates, albeit only on an arm's length basis. Finally, the (severe?) revenue limitation may induce holding companies to transfer bank eligible securities business (that is that *not* prohibited by the Glass–Steagall Act) from both their bank and non-bank subsidiaries into their section 20 firms to make the latter's operations viable. Such transfers would adversely affect the affiliated banks as their profitability (assuming the bank-eligible activities were profitable) and capital positions would deteriorate.

In considering the need for possible further changes in the arrangements governing the operations of section 20 subsidiaries, the GAO advised focusing on seven main areas: (i) the international perspective; (ii) organizational structure; (iii) the appropriateness of the firewalls and other limitations; (iv) the associated regulatory burden; (v) consumer protection; (vi) competitive equity; and (vii) reciprocity of treatment for securities firms.

In its comments on the international perspective, the GAO noted that the firewalls applied to Section 20 firms were not applied to the overseas operations of US bank subsidiaries or bank holding company subsidiaries.[78] While accepting that this enhanced the latter groups' international competitiveness, they questioned the logic, from a stability viewpoint, of operating such a dual control system which provided incentives for US banking organizations to shift business to foreign markets. Moreover, the retention of such controls on banks' domestic operations risks imparting a competitive advantage to foreign banking organizations, which can more readily undertake a full range of securities activities in the US (through direct subsidiaries, since 1990) and elsewhere because of their greater flexibility.[79]

With respect to organizational structure, the GAO makes it clear that it is not wedded to any particular structure but that it would like the following features to be preserved in any future arrangements: separate corporate identity for the firm engaging in the bank-ineligible activities; regulation of the banking and securities affiliates by a federal bank regulator and the SEC respectively; and regulation by the Federal Reserve of the financial holding companies that own the bank and securities affiliates.

Its concerns with the present structure relate chiefly to doubts about the likely degree of strengthening that the establishment of a section 20 firm will bring to insured depository institutions within a holding company structure. For example, as noted earlier, the viability of the section 20 firms may be dependent upon the transfer of profitable activities[80] out of the affiliated banks to provide a base of eligible revenue for the section 20 subsidiaries. Such transfers would cause the affiliated banks to become smaller, less diversified and possibly less profitable. Moreover, alternative structural arrangements would ensure that affiliated banks *automatically* benefited directly from the profitable operation of a section 20 subsidiary.[81] Finally, the GAO calls for clarification of the conditions under which a bank holding company can be required, under the Federal Reserve's Regulation Y, to use non-banking resources to support bank subsidiaries.[82] This, it is argued, would enable a clearer perspective to be drawn on how firewalls and Regulation Y work together in practice in strengthening banks affiliated with section 20 firms.

On the appropriateness of the firewall requirements, the GAO asserts that the purpose of individual firewalls is not always clear. For example, the prohibition on a bank issuing a letter of credit to support commercial paper underwritten by its section 20 affiliate implies that bank officials, in the absence of firewalls, cannot be trusted to make sensible pricing decisions. It is not intuitively obvious why this should be the case despite the Federal Reserve Bank's argument that the desire for fee income might otherwise lead to mispricing of the letter of credit by the bank affiliate. Additionally, as the American Bankers Association (ABA) points out, the prohibition precluding a bank or any subsidiary from supplying any form of credit enhancement for the ineligible securities to be underwritten by the section 20 firm is 'uneconomical and creates market inefficiencies and negative public perceptions' (Boren, 1990).

As for the appropriateness of the 10 per cent of gross revenue limitation, it is difficult to perceive of the chosen figure as anything other than an arbitrary interpretation of the 'engaged principally' provision of section 20 of the Glass–Steagall Act. Higher figures, perhaps anything up to 49.99 per cent, might serve equally well. Moreover, there is scope for further analysis of alternatives to the limitation on gross revenues for the ineligible earnings of section 20 firms.

The need to minimize the regulatory burden to be borne by subject institutions and indeed the economy is widely acknowledged but views differ markedly as to how this is to be achieved. Ideally, a more explicit cost-benefit style of analysis is required for each firewall and limitation implemented. Both the ABA and the Bank Capital Markets Association (BCMA) argued in their submissions to the GAO (US General Accounting Office, 1990, Appendices XII and XIII) that, taken together, the firewall requirements represented regulatory overkill. Indeed, in its testimony to Congress in 1990 (Boren, 1990), the ABA went so far as to ascribe the reason for most firms not embracing the freedoms allowed under the Federal Reserve Board's ruling of January 1989 (but, rather, operating under the – slightly? – less restrictive requirements of the April 1987 ruling) as the punitive set of 28 firewalls that would have to be accommodated. Collectively, the firewalls (and revenue limitation) are argued to have stifled business at birth, reduced benefits to customers (for example, through the restrictions placed on cross-marketing) and increased operating costs (see below). Further, it is argued, the concomitant increase in compliance costs could have been substantially reduced, with little adverse effects on risks,[83] if more reliance had been placed on the enforcement of basic banking and securities law and market safeguards. While acknowledging the increased regulatory burden borne by the banking organizations, the GAO, however, did not wholeheartedly agree that pre-section 20 safeguards were sufficient to ensure either that the new risks would be contained or that consumers would be adequately protected from the possible abuse of conflict of interest situations (see US General Accounting Office, 1989, for the reasons behind this reticence). In their words:

> When bank holding companies can demonstrate adequate capital, effective internal controls, and ability to manage new powers in a responsible manner, consideration can be given to reducing regulatory burden by relaxing some of the firewalls in light of the other regulatory controls that are in place and provided that efficient regulatory resources are available. (US General Accounting Office, 1990)

While conceding that the regulatory burden of its section 20 requirements may be onerous, the Federal Reserve Board justifies it by pointing to the benefits, in terms of stability, elimination of abuse and distancing of the federal safety net from securities subsidiaries, that have accrued. Moreover, it points out that it has already modified some of the firewall requirements imposed under the April 1987 ruling (US General Accounting Office, 1990, pp. 97–9) and in the light of experience will consider further modification once the section 20 firms have gained additional operating experience. The cost-effectiveness of regulation is thus very much a concern of the Board, although it is not willing to sacrifice the perceived benefits outlined earlier for a lowering of associated operating costs for subject institutions.

Consumer protection concerns are, of course, closely associated with the structure and substance of the firewall provisions. While banking industry lobbyists argue that additional protection is largely unnecessary, as noted earlier, sufficient doubt remains to justify the retention of at least some, if not the majority of, the current firewalls (notwithstanding the earlier comments that a few may increase rather than reduce risk for an affiliated bank or holding company). Although appropriate disclosure might go some way to obviating the need for retention of some of the prohibitions (it would necessitate more detailed monitoring if it was to prove effective, however), it is probably the case that the majority would still prove necessary if the Board's legitimate concerns are to be met. Nevertheless, some room for negotiation undoubtedly exists.[84]

The need to ensure competitive equity in regulation is equally complex. While bank officials assert that section 20 firms operate at a cost disadvantage relative to non-bank affiliated firms because of the capital requirements and firewalls they have to endure, securities firms claim that association with banks gives section 20 firms a cost advantage by virtue of their perceived proximity to the federal safety net. Although the Federal Reserve Board does not endorse the latter claim and, moreover, points to the other regulatory costs incurred by banking organizations, nevertheless, it is keen that regulatory arrangements for section 20 companies do indeed distance these companies from the federal safety net. Accordingly, it is far from clear whether present arrangements aspire to the principle of competitive neutrality or not.

Finally, in calling for reciprocal treatment of securities firms, the GAO is again focusing upon the competitive equity issue. It duly notes that comparable opportunities are not currently provided to domestic securities firms *vis-à-vis* diversification into domestic banking which, *ceteris paribus*, confers a competitive advantage on banking organizations able to reap the associated economies of scope.[85] But in practice the *ceteris paribus* requirement is, of course, violated. For example, banks are not permitted to give favourable treatment to an affiliate in issuing or pricing a letter of credit under section 23B of the Federal Reserve Act, a prohibition that reduces a bank's potential competitive advantage. Further, securities firms may derive comparative advantages over section 20 firms and their bank holding companies by virtue of: (i) the sanctioning of their affiliation with activities, such as insurance, which cannot generally be undertaken within bank holding company structures; (ii) their affiliation with non-bank banks which were authorized prior to the Competitive Equality Banking Act of 1987 (see note 8); (iii) their affiliation with overseas banks, which may increase their relative degree of flexibility in combining banking and securities business in both national and international markets; (iv) their parent holding companies not being subject to the same degree of regulation as bank holding companies, which fall under the jurisdiction of the Federal Reserve Board.

As is evident from the above discussion, the issues of reciprocity for securities firms and competitive equity are far from resolved. Suffice it to say, the Federal Reserve Board is keenly aware of and sensitive to such matters, although its regulatory objectives of safety and soundness and desire to eliminate abuses arising from the exploitation of conflicts of interest are likely to remain paramount.

(b)   *Views of the American Bankers Association (ABA)*   The ABA's case for extended powers for banks was succinctly stated in 1986:

> Without change, commercial banks will continue to lose market share and profitability as ever more banking functions are performed outside the traditional banking system. This, in turn, will significantly undermine the ability of present laws and regulations to ensure the stability of the financial system or the overall economy.   (ABA, 1986)

Recent developments, namely the sanctioning of securities operations for section 20 companies, certainly represent a step in the right direction as far as the ABA is concerned, but wrangles on detail persist. As noted earlier, the alleged benefits of certain firewalls have been contested and the cost-effectiveness of the regulatory framework questioned. While there is no need to rehearse the arguments here, it is illuminating to focus upon some of the features of the current arrangements which, it is argued, contribute most to increased operating costs for the banks and/or their holding companies. First, the prohibition on interlocking staff increases costs by duplicating staff functions and associated support systems thereby, incidentally, hampering the effective management of risks on a holding company-wide basis (Boren, 1990). Secondly, the requirement that unsecured extensions of credit between the parent or any of its non-bank subsidiaries and the section 20 affiliate be deducted from the parent's capital is deemed both costly (relative to the arrangements pertaining to their securities firm competitors) and unnecessary (Boren, 1990). Likewise, the prohibition against affiliated banks providing clearing services for their section 20 affiliates with respect to securities other than government securities is alleged to be both costly and unnecessary. Finally, the ABA criticizes the revenue limitation as being too severe, arguing that, even with the doubling of the limit to 10 per cent of gross revenue, their securities affiliates are often forced to make artificial business decisions. A higher limit, it is alleged, would allow banks' securities subsidiaries to better serve the capital-raising needs of local industry and result in a lowering of costs for capital issuers because of the concomitant increase in competition in the underwriting industry (Boren, 1990).

(c) *Views of the Securities Industry Association (SIA)*   As the trade association for the securities industry the SIA is not unexpectedly lukewarm, to say the least, about the Federal Reserve Board's promotion of the banks' interests through the section 20 route. Nevertheless, and in contrast with its earlier strategy of contesting in the courts every relaxation of the legislative barriers to the fusion of banking and securities services, the SIA has given grudging approval to some at least of the components of the reform initiated by the Board (although still not accepting that such an extension of bank powers is necessarily desirable in its own right). In particular, the SIA agrees that the new securities services should only be offered by wholly owned securities subsidiaries of banks or their holding companies and not direct (as the office of the Comptroller of the Currency has canvassed) by the bank subsidiaries themselves. Such a development, it is argued, might expose a bank's capital to greater risk of loss than the current arrangements (a point on which the GAO concurs – US General Accounting Office, 1990) and, moreover, would distort competitiveness by raising the public's expectations that the federal safety net would be widened to embrace such activities should they turn sour.

Setting aside the SIA's strong reaction to the Board's decision of September 1990 to allow the underwriting of corporate equities through section 20 affiliates, their remaining concerns relate to the adequacy of the firewall requirements to contain risk and prevent abuse and to continuing doubts about the isolation of the section 20 companies from the federal safety net.

On the former issue the SIA is unequivocal: the firewalls are inadequate. To preserve the integrity of the capital markets a flat prohibition on all tandem underwriting and placement activities and the providing of credit facilities by the bank and the section 20 affiliate is called for, and the SIA favours granting section 20 status only to commercial banking organizations which agree to move all their securities activities into their section 20 affiliates (Lackritz, 1990).

In a similar vein, it is argued that the current firewalls 'will prove inadequate "picket fences" for safeguarding against undue risks to the Federal deposit insurance system. Only structural changes enacted by Congress will serve to protect the federal deposit insurance fund, while allowing commercial banking organizations the synergies they seek in combining commercial and investment banking activities' (Lackritz, 1990). Whatever the chief concern of the SIA – the protection of the federal deposit insurance funds or the elimination of any possible competitive advantage for the banks deriving from the perceived proximity of their securities operations to the federal safety net – their message is again unequivocal: the firewall requirements are not stringent enough.

Finally, it should also be noted that the securities industry is fearful that the Board's current revenue limitation may permit bank holding companies to expand rapidly through the acquisition of existing securities firms. Whether or not banks choose this option remains to be seen.

In an endeavour to advance the debate about the most appropriate means for fusing banking and securities business in the US the SIA has put forward its own proposals for consideration. These, it is claimed, would allow banks to engage in the full spectrum of securities and securities-related activities within a holding company framework whilst providing the necessary safeguards for the federal deposit insurance funds and hence the taxpayer. They are also designed to maintain and promote a solvent and sound financial system and protect the investor from undue risk, while ensuring fair competition in the securities industry and international competitiveness for domestic firms.

The cornerstones of the plan are as follows (for a more detailed outline, see Lackritz, 1990, Appendix B):

(i)   require that a commercial banking organization carry on wholesale securities and securities-related activities outside of its federally insured units;

(ii)   permit a commercial banking organization to form an uninsured (or privately insured) financing company (an Investment Bank Finance Company – IBFC) which can accept wholesale deposits and make commercial loans;

(iii)   permit an IBFC to own securities subsidiaries in which all of the commercial banking organization's domestic and foreign wholesale securities activities and securities-related activities are conducted;

(iv)   permit full interaction between such securities subsidiaries and the IBFC;

(v)   institute specific 'no contact' rules prohibiting interaction between the commercial banking organization's federally insured banks and its IBFC/securities subsidiaries group;

(vi)   grant the IBFC/securities subsidiaries group of the bank holding company *and* broker-dealers not affiliated with a commercial federally insured bank direct access to the large dollar payments systems and, in times of generalized liquidity crisis, to the Federal Reserve window at a premium on a fully collateralized basis;

(vii)   require that the securities subsidiaries of a bank holding company's IBFC be regulated by the SEC and otherwise as if they were not affiliated with a commercial bank;

(viii) permit federally insured units of commercial banking organizations to own retail securities brokerages to carry on consumer securities activities on an agency basis and permit securities firms to own consumer banks.

(d)   *Views of the regulators*   The verdict of the *Federal Reserve Board* on developments to date with section 20 affiliates has already been covered in some depth in this chapter. Suffice it to say, the Board believes that commercial banks should be allowed to conduct a wider range of securities activities in order to strengthen their balance sheets[86] through an enhancement of their competitiveness,[87] and that the regulatory arrangements surrounding the activities of the section 20 affiliates are serving their purpose in insulating affiliated banks and holding companies from the operations of their section 20 subsidiaries, in distancing the federal safety net from their operations, in ensuring safety and stability, and in preventing conflict of interest abuses. The need for further modifications to the firewall arrangements will be considered in the light of developments and experience with the section 20 firms.

The *Office of the Comptroller of the Currency* (OCC) also favours reform of Glass–Steagall but, as noted earlier, canvasses the idea of abandoning the requirement that ineligible securities activities should only take place within a securities subsidiary of a bank holding company in favour of allowing direct subsidiaries of federally insured banks to offer the new securities services to the public (US General Accounting Office, 1990, Appendix X). As stressed in their testimony before the Senate Banking Committee in 1988, however, what they believe really matters is corporate separateness; subject to this, banks should be allowed to choose from among several structural forms of operation. Further, the OCC argues that more reliance might be placed on existing rather than new safeguards in order to minimize the compliance burden borne by the industry and the economy, and that alternative tests to gross income be explored for determining the meaning of 'engaged principally' under section 20 of the Glass–Steagall Act. They also advise that the limitation imposed on bank-ineligible securities activities is arbitrary and unnecessarily restrictive.

Finally, the *Securities and Exchange Commission* (SEC) is in agreement with the GAO on the necessity to incorporate within any legislative reform a requirement that banks conduct bank-ineligible securities activities in subsidiaries, subject to the regulatory scheme for broker-dealers designed by Congress to ensure investor protection. The SEC, however, would go further and require banks to conduct most of their new *and* existing securities activities in separate entities.[88] Additionally, the SEC is concerned that no completely comparable opportunity exists for securities firms to expand into banking opportunities. Accordingly, and for reasons of practicality, it calls for consideration to be given to amending the Bank Holding Company Act to permit securities firms to own banks without subjecting these firms and their holding companies to the full regulatory system applicable to banks and bank holding companies (US General Accounting Office, 1990, Appendix X1).

Reforms necessitating repeal of at least part(s) of the Glass–Steagall Act
One blueprint for financial reform which inevitably covers the subject of how to expand commercial bank powers has been put forward by the recent President of the Federal Reserve Bank of New York (Corrigan, 1987 and 1990). He also sponsors the bank holding company (BHC) structure (Corrigan, 1987), arguing that bank (or thrift) holding companies should be allowed to own and control one or more banks or thrifts and, in time, should be allowed to engage in a broad range of financial services (such as banking, insurance and securities services) through subsidiaries. They should not, however, be allowed to be owned or controlled by a non-financial concern nor be engaged in non-financial services. Such BHCs would be distinct from Financial Holding Companies (FHCs) which choose not to own or control insured banks or thrift institutions but otherwise offer the full range of financial services. The BHCs would be subject to a degree of consolidated supervision by the Federal Reserve.

The major virtues of this blueprint are perceived to lie in the fact that diversification opportunities are created for both banks and securities firms (that is, the domestic reciprocity issue is resolved)[89] in a manner which enforces the separation of banking from commerce, which is deemed necessary if the federal safety net is to be applied selectively to different parts or functions of the group. Strong Chinese Walls would also be used to provide protection against conflict of interest abuse, unfair competition and certain kinds of tie-ins, although care would be taken to ensure that firewall limitations on the mobility of funds and capital between affiliates were not so heavy-handed as to imperil international competitiveness or destroy the economic benefits sought after (Corrigan, 1990).

So much, then, for the reform packages already put forward (the US Treasury's 1991 package is considered below); but what of the alternative options? The polar options are continuing piecemeal reform within the confines of the Glass–Steagall Act, and a switch towards a European-style universal banking model. The former option, albeit within a 'section 20' framework, has already been discussed in depth so we can advance the analysis one stage further and consider piecemeal reform in a post Glass–Steagall-reform era. This would most likely proceed along similar lines to that proposed under the Financial Modernization Bill with banks being obliged to conduct their new securities activities (possibly together with much, if not all, of their old activities) through wholly owned non-bank subsidiaries of holding companies. A cautious approach would be adopted as to the speed and scope for the take-up of new activities, and functional regulation would involve the SEC and state insurance authorities in the regulation of securities and insurance activities respectively. This, in essence, is the model commanding majority support today in the US (see earlier discussion of the views of the GAO, FRB, ABA, SIA and SEC, for example).

The most radical alternative to this is to allow banks, subject to appropriate safeguards, to engage directly in whatever activities they wish – the so-called 'universal bank model' adopted in West Germany, Switzerland and elsewhere – although presumably, because of the strong opposition to the further merging of banking and commerce (Corrigan, 1990), the line in the US would be drawn at financial services.[90]

Between these two extremes a range of options is, of course, possible. One possibility is to allow banks to offer new securities and other activities through direct subsidiaries, as canvassed by the Office of the Comptroller of the Currency and suggested by the ABA for the non-underwriting activities of banks not owned by bank holding companies. Other options, variations and permutations could also be considered but, for analytical purposes, these three models, all of which necessitate legislative reform, will suffice to allow for a comparison of their relative merits.

The cost-benefit analysis of these three options must embrace, *inter alia*, the following considerations: (i) the risks created for affiliated banks and/or holding companies; (ii) the increased potential for conflict-of-interest abuse; (iii) the concentration risks created; (iv) competitive equity; (v) the potential economic benefits to be reaped; (vi) international competitiveness. Most of these issues are, of course, interrelated and require difficult trade-offs to be made by policymakers. For example, the greater the weight given to risk-minimization and avoidance of potential conflict of interest abuses, the lower the likely economic benefits in terms of increased competition, lower prices and greater choice for consumers, higher invisible earnings as a result of increased international competitiveness and stronger federally insured bank balance sheets. In operational terms, the trade-off turns on the extent to which reliance is placed for the handling of risks and the potential for abuse on new safeguards, such as firewalls, rather than on existing ones, for example: regulation of broker-dealers by the SEC, the Municipal Securities Rulemaking Board, the National Association of Securities Dealers and other SROs; regulation of bank and bank holding companies by the Federal Reserve Board and other federal and state regulatory agencies; internal controls; fiduciary requirements under common law. Similarly, but to a lesser degree, concerns with competitive equity (which brings in the reciprocity issue and the need to distance the securities operations from the federal safety net) may lead to a moderation in economic gains as a result, for example, of the reduced availability of synergies for the banks.

Within this context, the universal banking model, even if the range of new activities sanctioned is truncated at the financial services junction, clearly offers the best prospect for optimizing economic benefits but, alas, also poses the greatest 'risks', at least according to conventional wisdom (part of which was challenged earlier). In contrast, the holding company model reverses these prospects: it is a low-risk, low-return option. The intermediate option of allowing new activities to be provided through direct bank subsidiaries in effect embraces greater risk in the expectation of securing greater returns.

The likely outcome
The optimal combination of risk and return – and hence the choice of model – will, of course, depend upon the relative weights attached to these and other factors within the policymakers' objective functions. Suffice it to say at this current juncture in US history, with the financial services industry visibly under intense pressure, it is highly unlikely that the policymakers will flirt with danger, perceived or real. This was illustrated by Congress's rejection in November 1991 of the US Treasury's February 1991 proposals to reform Glass–Steagall by allowing financial service holding companies to own separately capitalized affiliates engaged in banking, securities, mutual fund and insurance activities. And even if new reform bills are presented in the near future, Congress is unlikely to support the more radical alternatives preferring, instead, a continuation of the policy of piecemeal reform within the confines of the existing legislative framework.

The options for reform in Japan

The alternatives
The major alternative routes[91] to reform appear to embrace the following:

(i)   require banks to offer securities business through wholly-owned, non-bank securities subsidiaries. This could involve the banks in offering securities business through direct non-bank subsidiaries, either multifunctional or functionally separated by type of non-banking business (the Canadian approach) or through subsidiaries of bank holding companies, the 'section 20' route adopted in the US for extending bank powers within the confines of the Glass–Steagall Act;

(ii) allow banks to offer securities facilities direct to the general public through their existing branch networks (the universal banking model);

(iii)   gradually extend the range of exceptions to the general prohibition on banks engaging in securities business (the so-called piecemeal approach). This, in fact, is the approach adopted to date, allowing diversification to financial institutions on a balanced basis within the confines of the existing legally segmented system.

Assessment of the reform options

A useful starting point is of *The Second Financial System Committee of the Financial System Research Counci Interim Report*, (Financial System Research Council, 1989) wherein the Committee argued that the following factors should be taken into account when assessing the relative merits of reform proposals:

(i)   Users' requirements. The relevant questions to be answered are: to what extent will reform promote competition, thereby contributing to an increase in consumer choice, an improvement in product quality and/or to cuts in product prices/service charges?; will reform promote innovation and contribute to the growth and vitality of markets?; will reform allow institutions to diversify away risk?

(ii)   Internationalization requirements. The relevant issues are the extent to which changes will facilitate market entry by overseas users, prevent the hollowing of domestic markets and permit the exercise of responsibilities commensurate with Japan's international standing. The compatibility of the reformed financial system with overseas systems is another important consideration.

(iii)   The maintenance of financial stability. Here the concern is with the continuing protection of depositors and maintenance of an orderly credit system. Solutions to any problems posed on either front must be found before reform can be contemplated.

(iv)   Preservation of the integrity of the capital market. Here the concern is to ensure that changes do not undermine public confidence in the operation of the capital market through, for example, inducing wide-scale abuse of conflict-of-interest situations.

(v)   Competitive equity.

Using this framework, the Second Financial System Committee evaluated five conceivable formulas (the 'five formulas' – see Table 9.5) for revising the Japanese financial system. It came out in favour of the wholly owned subsidiary route to reform,[92] which envisages either functionally separated subsidiaries or a single, multifunctional subsidiary possibly engaged solely in wholesale finance (that is, options B and C of the 'five formulas'), for the following reasons:

Table 9.5   The 'five formulas' for reform in Japan

A.   Piecemeal approach

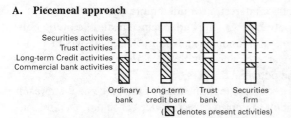

Securities activities
Trust activities
Long-term Credit activities
Commercial bank activities

Ordinary bank Long-term credit bank Trust bank Securities firm

(◪ denotes present activities)

To keep the basic system as it is and handle specific problems associated with particular financial instruments separately, allowing various types of banks and securities companies to gradually encroach on each other's business areas.

B.   Separated subsidiaries

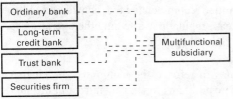

Ordinary bank — Trust bank / Securities firm
Trust bank — Securities firm
Securities firm — Ordinary bank / Trust bank

cf. same as Long-term credit bank

To authorize banks and securities companies to establish wholly owned subsidiaries in each of the specified financial areas (as in Canada).

C.   Multifunctional subsidiary

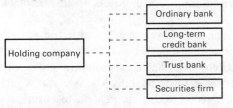

Ordinary bank
Long-term credit bank
Trust bank
Securities firm
— Multifunctional subsidiary

To allow each bank and securities company to newly set up a wholly owned subsidiary which can (exceptionally) engage in a wide range of securities and banking activities within a certain limited field (e.g., wholesale).

D.   Holding company

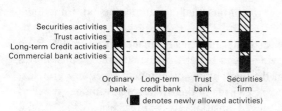

Holding company — Ordinary bank / Long-term credit bank / Trust bank / Securities firm

To allow banks and securities firms to create holding companies which have various types of financial subsidiaries as put forward in the US Proxmire Financial Modernization Bill.

E.   Universal bank

Securities activities
Trust activities
Long-term Credit activities
Commercial bank activities

Ordinary bank Long-term credit bank Trust bank Securities firm

(■ denotes newly allowed activities)

To introduce a European-type universal banking system, which does not distinguish between banking and securities businesses (examples of countries operating such a system are Germany and Switzerland).

Source: Financial System Research Council, 1989, p. 51.

(i)   Although the holding company route does offer the prospect of sub-
        stantial economic gains and does provide a degree of effective protec-
        tion against conflicts of interest, it would require repeal of Article 9 of
        Japan's Antimonopoly Law which is not deemed desirable in the light
        of the concentration of economic and political power which might
        result (Japan's prewar experience with the *zaibatsu* provides a salu-
        tary reminder of the potential dangers).

(ii)   Although the least disruptive, continuation of the piecemeal approach
        would make it difficult to improve user services or to build an interna-
        tionally acceptable or compatible financial system.

(iii)   Although the universal banking model (adoption of which would re-
        quire repeal of Article 65) offers the greatest potential economic gains,
        doubts persist about the authorities' ability to deal adequately with the
        resultant conflicts of interest and about the possibly destabilizing im-
        pact on the banking system and the wider financial system in Japan.
        However, in recognition of the possibility that, depending on the
        environment and nature of the new operations, the establishment of a
        new subsidiary might inflate overhead costs whilst bringing few ben-
        efits to users, the Committee recommended that consideration be given
        to discussing ways 'to ease regulations affecting the operating spheres
        of parent financial institutions' (p. 50).

Of the two subsidiary routes to reform, the Committee noted that both
approaches posed relatively few problems for Japan, at least in the short run.
Thus, either singly or as a combination (or, alternatively, institutions might
be left to select their mode of operation), both approaches were acceptable in
principle.

In comparing their relative merits, however, the Committee noted that the
multifunctional subsidiaries approach had the comparative advantage of lower
spending costs and greater flexibility and shared the customer service advantages of universal banking. Offset against this, however, is that it would be
more difficult than in the separated subsidiaries scenario to ensure sound
banking and prevent conflicts of interest; and it would further complicate
matters by introducing a new type of financial institution, the multifunctional
subsidiary.

Although noting in its Second Interim Report (Financial System Research
Council, 1990, p. 25) the widespread belief that the separated subsidiaries
route is the less desirable of the two options on competitive equity grounds,
because it might favour banks by virtue of their relative advantages in terms
of capital strength and privileged position *vis-à-vis* access to the official
safety net and information on their customers, the Committee nevertheless
favoured formula B over formula C on the grounds that it is represented the

Table 9.6 A comparison of the relative merits of different options for reforming Article 65

Option	Merits	Demerits
1. Banks' securities business to be conducted within wholly-owned non-bank securities *subsidiaries*[a] (i) where the subsidiaries are *direct subsidiaries* of the bank; or (ii) where the subsidiaries are *subsidiaries of bank holding companies*	1 (i) Legal separation maximizes protection of the payments and settlement system and minimizes the potential scope for abuse arising from conflict of interest situations, whilst allowing the parent access to new income sources. (The holding company route is clearly preferred on these grounds.) (ii) Allows for isolation of the securities operation from explicit and implicit government guarantees and facilitates functional supervision. (iii) Minimizes disturbances caused to the balance of competitive equity by preserving the existing vertical separation of the various types of business conducted by the parent companies. (The holding company route is the least preferred on this count.)	1 (i) Legal separation of the banking and securities business does not insulate the banking operation from all adverse reactions associated with the poor performance of the securities operation; moral responsibilities (with or without the coercion of supervisory authorities) and market realities will ensure that the fortunes of the two separate operations are inextricably linked. (ii) It is a high-cost option for the banks and one which limits the potential benefits to be reaped from economies of scope, according to the restrictiveness of the firewall structure adopted. (On efficiency grounds, the multifunctional, direct subsidiary option is clearly preferred.)
2. Banks allowed to offer securities facilities themselves direct to the general public through their branch networks (the so-called *universal banking* model, applied in Germany and elsewhere).	2 (i) Allows the banks maximum flexibility in the choice of operation, thereby maximizing the potential gains reaped from economies of scope and diversification as well as operational efficiency. (ii) Would best promote the internationalization of Japan's capital market as most financial centres are following the lead of Europe towards the adoption of universal banking principles. (iii) The best way of promoting competition in the financial services sector, with concomitant benefits for the economy and the consumer.	2 (i) Conflict-of-interest situations would abound, creating the potential for wide-scale abuse. (ii) Banking operations are more directly exposed to possible cross-contamination from securities operations, thereby possibly threatening the stability of the banking system and increasing taxpayers' exposure via the deposit insurance system and the official support programme. (iii) The risk of excessive concentration of power and business within bank hands is highest. (iv) Potentially highly disruptive for the domestic financial system, at least during a transitional phase. (v) Arguably,[b] this approach would best serve the interests of the banks, thereby upsetting the balance of 'competitive equity'.
3. Gradually extending the range of exceptions to the general prohibition on banks' involvement in securities activities (the so-called *piecemeal* approach).	3 (i) Minimizes market disturbances and turf disputes, thereby appeasing vested interests.	3 (i) At best, delays, and at worst, reduces the scale of, the enjoyment of economic benefits. (ii) Likely to artificially distort capital markets.

Notes
[a] These subsidiaries may be multifunctional (i.e., allowed to engage in a wide range of non-banking business) or restricted to engaging solely in securities business.
[b] This presupposes, of course, that the net effects of external regulations and supervision (embracing *inter alia*, monitoring and reporting, capital and liquidity requirements, reserve requirements, moral suasion, balance sheet restraints, implicit and explicit government guarantees, etc) are a positive benefit to banks, a situation which is not at all clear.

superior formula for mutual entry from the standpoints of achieving a level playing field, preventing harmful conflicts of interest, protecting depositors, preserving the stability of the banking system, and internationalizing Japan's financial system. Formula C's comparative advantage was deemed to lie in the maximization of efficiency gains and user benefits.

Such, then, represents the deliberations of the Second Financial System Committee of the Financial System Research Council; and to facilitate comparison with the parallel reform debate taking place in the US the comparative advantages and disadvantages of the reform options are restated in terms of the framework outlined at the beginning of this section in Table 9.6.

The outcome
Whatever the respective merits of the universal banking route to reform, the Japanese authorities (though, somewhat ironically, not the ruling Liberal Democratic Party), like their US counterparts, ruled it out of court because of their concerns for stability, depositor and consumer protection, and competition. Similarly, fears about the likely ensuing degree of concentration precluded sponsorship of the holding company option. Given an acceptance of the need for reform and an official eschewal of a continuation of the piecemeal approach, this left of the five options considered only the subsidiary routes for further consideration; and, for the reasons given earlier, it is the separated rather than the multifunctional subsidiaries formula which received the seal of approval. Accordingly, in June 1992 the Diet agreed on proposals incorporated within the Financial System Reform Bill to allow banks and securities companies to engage in each other's areas of activity through wholly owned, separately capitalized subsidiaries. Brokerage, however, will still be denied to the banks – at least for the time being – and an 'appropriate' set of firewalls (details yet to be worked out) will be placed between the parents and their subsidiaries. If Congress drags its feet much longer in introducing reform in the US, it is therefore likely that Japan, contrary to earlier expectations, will move first, for the reforms are planned for implementation in the first half of 1993.

Conclusions
In spite of the common acceptance of the need for reform of the legislative and administrative frameworks governing the separation of banking and securities business in home markets, it is highly likely that significant differences in the US and Japanese approaches to the subject will persist, even in a post-reform era. This is because of Japan's eschewal of the holding company formula which, in all likelihood, is the *only* solution likely to be adopted in the US in the foreseeable future, if indeed one is adopted at all. Although the universal banking model is rejected in both countries, for similar reasons,

the Japanese parliament proved to be more open to persuasion than Congress in respect of the pressing need for fundamental reform. In part, this reflected the unwillingness of the Japanese authorities to match the pace of piecemeal reform achieved in the US, but also Japan's determination to internationalize its financial system and improve the efficiency of its financial markets and institutions. Great care will be taken, however, to ensure that this will not be achieved at the expense of instability or loss of confidence in the system. Appropriate safeguards, erring on the side of caution, will thus be employed which will again serve to differentiate the Japanese from the US approach, existing or prospective. Accordingly, competitive anomalies are likely to persist in the foreseeable future, both at the interface of indigenous and foreign firms' operations in home markets and in overseas markets, although continuing political and competitive pressures will serve to ensure that regulatory convergence remains on the political agenda.

Notes

1. While the OCC charters and supervizes national banks, the Federal Reserve is responsible for regulating and supervizing bank holding companies and the foreign operations of banks which are members of the Federal Reserve System (i.e. member banks). The Federal Deposit Insurance Corporation (FDIC), in turn, regulates state non-member banks.
2. They may invest up to 10 per cent of capital and surplus in such securities.
3. These section 23B limitations have also applied to all FDIC-insured banks since 1987.
4. Both premises of this assumption can, of course, be challenged: the former on standard portfolio theory grounds (Jensen, 1972) that diversification can, in principle, reduce risk if this is measured as the variability in portfolio returns; and the latter on the grounds that there are alternative and more cost-effective means of shielding consumers of financial services from conflict of interest abuse (Hall, 1987).
5. More precisely, national banks. Section 5(c) extends the prohibition to state-chartered member banks.
6. The Competitive Equality Banking Act of 1987 temporarily extended the prohibition to FDIC-insured non-member banks until 1 March 1988.
7. Section 20, however, by prohibiting the affiliation of a member bank with any firm engaged *principally* in underwriting or dealing in securities, does limit the number of cases in which a holding company structure can be operated comprising, *inter alia*, both an investment banking firm and a commercial bank. Such a structure is prohibited unless either the commercial bank concerned is not a member of the Federal Reserve System or the principal activity of the securities firm is not investment banking.
8. Although the lifting, in March 1988, by the Federal Home Loan Bank Board (now known as the Office of Thrift Supervision) of a five-year moratorium on the establishment of affiliations with securities firms allowed savings and loan associations to take further advantage of the situation, the loophole for non-member banks was, temporarily at least, blocked. This was due to the enactment of the Competitive Equality Banking *Act* in August 1987 which extended the Glass–Steagall restrictions to all FDIC-insured banks until 1 March 1988. It also, temporarily again, prohibited securities houses from becoming bank affiliates, and blocked the non-bank bank (that is, a bank that does not satisfy the definition of a bank given in the Bank Holding Company Act of 1956 (BHCA), namely, that in general it engages in *both* receiving demand deposits and making commercial loans) loophole, which allowed non-bank penetration of banking, by requiring FDIC-insured non-bank banks to conform to the provisions of the BHCA

(which confined the operations of bank holding companies and their affiliates to banking operations, as defined in the Federal Reserve Board's Regulation Y – see below).

9. It was, however, discouraged by the Comptroller of the Currency and, at any rate, was not possible until fixed-rate commissions were abolished in 1975. Moreover, a bank's legal ability to offer full-service brokerage was in question until the issue was resolved in favour of the banks by a Supreme Court ruling in January 1988 (Kaufman and Mote, 1990).

10. Municipal revenue bonds were added to the list of securities which could be underwritten by commercial banks in 1968.

11. For now, it is sufficient to note that their securities operations are subject to the broker-dealer provisions of the Securities Exchange Act of 1934. Moreover, the International Banking Act of 1978, although grandfathering the exemption from Glass–Steagall of the existing securities operations of foreign banks, did place restrictions on the grandfathered affiliates, preventing them from entering new activities and from acquiring more than 5 per cent of any going concern. This action has greatly reduced their competitiveness, thereby reducing their comparative advantage *vis-à-vis* US member banks, although their ability since 1990 to underwrite securities in the US in subsidiaries of the banks themselves (rather than of bank holding companies) has served to increase their comparative advantage again.

12. Although the Federal Reserve also has authority over some of the foreign activities of national banks.

13. It was the UK bank, National Westminster, which first opened this door when the Supreme Court in January 1988 allowed the Federal Reserve Board's 1986 decision to stand which allowed the establishment of a securities subsidiary to both conduct discount brokerage operations and provide investment advice.

14. This followed expiration of the moratorium imposed by Congress on the granting by banking regulatory agencies of new securities powers to bank holding companies and their affiliates and the Court of Appeal's decision in February 1988 (upheld by the Supreme Court in June 1988) to uphold the Federal Reserve Board's April 1987 decision to allow bank holding companies, subject to meeting certain requirements, to engage in such activities through wholly owned subsidiaries. The Board determined that the types and levels of activities proposed by the bank holding companies complied with the provisions of the Glass–Steagall Act and that the bank-ineligible securities activities met the requirements of the Bank Holding Company Act of 1956, as amended.

15. Following a Federal Appeals Court ruling in September 1989, these assets can now come off the bank's own balance sheet.

16. These limitations and requirements became clear in January 1989, when the Board of Governors announced that it had approved applications (submitted during 1987) by five commercial banks to underwrite such forms of corporate debt through subsidiaries. Approval was subject to the following: (i) that no more than 5 per cent (raised to 10 per cent in September 1989) of total gross revenues on average over any two-year period be earned from this source by the bank's underwriting subsidiary; (ii) that specified capital adequacy requirements be met (e.g., that the parent holding company had a risk asset ratio substantially in excess of the fully phased-in BIS-required minimum of 8 per cent – excluding the capital invested in the subsidiary); (iii) that firewalls be erected between the securities and lending business to ensure, *inter alia*, the physical separation of staff and premises and to curb abuse that might arise from cross-lending, cross-marketing or cross-purchases/sales of securities (limitations are also placed on credit extensions by lending affiliates to customers of the underwriting subsidiary). (For full details, see US General Accounting Office, 1990, pp. 94–8.)

17. In fact the Board had approved applications by a number of bank holding companies to underwrite and deal in corporate debt *and* equity securities, but a one-year moratorium was placed on equity securities activities.

18. The new, tougher set of firewalls must be applied to all ineligible securities activities carried out by the section 20 subsidiaries and not just to corporate debt and equity operations.

19. Three more banks – Bankers Trust of New York, the Royal Bank of Canada and the Canadian Imperial Bank of Commerce – were empowered to underwrite and trade in US equities through section 20 subsidiaries in January 1991.

20. That is, those corporations chartered by the Board of Governors under section 25(a) of the Federal Reserve Act (the Edge Act) for the purpose of engaging in international or foreign banking or other international and foreign operations.

21. The Federal Reserve also interprets it to apply to state-chartered member banks.

22. Regulation K, and especially the quantitative limitations on securities underwriting and dealing activities, is currently under review by the Federal Reserve.

23. The Federal Reserve is responsible for regulating and supervizing the foreign operations of member banks and bank holding companies. It also charters, regulates and supervizes Edge Act corporations. The OCC charters and supervizes national banks; the FDIC regulates state non-member banks (although their international operations are relatively limited).

24. The Riegle–Garn Bill, which was approved by the Senate Banking Committee in June 1990, sought to shift this towards reciprocal national treatment but it was not enacted prior to adjournment. Continuing pressures for similar legislation may yet result in such a change of policy – although the Federal Reserve has threatened to block it – which would require foreign countries to grant US banks and securities firms 'the same competitive opportunities (including effective market access)' (Key, 1990) as are available to the countries' domestic banks.

25. A similar policy is adopted in respect of foreign securities firms' US operations although, with respect to operation of a primary dealership in government securities, a policy of reciprocal national treatment (under the Omnibus Trade and Competitiveness Act of 1988) is applied.

26. Prior to the IBA, US agencies and branches of foreign banks were licensed and supervized only by individual states; there was no federal regulatory framework for foreign banks only operating agencies or branches (i.e., not subsidiaries). As a result, foreign banks enjoyed a competitive advantage *vis-à-vis* US banks because:

    (i) they could establish full service branches in more than one state (as long as branches were permitted by state law);
    (ii) they were not required to hold (non-interest-bearing) reserves with the Federal Reserve system;
    (iii) only those foreign banks operating commercial bank subsidiaries in the US were subject to the provisions (section 4) of the BHCA restricting non-banking activities, which allowed foreign banks to operate both securities affiliates and deposit-taking branches in the US.

27. Exemptions from section 4 of the BHCA are, however, available to 'non-controlled' foreign affiliates in respect of their non-securities, non-banking financial activities (e.g., insurance) if the foreign banking organization meets the so-called 'qualified foreign banking organization' (QFBO) test of the IBA.

28. Defined under Article 2.8 as:

    (i) the buying and selling of securities;
    (ii) acting as a broker, or agent or a proxy with respect to the buying and selling of securities;
    (iii) acting as a broker, or agent or a proxy with respect to entrusting of buying or selling transactions on the securities market;
    (iv) underwriting securities;
    (v) effecting secondary distribution of securities;
    (vi) handling an offering or secondary distribution of securities.

29. The sale of medium-term public bonds was sanctioned in October 1983.

30. Although banks were still required under both the Banking Law and the Securities and

Exchange Law to obtain a licence prior to engaging in the retail sale of newly issued public bonds.

31.   The move was taken for a number of reasons. These included an official desire to: (i) promote wider ownership of government bonds; (ii) reduce the banks' funding burden due to their extensive government bond underwriting activities; (iii) allow banks to reduce capital losses on their government-bond holdings; and (iv) allow banks to reap economies of scope (e.g., through offering new savings instruments). Prior to this move, liquidity in the government bond market was provided by the Bank of Japan through its willingness to purchase them one year after issue.

32.   Initially, such activities were restricted to bonds with maturities of less than two years but in 1985 this restriction was removed.

33.   Because commercial paper was defined in legal terms as a promissory note it lay outside the scope of the Securities and Exchange Law restrictions, thereby allowing banks to engage freely in activities in this market since its inauguration in 1987. (Japanese banks have been permitted to issue and deal in certificates of deposit since 1979.)

34.   Under the regulatory framework established in 1988 as an amendment to the Securities and Exchange Law (reviewed in 1991):

(i)   Japanese banks (and securities firms) are allowed to trade government bond futures on the Tokyo stock exchange (the market was established in October 1985) and, since 1989, have been allowed to *broke* government (domestic and foreign) bond futures but not stock index futures. (Nor are they allowed to broke the underlying cash government bonds although, in practice, this is done by passing client orders once they are through their own accounts.)

(ii)   Japanese banks have unlimited access to the domestic financial futures exchange to trade both futures and options, both on their own account and as brokers.

(iii) Japanese banks (and securities firms) are allowed to use overseas options and futures markets but may not act as brokers in foreign currency or stock index options.

35.   Banks are currently engaged in discussions with the MOF with a view to gaining permission to securitize other forms of consumer debt.

36.   Co-managements are less desirable as they are less profitable.

37.   For example, that set up by the Industrial Bank of Japan in the US in September 1990, known as the Bridgeford Group.

38.   For example, the Long-term Credit Bank of Japan bought a stake in Aubrey G. Lanston in 1986.

39.   For example, Dai-Ichi Kangyo opened a brokerage subsidiary in New York to deal in and underwrite bank-eligible securities in 1989.

40.   For example, the Industrial Bank of Japan took a 20 per cent stake in D'Accord, a US leasing specialist, in May 1989.

41.   For example, Bank of Tokyo Capital Markets has made markets in Ecu-denominated Treasury bills since November 1989.

42.   Sumitomo Bank's London securities offshoot was the first to obtain such a licence in July 1986; and since then many other Japanese commercial banks (e.g., Dai-Ichi Kangyo, Fuji, Mitsubishi, Sanwa, Mitsui) have also acquired licences.

43.   Overseas banks' Japanese securities subsidiaries were first sanctioned in December 1985, with overseas securities companies achieving success in 1986.

44.   A notorious example of this was the stalling by the Bank of England, on the prompting of the Treasury, of the award of primary gilt dealerships to Japanese firms until the dispute over the admission of certain British firms to the membership of the Tokyo Stock Exchange had been resolved. The dispute was duly settled in 1990.

45.   In fact the foreign investment banks concerned – Warburgs, Jardine Fleming, Merrill Lynch, Goldman Sachs, Morgan Stanley and Vickers da Costa – were informed of their successful applications in November 1985.

46. The British firms Barclays de Zoete Wedd, Kleinwort Benson, Schroders, Baring Brothers and County Natwest are all now members.
47. Dealing licences in Japanese government bonds were first granted to foreign concerns in 1986.
48. Permission for foreign banks to establish trust banking subsidiaries in Japan required waivers from the Japan Fair Trade Commission.
49. Foreign *commercial* banks were first admitted as participants in 1986.
50. Corporate pension fund management was first opened up to foreign companies (banks) in 1985, with a requirement that it be conducted within wholly owned trust bank subsidiaries. Investment management (excluding pension fund business) licences were first granted to foreign companies in 1987 and investment trust (i.e., mutual) fund management licences in 1990. Public pension fund management was not permitted (for foreign trust banks) until 1989.
51. Apart from the MOF's acquiescence in, if not promotion of, Japanese banks' securities aspirations, a number of important decisions were also taken which furthered the securities companies inroads into banking. Thus, while they cannot take deposits or make loans other than for securities purchases in Japan, they can nevertheless: make loans collateralized by local government bonds; buy and sell yen-denominated certificates of deposit (CDs), foreign CDs and commercial paper; operate in the yen-based bankers' acceptance market; offer money market funds; and deposit accounts linked to medium term government bond investments, which compete with banks' short term deposit accounts; trade freely in stock exchange futures as well as on the financial futures exchange (except spot currency option trading).
52. Nomura, for example, obtained a deposit-taking licence in London in 1986, and has stakes in Banco Santander, the Spanish bank, and Matuschka, the German investment bank. It also has a Swiss banking licence.
53. It is becoming increasingly difficult for the authorities to champion the principle of separation, given their attitudes to the overseas activities of their own commercial banks and the treatment granted to overseas firms in the Japanese market place. Competitive distortions, which weigh against their own firms in domestic markets, abound as a result of the asymmetry in regulation of domestic and foreign financial firms.
54. Some of the remaining irritations facing the City banks comprise: (i) the prohibition on participation in the retail sector of the equity brokerage business; (ii) the inability to directly underwrite corporate bonds; and (iii) the frequent need to use trust banks for both underwriting public bond issues and for selling shares to the public.
55. Before the Second World War, the separation of banking and securities business was not enshrined in law in Japan. Under the Banking Law of 1927, banks were permitted to invest in equities and public bonds on their own behalf, to act as securities agents (e.g., accept money for equities payment, pay principal and interest for securities, etc.) and to lend securities. Indeed, the large banks played a significant role in public bond underwriting, particularly in government bonds, where the underwriting syndicate was composed exclusively of banks.
56. And, as noted earlier, section 20 blocks the loophole of securities firms using subsidiaries or affiliates to take deposits.
57. Under exceptions to the general prohibitions on engaging in securities business incorporated in the Glass–Steagall Act in the US and Article 65 of the Securities and Exchange Law in Japan.
58. Although this is not because of legal impediments but rather the MOF's refusal to grant such powers because of the fine balancing act it is trying to perform in respect of the mutual interpenetration of banking and securities markets by the relevant firms.
59. Pre-1940 experience with the *zaibatsu*, the all-powerful financial and industrial conglomerates, also still weighs heavily with administrators who fear the consequences of full-scale deregulation.
60. This excludes the possibility that regulators are susceptible to special pleading from interested parties, keen to maintain barriers to entry to their industries.
61. It is the *risk-adjusted* rates of return which are relevant.

62. Benston (1990, p. 149) contends that this is not the most appropriate measure of risk but rather 'the probability that a bank will become insolvent and impose costs on the FDIC, other banks, and the economy'.

63. This is assuming that banks, in a deregulated environment, would not be allowed to offer securities services directly, a policy which finds favour with Benston (1990, ch. 2) as a means of minimizing risk.

64. This is part of the rationale for the so-called prudential controls widely applied to banking organizations around the world.

65. Existing bank eligible securities activities and traditional commercial banking activities probably already expose banks to the levels of individual risk that new activities entail.

66. The introduction of actuarially sound, risk-based premiums would preclude the extension of the safety net through the medium of federal deposit insurance. Similarly, expeditious use of risk-based capital requirements and resolution policies could be used to avoid extension of the safety net through the other mediums.

67. For example, forcing a reorganization *before* their economic capital falls below zero (Benston, 1990, p. 184).

68. That is, institutional measures designed to prevent the leakage of information acquired in the course of performance of business in one section of an organization to other sections of the organization.

69. Kaufman and Mote (1990) also contend that under existing arrangements governing banks' involvement in securities business, the smaller banks are discriminated against.

70. The concern about the comparative advantages (*vis-à-vis* securities companies) possessed by commercial banks is more marked in Japan compared with the US because of the differing institutional and legal frameworks applying in the two countries. Thus, Japanese commercial banks, unlike their US counterparts, can hold client firms' shares up to a certain degree (i.e., up to 5 per cent of total outstanding stock), capital ties which are often considerably strengthened through the holdings of said stock by the banks' affiliates, which are not governed by the 5 per cent limitation (although *group* holdings are restricted by the exercise of moral suasion by the MOF – see text). While companies have traditionally welcomed these ties as a means of stabilising shareholdership, thereby allowing them to concentrate on maximizing long-term returns rather than being concerned with short-term defensive moves to stave off predators, etc., some nevertheless regard the situation as unhealthy.

    Similarly, institutional arrangements in Japan result in many bank officials sitting on the boards of directors of client companies and corporate customers looking to their bankers for lender-of-last-resort-facilities in tough trading conditions under the so-called 'main bank' relationships. These features, together with privileged access to the official safety net, help to explain the widespread concern felt about the power of banks in the Japanese economy and why many call for, at the very least, *quid pro quo* diversification opportunities (e.g., in banking, trust, FOREX and other business areas) to be given to securities companies under any reform package.

71. Deregulation in Japan, for example, has led to a narrowing of margins because of an increase in bank deposit rates; and the banks have also lost deposit business because of the abolition of the tax exemption on *maruyu* savings accounts (money flowed out into unit trusts) and lending business because of the decision, taken in 1989, to allow companies access to the short-to-medium (i.e., up to four years maturity) term domestic bond market.

72. Not least because of their desire to take full advantage of the opportunities afforded by the European single market after 1992 but also because of their wish to minimize distortions in their domestic financial markets.

73. Taking the example of Japan, again, foreign banks (including US banks, which are prohibited from engaging in such activities at home) are able to engage in securities and trust business in Japan which is not open to Japanese banks; and, through subsidiaries, both Japanese banks and securities firms can engage in activities in overseas markets which are prohibited domestically.

74. An added benefit for the Japanese government of more efficient money and capital

markets is that this would facilitate the conduct of official monetary policy through open market operations.

75. This section is taken from Hall (1991).

76. Those section 20 firms operating under the Board's orders of January 1989 have to establish no fewer than 28 firewalls.

77. Under the Securities Exchange Act of 1934, the section 20 subsidiaries must register as broker-dealers, thereby becoming subject to SEC regulation. This requires, *inter alia*, the section 20 subsidiaries to comply with the SEC's net capital rules and to join an SEC-approved industry self-regulating organization (SRO). As the primary regulator, however, the Federal Reserve Board is required to enforce the firewall provisions and capital adequacy and other requirements imposed and it has also demanded the quarterly submission to the Federal Reserve Bank of New York of the FOCUS reports filed by the firms with their SROs together with other information as detailed. The Board will also, of course, continue to regulate and supervise the bank holding companies according to the provisions of the Bank Holding Company Act of 1956.

78. In an earlier study into these operations (US General Accounting Office, 1988) the GAO expressed concerns about the low level of profitability, the lack of management controls and the inadequacy of credit and risk assessment procedures.

79. Moreover, some bank holding companies have argued that the inability of banks to provide credit enhancements for securities underwritten by affiliates gives some foreign banking organizations a competitive advantage over US bank holding companies.

80. This is certainly an option for money centre banks but less easy for regional bank holding companies which are much less involved in operations in government securities.

81. Under current arrangements, the disbursement by the holding company to an affiliated bank of profits earned by a section 20 subsidiary is at the discretion of the holding company. If, however, the Federal Reserve Board dropped its insistence that ineligible securities activities take place only within a securities subsidiary of a bank holding company to allow, for example, securities underwriting in direct subsidiaries of federally insured banks, any profits earned by the subsidiary would automatically benefit the bank. The corollary, however, is that losses incurred by the subsidiary would automatically fall upon the affiliated bank, thereby depleting its capital. Moreover, as pointed out by the Securities Industry Association (Lackritz, 1990), the more direct linking of the securities subsidiary to the federal safety net might convey an unwarranted competitive advantage to firms associated with banks.

82. Under the Financial Institutions Reform, Recovery and Enforcement Act (FIRREA) of 1989 affiliated insured depository institutions are held liable for each other's losses but this does not extend to holding companies unless they themselves are depository institutions.

83. Including the risk that firms might exploit the new conflicts of interest created.

84. Apart from the examples of inappropriate restrictions cited earlier, doubts also persist about the wisdom of the prohibition on banks marketing securities underwritten by their section 20 affiliates. Although this, in part, is designed to prevent confusion arising amongst customers concerning which products are federally insured and which are not, confusion already exists because a bank is able to sell securities products to its customers from a bank-owned discount brokerage subsidiary, and under far less stringent rules than those applied to section 20 companies. Unless and until the latter situation is tackled, the retention of this firewall does seem something of an absurd anomaly.

85. The SEC has suggested that consideration be given to amending the Bank Holding Company Act of 1956 to allow securities firms to own banks without subjecting the securities firms and their holding companies to the full regulatory system applied to banks and their holding companies. The GAO, however, is opposed to this idea as it supports the retention of controls over the entire holding company comparable to the Federal Reserve's controls over bank holding companies.

86. The Chairman of the Board favours repeal of Glass–Steagall because 'technology and globalisation have continued to blur the distinctions among credit markets. Outdated

constraints endanger the profitability of banking organisations and their contribution to the US economy' (Greenspan, 1988).

87. In the light of the excess capacity and low level of profitability prevailing in many securities markets, some question the wisdom of allowing banks wider access to securities activities. The potential benefits, however, do not necessarily derive from the absolute level of profitability of securities operations; portfolio diversification and economies of scope offer the prospect of increased risk-adjusted portfolio returns, while the joint offering of banking and securities services is thought likely to lead to a cyclical smoothing of reported profits.

88. The revised version of the Financial Modernisation Bill would have required banks, if Congress had voted to allow them to underwrite equities, to transfer all their securities activities into securities subsidiaries with the exception of public and revenue bond business.

89. This is consistent with the provisions of the Proxmire–Garn Financial Modernization Bill of 1987 which envisaged the formation of diversified financial holding companies, which would devote 80 per cent or more of their consolidated assets to securities business and other bank-related activities. Securities companies would have been allowed to own banks through such holding companies under the proposals without falling within the purview of the Bank Holding Company Act of 1956; and they would have been permitted to continue to carry out insurance and real-estate activities, within certain limits, parallel with their securities business.

90. It is interesting to note that the US Treasury, in its banking reform package presented in February 1991, did *not* rule out the ownership of financial service holding companies by industrial or commercial companies.

91. It is assumed that we are concerned here with fundamental reform (i.e., allowing banks in principle to engage in all forms of securities activities) rather than with a minor relaxation of the rules to allow, for example, banks greater freedom in the area of private placements of securities products or to receive, as trust banks already do, commission on stock exchange transactions carried out on an agency basis (as permitted under Article 65). Other options, such as allowing interpenetration of banking and securities business through the routing of business through the banks' and securities houses' overseas operations, with associated privileges, are considered in Dale (1990).

92. This would require either new legislation exempting wholly owned subsidiaries from the scope of the Antimonopoly Law or companies seeking special permission from the Fair Trade Commission.

References

American Bankers Association (ABA) (1986), *The Public Policy Perspective: Expanded Products and Services for Banking* (Washington, D.C.: ABA).

Benston, G. J. (1990), *The Separation of Commercial and Investment Banking: the Glass–Steagall Act Revisited and Reconsidered* (London: Macmillan).

Boren, A. R. (1990), 'The activities of securities subsidiaries of bank holding companies', Statement made on behalf of The American Bankers Association before the Subcommittee on General Oversight and Investigations Committee on Banking, Finance and Urban Affairs of the US House of Representatives (Washington, D.C., May).

Corrigan, E. G. (1987), *Financial Market Structure: A Longer View* (New York: Federal Reserve Bank of New York).

Corrigan, E. G. (1990), 'Reforming the US financial system: an international perspective', *Federal Reserve Bank of New York Quarterly Review*, vol. 15, no. 1, pp. 1–14.

Dale, R. (1990), 'Japan's banking regulation: current policy issues', in C. A. E. Goodhart and G. Sutija (eds), *Japanese Financial Growth* (London: Macmillan), pp. 33–45.

Federation of Bankers' Associations of Japan (FBAJ) (1989), *The Banking System in Japan* (Tokyo: FBAJ).

Financial System Research Council (1989), *On a New Japanese Financial System*, interim report by the Second Financial System Committee of the Financial System Research Council (Tokyo: Federation of Bankers' Associations of Japan).

Financial System Research Council (1990), *On a New Japanese Financial System*, second interim report by the Second Financial System Committee of the Financial System Research Council (Tokyo: Federation of Bankers' Associations of Japan).

Financial System Subcommittee (1987), *Report on the Specialised Financial Institution System in Japan* (Tokyo: Federation of Bankers' Associations of Japan).

Fundamental Research Committee of the Securities and Exchange Council (1990a), *Restructuring the Legal Framework to Deal with the Securitisation of Finance*, First Subcommittee Report (Tokyo: Capital Markets Research Institute).

Fundamental Research Committee of the Securities and Exchange Council (1990b), *Restructuring Japan's Capital Market: Toward an International Market*, Second Subcommittee Report (Tokyo: Capital Markets Research Institute).

Greenspan, A. (1988), *Remarks before the 24th Annual Conference on Bank Structure and Competition*, organized by the Federal Reserve Bank of Chicago (Chicago: Federal Reserve Bank).

Hall, M. J. B. (1987), 'Reform of the London Stock Exchange: the prudential issues', *Banca Nazionale Del Lavoro Quarterly Review*, June, pp. 167–81.

Hall, M. J. B. (1989), 'The BIS capital adequacy "Rules": a critique', *Banca Nazionale Del Lavoro Quarterly Review*, no. 169, pp. 207–27.

Hall, M. J. B. (1991), 'Banking reforms in the US: Part II', *Journal of International Banking Law*, vol. 6, no. 1, pp. 28–37.

Japan Securities Research Institute, *Securities Market in Japan* (Tokyo: JSRI).

Jensen, M. C. (1972), 'Capital markets: theory and evidence', *Bell Journal of Economics and Management Science*, vol. 3, no. 2, pp. 357–98.

Kaufman, G. G. and Mote, L. R. (1990), Glass–Steagall: repeal by regulatory and judicial reinterpretation', *Banking Law Journal*, September–October, pp. 388–421.

Key, S. J. (1990), 'Is national treatment still viable?: US policy in theory and practice', *Journal of International Banking Law*, vol. 5, no. 9, pp. 365–81.

Lackritz, M.E. (1990), 'Statement of the Securities Industry Association on the GAO report entitled "Bank powers: activities of securities subsidiaries of bank holding companies" before the Committee on Banking, Finance and Urban Affairs of the US House of Representatives', Washington, D.C., May.

Schneider, H. M. (1990), 'Testimony on behalf of the Bank Capital Markets Association on the GAO Report on "Activities of securities subsidiaries of bank holding companies": hearings by the Subcommittee on General Oversight and Investigations House Committee on Banking, Finance and Urban Affairs', Washington, D.C., May.

Suzuki, Y. (1986), *Money, Finance and Macroeconomic Performance in Japan* (New Haven, Conn.: Yale University Press).

Trenchard, Thomas, 2nd Viscount Trenchard (1990), 'Japan', in W. Kay (ed.), *Modern Merchant Banking*, 3rd edn (London:Woodhead-Faulkner) ch. 18.

US General Accounting Office (GAO) (1988a), *Bank Powers: Issues Related to Repeal of the Glass–Steagall Act* (Washington, D.C.: GAO).

US General Accounting Office (GAO) (1988b), *International Finance: US Commercial Banks' Securities Activities in London* (Washington, D.C.: GAO).

US General Accounting Office (GAO) (1989), *Banking: Conflict of Interest Abuses in Commercial Banking Institutions* (Washington, D.C.: GAO).

US General Accounting Office (GAO) (1990), *Bank Powers: Activities of Securities Subsidiaries of Bank Holding Companies*, Report to the Chairman, Subcommittee on General Oversight and Investigations, Committee on Banking, Finance and Urban Affairs, House of Representatives, Washington, D.C.

US Treasury (1991), *Modernizing the Financial System: Recommendations for Safer, More Competitive Banks* (Washington, D.C.: US Treasury).

List of statutes

UK

Bank of England Act 1946
Banking Act 1979
Banking Act 1987
Cheques Act 1992
Consumer Credit Act 1974

USA

Bank Holding Company Act 1956
Bank Mergers Act 1960
Bank Mergers Act 1966
Bank Survey Act 1970
Banking Act 1933
Banking Reform Act 1991
Change in Bank Control Act 1978
Community Reinvestment Act 1977
Competitive Equality Banking Act 1987
Consumer Credit Protection Act ('Truth in Lending Act') 1969
Deposit Insurance Reform Act 1991
Depository Institutions Deregulation and Monetary Control Act 1980
Douglas Amendment to the Bank Holding Company Act 1956
Edge Act 1913
Electronic Funds Transfer Act 1980
Equal Credit Opportunity Act 1974
Expedited Funds Availability Act 1988
Fair Credit Billing Act 1974
Fair Housing Act 1968

Federal Deposit Insurance Act 1933
Federal Deposit Insurance Act 1966
Federal Deposit Insurance Corporation Improvement Act 1991
Federal Reserve Act 1913
Federal Trade Commission Improvement Act 1975
Financial Institutions, Recovery, Reform and Enforcement Act 1989
Financial Institutions Regulatory and Interest Rate Control Act 1978
Foreign Bank Supervision Enhancement Act 1991
Garn-St. Germain Act 1982
Glass–Steagall Act 1933
Home Mortgage Disclosure Act 1975
International Banking Act 1978
McFadden Act 1927
National Bank Act 1864
Proxmire-Garn Financial Modernization Bill 1987
Real Estate Settlement Procedures Act 1974
Riegle-Garn Bill 1990
Securities Exchange Act 1934

Japan

Anti-Monopoly Law 1947
Bank of Japan Law 1942
Banking Act 1890
Banking Law 1927

Banking Law 1981
Deposit Insurance Law 1971
Financial System Reform Act 1992
Foreign Exchange and Foreign
  Trade Control Law 1947
Foreign Exchange Bank Law 1954
Investment Advisory Law 1987
Labour Bank Law 1953
Law Concerning Amalgamation and
  Conversion of Financial
  Institutions 1968
Law Concerning Bond Issue by
  Banks 1950
Law Concerning Concurrent
  Operation of Savings Bank
  Business or Trust Business by
  Ordinary Banks 1943
Law Concerning Concurrent
  Operation of Trust Business by
  Ordinary Banks 1981
Law Concerning Special Account of

Government Bonds Consolida-
  tion Fund 1975
Law Concerning the Reserve
  Deposit Requirement System
  1958
Loan Trust Law 1952
Long-Term Credit Bank Law 1952
National Bank Act 1872
Norinchukin Bank Law 1923
Postal Savings Law 1981
Savings Bank Act 1890
Savings Bank Law 1921
Securities and Exchange Law 1948
Shinkin Bank Law 1951
Shokockukin Bank Law 1936
Sogo Bank Law 1951
Special Taxation Measures Law
  1986
Temporary Interest Rate Adjustment
  Law 1947
Trust Business Law 1922

Index

accounting arrangements
Japan 153
UK 37
USA 66–7
administrative guidance (Japan) 86, 88, 91, 151, 156, 158, 169
agricultural co-operative (Japan) 14, 15
American Bankers Association 55, 61, 66, 72, 78, 84, 244, 245, 247, 252, 266
antitrust laws
Japan 91, 116, 147, 164
UK 39–40
USA 59, 79
Antimonopoly Law 1947 (Japan) 91, 152, 227, 256, 266
1977 amendment 230
Argy, V. 170
auditing arrangements
Japan 153
UK 32, 43
USA 66

Bank Accounts Directive (EC) 190, 195, 215
Bank Capital Markets Association (USA) 245, 267
bank examination procedures
comparison 176–9
Japan 146, 150–51, 158, 169
UK 32
USA 61–5
Bank for International Settlements 18, 19, 154, 170, 188–213, 215, 226
Bank Holding Company Act 1956 (USA) 57, 58, 75, 79, 83, 218, 220–22, 225, 226, 250, 259, 260, 261, 265, 266
Douglas Amendment 77, 78
Bank Insurance Fund (USA) 71, 74, 77, 82
Bank Mergers Act 1960 (USA) 59
Bank Mergers Act 1966 (USA) 59

Bank of Credit and Commerce International affair 32, 41–3, 45, 64–5, 83, 179
implications for UK banking regulation and supervision 42–4, 46–7
implications for US banking regulation and supervision 64–5, 83–4
Bank of England 3–4, 5, 176–83, 190–217
Board of Banking Supervision 32, 43
conduct of monetary policy 29–31
prudential regulation and supervision 31–48
Bank of England Act 1946 4
Bank of Japan 13, 14, 15–16, 93, 96, 116, 117, 134–40, 144, 148, 150, 151, 158, 162, 163, 170, 262
Bank of Japan Law 1942 15
Bank of Tokyo 15, 19–20
Bank of Yokohama 232
bank ownership 'rules'
comparison 181
Japan 163–4
UK 40–41
USA 60
Bank Survey Act 1970 (USA) 61
Banking Act 1933 (US) 49, 57, 60, 79, 219
Banking Act 1979 (UK) 31
Banking Act 1987 (UK) 4, 31, 32, 33, 37, 44
control of shareholders 40
minimum criteria for authorization 33
Banking Law 1929 (Japan) 263
Banking Law 1981 (Japan) 91–3, 151, 152, 153, 159, 227–9, 230, 235, 261
Banking Reform Act 1991 (USA) 64
banking scandals
Japan 163, 169
UK 37, 39
see also Bank of Credit and Commerce International affair